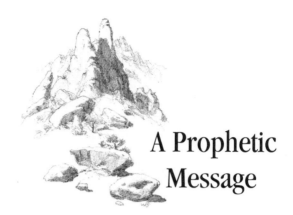

# A Prophetic Message

Published by Stanley W. Paher
NEVADA PUBLICATIONS
P.O. Box 15444, Las Vegas, Nevada 89114
(775) 747-0800

Illustrations by ROY PURCELL

Produced at WHITE SAGE STUDIOS,
Virginia City, Nevada

# A Commentary on
# DANIEL

# A Prophetic Message

# by Homer Hailey

**NEVADA PUBLICATIONS**
Las Vegas, Nevada

# Table of Contents

IN MEMORIAM
1903 – 2000

DEDICATED TO:

Todd, a blessing to all
Cody, the Champ
Dylan, my Little Buddy
Johanna, our Little Princess

Ruby Stroup's Grandchildren
to whom I am totally devoted.

# Foreword

"**H**omer Hailey is an old man."

This is a statement of utmost respect. As these words are being penned, we have honored Homer Hailey's ninety-seventh birthday. Yet even now his pen flows rich with the wisdom gleaned during nearly a century of diligence to the study of God's Word. Though his physical heart is weak, his spiritual heart churns all the stronger. His passion for the righteousness of God's Servant is as intense as a fiery furnace and you will be set on fire by his passion in this commentary on Daniel. Students of Hailey's earlier works in the prophetic and wisdom literature (such as Isaiah, the Minor Prophets and Job) will recognize another masterpiece of elucidation herein. His style is not so much one of dry commentary as it is master teacher, a style that endears itself to us common Bible students.

For me, Homer Hailey has always been an old man. The first year I sat at his feet learning of Job and Isaiah (I was twenty), would be his last year in a collegiate classroom. (Draw what conclusions you might.) He retired from classroom teaching nearly thirty years past. Yet even now, when I read his words teaching us of Daniel, it sounds exactly as he sounds in person. The literary intonation, phrasing, passion and even dry wit rings through, true to the man. Listening to Homer preach is like listening to a recording of the Bible. Even his ordinary speech about a common event of the day is like listening to a prophet. One is never quite sure whether he is quoting scripture or just speaking in the language of scripture. This same feature characterizes his writing style even more. Both his speech and pen have that reassuring luster of wizened antiquity.

Yet Homer was not always old. As a young boy he migrated with his family to the American desert in a covered wagon. Growing up, he knew six-shooters and cattle drives first hand. But as a young man his attentions turned to an education in the Bible. He soon distinguished himself as a student of God's word and especially as a student of the prophets. Over the next seventy years or so, his world radically changed: from that typified by the freedom of an open range, to a life in virtual exile. He witnessed the trampling of his cultural and spiritual roots as this nation grew from a neophyte-nation born of faith in the word of God to the dominant world empire it is today which yet knows not God. As the nation went, so went Christ's church in many ways. The nation and even the church in some dimensions became like the Israel of old which trampled God's people among it. One can see the tears in Homer's eyes through his words, as though he sees the wine-press of God's coming judgment treading out retribution on his own. He has looked into the mouths of the lions who would see him silenced for his refusal to abandon his convictions. Even now in Daniel he will speak without shame of a sense of angels present. And he will be criticized for it - again - by those who find his insights a challenge to be rebuked rather than plumbed. He has preached hard and at great personal risk right along with the prophets of the Old Testament concerning the downfall of the nation in our self-aggrandizement and desertion from God's law. Yet for all that, he writes still, in hope of just another day of service in the Lord's work. In short, Homer is a Daniel. Consequently, he would never see himself for the humble Daniel that he is in our time. Read this book and you will discover a writer who has seen the furnace from inside, several times in his long life, and come through it stronger in the Lord's service each time. From that perspective he introduces us to Daniel almost as if he were his personal friend. I suppose that comes from a life lived in the Book.

Daniel, like Homer, was an unusually old man, probably in his nineties after surviving seventy years of exile in Babylon. He could but dimly remember the Temple from his youth (if its prominence in his book is any indication). He had known Kings of two empires, and prayed through the trials brought by pagans practicing their treachery on him. He saw the prophecy of Jeremiah fulfilled as Cyrus decreed the captives' return. But the aged Daniel prefers to let others lead the return. He chooses to write for posterity as God directs him across a stage of visions. First, he looked back on his early years. As with Homer, the history of the early years of Daniel's life makes for fascinating reading. (See Ed Harrell's "The Churches of Christ in the 20th Century: Homer Hailey's Personal Journey of Faith".) So likewise we relish the first half of Daniel. Child and adult alike delight in the escapades of Daniel in the court of Babylon. With characteristic clarity Homer leads us through the lessons to be learned from Daniel's faithful life in times of adversity, drawing hope from disaster. But the old man Daniel was also a scary visage. Fire couldn't burn his friends and lions wouldn't eat him. He was a seer, the master seer among the Chaldeans. He had the private ear of Emperors, not to mention God Almighty!

Daniel "saw things." He interpreted dreams for Nebuchadnezzar. He had Divine visions of monsters! "Nightmares" we might be inclined to call them, were we the recipient of such an inspired gift. Not to put too fine an edge on it, but Daniel's visions were weird. Typically, at chapter seven the average Bible class calls it quits to study something easy, such as John's Apocalypse (also a masterpiece of exposition by Hailey). But fear not, as Daniel trusted God to interpret Nebuchadnezzar's dreams, so Homer prayerfully trusts God's word to interpret Daniel for us. Homer leads us with confidence into the night visions, the war rooms, the throne scenes and heavenly places to see our way clear through Daniel's visions of the coming of the Son of Man. Homer tells us when he is uncertain, yet always falls back on the unity of scripture to interpret the difficult passages, using the Bible to interpret the Bible. He shows us the thread that connects the prophet's words to their fulfillment in the coming of the Ancient of Days in the Kingdom of Jesus Christ. In fact one wonders after reading Hailey's Daniel if it isn't time to pull Hailey's Revelation off the shelf and take a fresh look at the elder John's visions in light of a better understanding of Daniel's book.

His treatment of the seventy weeks (with the aide of Phil Roberts in an Appendix) will help the Bible student avoid many of the wild speculations and spurious interpretations thrust on such passages by those seeking to validate some modern prophetic theory, or those struggling to force-fit a prophetic time frame into a fixed calendar. After reading Hailey on Daniel one wonders if it is appropriate anymore to speak of four hundred years of silence between the testaments. If Hailey's interpretations are on the mark, and so it seems, God was not so much silent as He was cryptically apocalyptic concerning the events that would unfold in those war torn centuries. True, no prophet spoke aloud in Israel during those years, but they being dead yet spoke. Still today, the voice of Daniel speaks with vivid confidence of the living God's sovereignty over all, and care for those who place their trust in Him.

Thank you once again, Homer Hailey, for leading us through difficult straits to see the glory in God's Word. It is quite an honor for me to be offered the opportunity to express our collective thanks.

*Hill Roberts*
Huntsville, Alabama

# Preface

This is not a critical commentary of the book of Daniel, but it is an effort to interpret the book in relation to present day needs. We stand on the threshold of a new century, and view the exit of the twentieth as it passes into that vast eternity outside of time.

No pretense is made to prophesy the future, attempting to foretell specifically what it holds for us, for only God can do that. God has not appointed any man to prophesy since the last of the New Testament prophets. But in the light of what He said through the Old Testament prophets and the consequential judgments on the pagan nations, we can deduce some conclusions respecting social, political, and religious conditions of today as we face the new century. These conclusions rest upon two infallible principles of the eternal God. First, His unchangeable nature: "For I, Jehovah, change not" (Mal. 3:6; James 1:17). Second, His judgments are always righteous and against sin, for, the Judge of all the earth does right (Gen. 18:25); and, "I know, O Jehovah, that thy judgments are righteous" (Ps. 119:75a; Isa. 26:9). The New Testament writers affirm the same message: "And we know that the judgment of God is according to truth against them that practice such things [as practiced by the Gentiles (Rom. 1:29- 32)]" (Rom.

2:2); and, "Yea, O Lord God, the Almighty, true and righteous are thy judgments" (Rev. 16:7). Our conclusion points only to what God can do, and in no way determines what He will do.

Neither is this a scholarly discussion of "the problems of Daniel." When one announces that he is going to discuss the book of Daniel, or deliver a series of lessons on the book, the question is often asked, How do you propose to handle the problems of Daniel? Admittedly, some problems exist, but I leave these for other scholars to solve. My view may be an over simplification, but here is a sample.

The problem of identification. Who was Daniel? Was he a fictitious character, or was he God's prophet in the sixth century B.C.? Liberal scholars have gone to great lengths to discredit Daniel as a prophet of the sixth century so that they could bring the date of the book bearing his name down to the second century B.C. Also, they attempt to establish multiple authorship in order to deny that Daniel was the sole author. One who believes that the Bible is a document written by inspired men, the answer is simple. Daniel was named as a younger contemporary twice because of his righteousness (Ezek. 14:14, 20); and once by the same prophet because of his wisdom (28:3). Two New Testament writers quote Jesus who called him "Daniel the prophet" (Matt. 24:15; Mark 13:14 KJV). Furthermore, Jesus and Paul testified that at the mouth of two witnesses or three, "Shall every word be established" (Matt. 18:16; II Cor. 13:1). This is sufficient testimony to resolve "the problem of identification." The book was written by Daniel the prophet of the sixth century B.C.

Second, there is the problem of languages in which the book was written. Why was it written in Hebrew, 1:1 - 2:4a, and in Aramaic, 2:4b - 7:28, and back to Hebrew, 8:1 - 12:13? Keil reasons that since the portion written in Aramaic pertained to the world kingdoms, Daniel wrote in the language of the world kingdoms. After reading the attempts of several other commentators to explain why it was so written, it seems obvious that we do not know. Since the Bible does not offer an explanation, one realizes that we cannot know.

Third, there is the problem of explicit and clearly delineated prophecies regarding events between the covenants, especially are these found in chapters 10 and 11. When Aaron and Miriam spoke against Moses, the Lord came down in a cloud and called the three to meet Him at the tent of meeting where He said to them: "Hear now my words: if there be a prophet among you, I Jehovah will make myself known unto him in a **vision**, I will speak with him in a **dream**. My servant Moses is not so; he is faithful in all my house: with him will I speak mouth to mouth, even **manifestly**, and not in dark speeches" (Num. 12:6-8). Accordingly, some prophecies were clearly manifested, while others had their meanings concealed. Again, God said to Moses, "I will raise them up a prophet from among their brethren, like unto thee; and I will put my words in his mouth, and he shall speak unto them all that I shall command him. And it shall come to pass, that whosoever will not hearken unto my words which he shall speak in my name, I will require it of him" (Deut. 18:18-19). Peter applied this prophecy to Jesus (Acts 3:22-23); but it also applied to all prophets whom God raised up as stated by God to Moses: "When a prophet speaketh in the name of Jehovah, if the thing follow not, nor come to pass, that is the thing which Jehovah hath not spoken: the prophet hath spoken it presumptuously, thou shalt not be afraid of him" (18:22). What Daniel said prior to chapters 10 - 11 came to pass, as did chapters 10 - 12. We conclude that since it was attributed to Daniel by Ezekiel and Jesus, and all that was foretold came to pass, Daniel is the author of the entire book.

Peter said that no prophecy of scripture was of private interpretation, "For no prophecy ever came by the will of man: but men spake from God, being moved by the Holy Spirit" (II Pet. 1:20-21). And the writer of Hebrews said, "God, having of old time spoken unto the fathers in the prophets by divers portions and in divers manners, hath at the end of these days spoken unto us in His Son" (Heb. 1:2). It seems obvious that the problem is not with the book of Daniel, but with the readers of Daniel. God could have inspired Daniel to prophesy clearly as well as "in dark sayings." This effort is devoted to understanding Daniel, and making application of his teaching to this present time, rather than trying to solve "the problems of Daniel."

However, there are some problems that are not easily resolved that require further discussion.

Now for a positive word. This book is written in hope that it will aid Christians in establishing a sustaining faith to meet the problems that could be faced in the evil day of national judgments. For, like Israel and the ancient world kingdoms, the people of this century are guilty of having lived recklessly in a fool's paradise. Concerning this attitude Amos said, "Ye that put far away the evil day [of judgment], and cause the seat of violence [reckoning] to come near" (Amos 6:3), which judgment, according to God's character, is inevitable.

In time of national judgment, the people of God suffer with the wicked of that nation. Jesus said that the Father in heaven, "Maketh his sun to rise on the evil and the good, and sendeth rain on the just and the unjust" (Matt. 5:45). But the flood brought on by the rain carries away the saint's possessions as well as that of the sinner; likewise, hurricanes may demolish the house of the good as it does the house of the evil. But there is a difference. The Christian looks beyond the storm and sees God working out His eternal purpose. He sees God as his Father and Jesus as his Saviour, each deeply caring for His own. He looks beyond the temporal to the eternal, and thanks God for the faith and hope that enables him to hold fast and not despair. God controls his universe and will carry the Christian through every crisis that comes.

Together with Daniel, the faithful people of Israel were in Babylon with the wicked because God's judgment came upon their nation. The prophet Ezekiel preached to captives that they should turn back to God, while Daniel was fulfilling God's mission for him by serving in positions of state. He influenced the rulers, and wrote for future generations, assuring both that God rules over all. His work was to encourage his generation, and assure future generations. What he saw in visions of the present and future, were intended to encourage his people. We see those of his day fulfilled in Christ and the present kingdom which are intended to encourage us. Faith in

God guarantees ultimate victory over all forces.

A basic presupposition is that the providence of God directs and controls the destiny of both individuals and nations. Faith in His providence should be a strong factor in every Christian's life. Providence is not miraculous; it is God working through His spiritual and physical laws in people and events. One may not understand how God brings events to pass, but he can understand the visible results when they come to pass. As affirmed in the book *God's Judgments and Punishments*, by Homer Hailey, He raises up nations, uses them for good or for judgments, and finally, because of their wickedness He destroys them by raising another nation which He uses to that end. And yet, He never violates the sanctity of the human will and choice, but uses both. And so with individuals, God elevates them to powerful positions and uses them to accomplish His purpose.

## Methodology

The methodology of Daniel is the same as that followed by Isaiah. Isaiah's book is divided into two sections: Part One, chapters 1-39; and Part Two: chapters 40-66. In Part One the prophet dealt with certain aspects of Israel's future, the judgment of Israel and of the nations, in which judgments the heathen nations were destroyed. In Part Two he dealt with Israel's future and with factors that prepared the people for the captivity, how to endure the humiliation of it, and the return from Babylonian captivity under Cyrus, whom God would raise up.

Daniel followed a similar pattern. In Part One, chapters 1-6, he dealt with certain factors of Israel's future; the rise, judgment, and destruction of future empires. These oppose the kingdom of God, but God is faithful to the captives. In Part Two, Daniel dealt with his dreams and visions that were intended to prepare the people to meet the oppositions of those empires. As in Isaiah, so in Daniel—faith in God and His promises would bring victory. As Isaiah pointed to the Messiah who would come, so Daniel pointed to His coming in the time of the most terrible and strongest nation yet seen in the world. Just as there had been a faithful remnant through each of the empires discussed by Daniel, there would be a faithful and triumphant remnant when the Messiah came during the fourth empire. As Isaiah sought to prepare Israel for judgmental captivity, so Daniel sought to prepare the ones in the judgmental captivity for future trials that would come upon the nation. Similarly, the need is to prepare today's saints to face the national judgments of God that will eventually befall us.

In writing a book such as this, one finds himself indebted not only to those writers who preceded him, but also to friends who helped and encouraged him. I am grateful to Arvid McGuire, who corrected the sentence structure and punctuation where needed, to Margie Garrett, who has read and made valuable suggestions to my books for the last thirty years, and to Ruby Stroup who painstakingly typed the manuscript and provided valuable suggestions as we worked together. I am also indebted to Doris Redo for reading the manuscript for typographical errors. My profound thanks goes to F. LaGard Smith and Stanley W. Paher, who helped and encouraged me in this endeavor. Thank you also goes to Hill Roberts for writing the Foreword and to Phil Roberts for letting me use his information on the Seventy Weeks that was a vital addition to this study. Thanks to all of the above named individuals for their labor of love, sacrifice of time, and contribution to the completed work. If I have overlooked anyone whose help I should have mentioned please charge it to the forgetfulness of a 97 year old man. His longevity excels his memory.

*Homer Hailey*

# Babylon and the Beginning of the Persian Period

In the midst of an immoral pagan society, the prophet
Daniel served the true God of heaven and comforted His
people. Daniel refused to defile himself with royal food
and wine, and he and his companions refused to bow
before the Babylonian king's image of gold.

# CHAPTER I

# Daniel in Babylon

Nabopolassar king of Babylon (626-605 B.C.) began his rise to power as a petty chieftain in southern Chaldea. At the death of the king of Assyria, which kingdom had ruled Chaldea, he overthrew the Assyrians, driving them out of Babylon, and took control of the city (625 B.C.). His son Nebuchadnezzar, whom Nabopolassar made commander of his army, marched against Nineveh, some 250 miles north of Babylon, defeating the Assyrian army; the remnant fled west to Haran (612 B.C.). Three years later (609 B.C.) a decisive battle defeated the Assyrians.

This was the battle that Pharaoh-Necho sought to reach when Josiah attempted to stop him and was killed at Megiddo. The Egyptian army was hindered by Josiah at Megiddo, but later marched north and took the city of Carchemish. The Egyptians taunted the Babylonians until a final battle erupted between Nebuchadnezzar's army and that of Necho in which the Egyptians were defeated.

According to four cuneiform tablets, discovered in the British museum by D. J. Wiseman in 1956, the Egyptians received a crushing defeat inflicted upon them at Carchemish in 605 B.C. "One result of this victory [at Carchemish] was that the Babylonians seem to have demanded hostages of

Judah as evidence of good faith toward Babylon, and it was this group which went into captivity [as hostages] in that third year of Jehoiakim (Dan. 1:1, 3), including the young man Daniel" (*ZPEB* II 22).

Nebuchadnezzar and his army pursued Necho and his army south as far as Judea where he received the news that his father had died. In rushing to Babylon to secure the throne for himself, Nebuchadnezzar took Daniel and his three friends, along with other hostages. Hear the words of Daniel, "And the Lord gave Jehoiakim, king of Judah, into his hand." This marked the beginning of God's use of Nebuchadnezzar and the Chaldeans in His conquest and destruction of the nations as foretold by the prophets.

## How Daniel Came to be in Babylon
## (vv. 1-2)

**Verse 1** *In the third year of the reign of Jehoiakim king of Judah came Nebuchadnezzar king of Babylon unto Jerusalem, and besieged it. 2 And the Lord gave Jehoiakim king of Judah into his hand, with part of the vessels of the house of God; and he carried them into the land of Shinar to the house of his god: and he brought the vessels into the treasure-house of his god.*

vv. 1-2. The opening sentence in the book of Daniel has given occasion to liberal critics to attack the authenticity and accuracy of information about the author. It tells of the coming of Nebuchadnezzar, king of Babylon, and his besieging the city of Jerusalem in the third year of the reign of king Jehoiakim, which presents a problem. The difficulty is that Jeremiah equated the fourth year of Jehoiakim's reign with the first year of Nebuchadnezzar, king of Babylon (Jer. 25:1). It was in this prophecy of Jeremiah that God foretold the bringing of Nebuchadnezzar and "the families of the north" against all the nations (vv. 8-26), which included "Jerusalem and the cities of Judah" (v. 18). Also, Jeremiah has Nebuchadnezzar at Carchemish in the fourth year of Jehoiakim's reign.

A discussion of the problem and proposed solutions is too involved to attempt such in a commentary of the purpose and intent of this one. Leupold devoted almost ten pages in his commentary, *Exposition of Daniel,* to a discussion of the problem. In an appendix in Young's commentary, *The Prophecy of Daniel,* he devoted three and a half pages and Wilson, in his *Studies in the Book of Daniel,* Book One, devoted an entire chapter (17 pages) to a discussion of the matter. For a fuller statement of the problem the reader is referred to these.

It should be observed that the king of Babylon "came...unto Jerusalem and besieged it," not that he took the city or that it fell to him. Furthermore, all that is said of Jehoiakim was that the Lord gave the king of Judah "into his hand"; he was now subject to the king of Babylon. Furthermore, the Lord gave "part of the vessels of the house of God" into his hand; these Nebuchadnezzar carried to Babylon and put them in the house of his god; not in the house of his own treasure. This seems to indicate a deep religious disposition on the king's part. He was an idolater and a worshipper of many gods. His respect for God and his understanding of God's nature will be evident as the history of the rise of Nebuchadnezzar and the Babylonian empire unfolds.

## Daniel and His Friends Selected for Training
### (vv. 3-4)

**Verse 3** *And the king spake unto Ashpenaz the master of his eunuchs, that he should bring in certain of the children of Israel, even of the seed royal and of the nobles; 4 youths in whom was no blemish, but well-favored, and skillful in all wisdom, and endued with knowledge, and understanding science, and such as had ability to stand in the king's palace; and that he should teach them the learning and the tongue of the Chaldeans.*

v. 3. Other than that Daniel was "of the seed royal and of the nobles," nothing is revealed, especially of his ancestry and background. However, although the ages of the four hostages is not stated, it is not unreasonable to assume from Nebuchadnezzar's requirements for their appointment as students (v. 4), that they were at least sixteen to twenty years of age. Also, the word "youths," translated "children" KJV, is from a word that allows the same conclusion. "The word is from the Hebrew *yeled* [translated] **child, young man, son, boy, fruit** (RSV...adds youth)" (*TWOT* I 379). It's range of usage is from the unborn fetus "fruit" (Ex. 21:22), to "young men" who had grown up with Rehoboam (I Kings 12:8) who was forty-one years of age at the time (I Kings 14:21). The "youths" of Daniel 1:4 could have been any age between 14 and 41.

Assuming the age of seventeen, as some have, they would have lived fourteen years of Josiah's reign of reform, and three years of Jehoiakim's reign of wickedness. As children of faithful God-fearing Jews, they were taught the law from babyhood; and possibly they could have heard some of the preaching of Jeremiah and other prophets. And being of "the seed royal," they would have had opportunity to hear discussions of the fall of Assyria at the hands of the Babylonians, and their final defeat at Haran and Carchemish. They were in a position to develop a youthful world-view on which to become useful men in the king's court.

Aside from being mentioned by two others, Daniel's name occurs only in the book bearing his name. The two occurrences are: three times in Ezekiel, a contemporary prophet in the land of Chaldea, in connection with Daniel's righteousness, wisdom, and knowledge (Ezek. 14:14, 20; 28:3); and by Jesus, who said, "When therefore ye see the abomination of desolation, which was spoken of through Daniel the prophet, standing in the holy place...then let them that are in Judea flee unto the mountains" (Matt. 24:15-16; Mark 13:14, KJV). This testimony of Jesus is sufficient for any one that believes the Bible to be the word of God, inspired by the Holy Spirit (II Pet. 1:20-21), to accept Daniel as a prophet of God. For the view of a liberal modernist, see the note below. [1]

---

[1] "The historical background of Daniel as was discovered immediately after its publication, is not that of the sixth, but of the second century" (p. 755). In

v. 4. Nebuchadnezzar was not only a great military leader who set out to conquer the world, but he was also a wise administrator. Jehovah said that He made the heavens and the earth, and that He gives to whom He will; and that He was giving all the lands into the hand of Nebuchadnezzar (Jer. 27:5-6). This began when he brought Daniel and those with him to Babylon. In anticipation of the need for court officials from the various conquered peoples, he selected and prepared qualified men to meet the court needs of the various conquered nations. That the four Hebrew youths were not the only ones being trained is indicated by their being compared to "the youths that did eat of the kings dainties" (Dan. 1:13).

It is impossible to determine whether Ashpenaz and the men over whom he was master were eunuchs in the generally accepted meaning of the word, or court officials; for in the Old Testament the word is used of both. Being of "the seed royal," one, or all of them, may have been descendants of king Hezekiah, for twice it is recorded that his yet to be born sons would be taken away, "and they shall be eunuchs in the palace of the king of Babylon" (Isa. 39:7; II Kings 20:17-18). It may be seriously doubted that the four were eunuchs when selected (Lev. 22:24; Deut. 23:1); and there is nothing said about their being made eunuchs or of their posterity. So, the question remains unanswered. However, the use of eunuchs in the literal sense may have been a wise practice. For they would not be detracted from their work because of home responsibilities; and they could be trusted around women at any place in the palace.

The king was very explicit in stating a "measuring line" by which they were selected, except for the word "youths." They shall be "youths," but like "eunuchs," as pointed out above, the

---

writing of the author's discrepancies in the book of Daniel, Pfeiffer observed (p. 757) "In the author's muddled mind" certain conquests occurred. He makes a further observation, "In conclusion, the author's information on the period preceding Alexander is extremely vague, being partly drawn from his imagination and partly from unreliable sources" (P. 758). And a final quotation, "What lies beyond December 165 is not historical reality but apocalyptic dream" (p. 759). Robert H. Pfeiffer, *Introduction to the old Testament* (New York: Harper & Brothers Publishers, 1948).

word *yedel* covers a large area of definite ages, ranging from a fetus (Ex. 21:22) to young men of Rehoboam's age (I Kings 12:4-10). The following two characteristics pertain to their physical appearance, "in whom was no blemish": physical defect; "but well-favored": handsome of features and physically impressive. Since they were to stand in the king's court, two additional qualities would add to their impressiveness. "Skilled in all wisdom, and endued with knowledge." Inasmuch as these were youths, their potential was elementary which could be developed. Possibly the phrase refers to ordinary intelligence, skill, and common sense. In handling the affairs of a vast empire being built by Nebuchadnezzar, his representatives, wise men or counselors, would need insight and comprehension of governmental affairs. Lack of wisdom, insight into causes and consequences, hinders the use of knowledge essential to proper government. "And understanding science and such as had ability to stand in the king's palace." This seems to be a summary of their wisdom and knowledge, that they had the ability to fulfill their purpose, i.e., to stand in the king's palace, "And that he should teach them the learning and the tongue of the Chaldeans." The "tongue" referred to the language, the ability to use it was essential to the position held by these men now and in future days." [2]

## (vv. 5-7)

**Verse 5** *And the king appointed for them a daily portion of the king's dainties, and of the wine which he drank, and that they should be nourished three years: that at the end thereof they should stand before the king.* **6** *Now among these were, of the children of Judah, Daniel, Hananiah, Mishael, and Azariah.* **7** *And the prince of the eunuchs gave names unto them: unto Daniel he gave the name of Belteshazzar; and to Hananiah, of Shadrach; and to Mishael, of Meshach; and to Azariah, of Abed-nego.*

[2] "An excellent summary of the inclusiveness of this "learning" is well summarized by T. G. Pinches, in *The International Standard Bible Encyclopedia* (I 592).

v. 5. These were fed from the king's table which included a daily portion designated by the king. Their food and wine was from the same menu as his. The course of study and provision for their support would continue for three years, at the end of which time they would stand before the king, either for examination, or to begin the service for which they were trained.

vv. 6-7. Though there may have been others, these four named were from the tribe of Judah. Ashpenaz (presumably) gave them new names. Here is a list of the meaning, and probable meaning of the Hebrew and new Babylonian names:

Daniel: "God has judged" (Young); Belteshazzar: "Protect his life" (Young). [3]

Hananiah: probably "Jehovah has been gracious" (Young); Shadrach: "Command of Aku (Aku being the moon god)" (Leupold). [4]

Mishael: "Who is what God is?" (Young); Meshach: "Who is what Aku (the moon god) is" (Leupold).

Azariah: "Jehovah has helped" (Young); Abed-nego: "Servant of Nebo," Nego being a corruption of Nebo (Leupold).

The names of the four sons of Judah indicated a relationship to Jehovah. One's name stands for all that he is. So apparently Ashpenaz renamed them to break that connection with the God of the Jews and make a new one relating them to the Babylonian deities.

In the fiery furnace episode (3:12-30), Shadrach, Meshach, and Abed-nego, the Chaldean names of the three, were used. But when Daniel asked for their help in prayer to God (2:17) he used their Hebrew names, Hananiah, Mishael, and Azariah. Daniel kept his Hebrew name Daniel throughout the book. If he used the Babylonian name given to him he would clarify it by saying "Daniel, whose name was Belteshazzar" (2:26, 4:8, etc.). The king used the name, Belteshazzar

---

[3] Edward J. Young, *The Prophecy of Daniel* (Grand Rapids, Michigan: Wm. B. Eerdmans Publishhing Co., 1949).

[4] H. C. Leupold, *Exposition of Daniel* (Columbus, Ohio: The Wartburg Press, 1949).

in the fourth chapter. Daniel kept his Hebrew name as faithfully as he did his diet. He wanted to maintain his identity with God.

Under His divine providence, God was preparing a prophet, Daniel, to represent Him before the throne of the heathen kings of two pagan empires. And by the same providence He was preparing the three friends to represent true faith in Him in time of severe trial.

## Faith and Providence
## (vv. 8-13)

**Verse 8** *But Daniel purposed in his heart that he would not defile himself with the king's dainties, nor with the wine which he drank: therefore he requested of the prince of the eunuchs that he might not defile himself.* **9** *Now God made Daniel to find kindness and compassion in the sight of the prince of the eunuchs.* **10** *And the prince of the eunuchs said unto Daniel, I fear my lord the king, who hath appointed your food and your drink: for why should he see your faces worse looking than the youths that are of your own age? so would ye endanger my head with the king.* **11** *Then said Daniel to the steward whom the prince of the eunuchs had appointed over Daniel, Hananiah, Mishael, and Azariah:* **12** *Prove thy servants, I beseech thee, ten days; and let them give us pulse to eat, and water to drink.* **13** *Then let our countenances be looked upon before thee, and the countenance of the youths that eat of the king's dainties; and as thou seest, deal with thy servants.*

v. 8. Daniel's purpose of heart regarding the food provided from the king's table, and his request of the prince of the eunuchs, indicated a maturity in harmony with the age suggested, between sixteen and twenty. Also, both his purpose and request reveal a faith determined to serve God although he was a captive in a foreign land. Whether the resolve was based on his knowledge of God's law concerning clean and unclean foods (Lev. 11; Deut. 14:3-21), or the fear that the meats had been sacrificed to idols, is uncertain. If the latter, he would be concerned that in eating of the sacrifice he would be having communion with the idol, that is, with the demon god that the idol represented, which would be sin (cf. Paul's statement, I Cor. 10:18-21). Probably both may have been in his mind. The petition was made in the form of a humble request, not a demand.

v. 9. Daniel's faith was rewarded by God's providence who made him find favor in the sight of the prince of the eunuchs.

v. 10. In spite of his compassion, the man responsible for Daniel feared for his life if he failed to carry out the king's command. Did his response of endangering his head if the experiment failed mean the bearing of the blame, or did it involve capital punishment, the losing of his head? Nebuchadnezzar commanded fear and respect, but not to the extent that his servant felt he could not deviate from his orders as long as the end result was the same. The prince of the eunuchs treated Nebuchadnezzar as though he would show no bigotry or tyranny so long as the best mental and physical health was attained.

vv. 11-12. The prince of the eunuchs appointed a steward to care for Daniel and his three friends - *Melsar* (KJV), "**guardian**, a Babylonian title, meaning dubious" (*TWOT* I 511). Apparently he was an officer of lower rank than the prince. In the same humble spirit that he had previously manifested, Daniel proposed that the steward feed them pulse for food and water to drink for ten days as an experiment. "Pulse" is from a Hebrew word which "refers to the action of sowing seed in the fields"; therefore, that which is sown. In this instance it means "vegetables" (*TWOT* I 252); and possibly grain. Of the "ten days," Keil says that it refers to "completeness or conclusion," and may refer to a long or short time. He says that here it is used of a short time, "because ten days are sufficient to show the effect of the kind of food on the appearance" (K & D *Daniel*). However, an indefinite or full time seems necessary and is preferable.

v. 13. At the end of the ten days they would compare the results between the four Hebrews and the young men who ate of the king's dainties and decide the matter.

## Results of the Experiment
## (vv. 14-16)

**Verse 14** *So he hearkened unto them in this matter, and proved them ten days.* **15** *And at the end of ten days their countenances appeared fairer, and they were fatter in flesh, than all the youths that did eat of the king's dainties.* **16** *So the steward took away their dainties, and the wine that they should drink, and gave them pulse.*

vv. 14-16. The steward gave heed to the suggestion of Daniel and tested them for the "ten days" by giving them the simple fare requested (v. 14). The fairer countenances would mean that their faces were free from blemishes and "acne" which mar the faces of so many youths. And of "fatter," the word "is used to describe healthy human beings" (*TWOT* I 128); in every way these four showed improvement over the youths who ate of the kings dainties (v. 15). The steward was convinced and took away the dainties and the wine, and continued to provide the simple food requested (v. 16).

From this example the citizens of our nation should learn a lesson. In my book, *National Judgments*, it was observed that our nation is entering a century faced with heavy doctor bills because of the poor general health of the people. And much of the poor health is due to the poor quality of food that is consumed. Much of the soil on which our food is grown is depleted of the minerals and other substances essential to the production of nutritious life-giving and sustaining foods. Chemical fertilizers, inorganic minerals, and insecticides are being substituted which may produce quantity, but not quality. Add to this poor food quality the billions of dollars spent on medicines and drugs in an effort to regain health, which so often burdens the body with the additional task of disposing of their poisonous effects. And instead of water, consider the untold barrels of carbonated "soft drinks" that are being consumed which, likewise, impair one's health. The four Hebrew youths refused the king's wine and asked for water, which, if the wine were mixed with water (as it was in most instances in those days) might be less injurious than the soda water of today. The remedy is more organic gardens, more careful selection of the foods consumed, and the elimination of the dead "foodless" foods on which so many attempt to survive today. Does the reader respond to this by pointing to the number of "old" people today and the longevity of their lives? If so, remember they began life consuming an entirely different diet than that of the present generation.

## God's Providence and Man's Knowledge and Wisdom (vv. 17-21)

**Verse 17** *Now as for these four youths, God gave them knowledge and skill in all learning and wisdom: and Daniel had understanding in all visions and dreams.* **18** *And at the end of the days which the king had appointed for bringing them in, the prince of the eunuchs brought them in before Nebuchadnezzar.* **19** *And the king communed with them; and among them all was found none like Daniel, Hananiah, Mishael, and Azariah: therefore stood they before the king.* **20** *And in every matter of wisdom and understanding, concerning which the king inquired of them, he found them ten times better than all the magicians and enchanters that were in all his realm.* **21** *And Daniel continued even unto the first year of king Cyrus.*

v. 17. The writer contrasted what God gave the four Hebrew youths and the special gift that He gave to Daniel. God's gifts included inherited and applied abilities (v. 4a), and their individual efforts and application under their tutors. The true believer looks upon his abilities and achievements as gifts from God. These include skill, proficiency, expertness, and dexterity in all learning of literature and language of the Chaldeans (v. 4b). Daniel's gift of "understanding in all visions and dreams" went beyond that of the other three; it involved a special miraculous gift of interpreting Nebuchadnezzar's dreams recorded in chapters 2 and 4, as also his own visions.

v. 18. "At the end of the days which the king appointed" was at the end of the three years (v. 5). At that appointed time the prince of the eunuchs brought in before the king all that had been selected from the various provinces (v. 10).

v. 19. The king "communed," spoke or interviewed, the group; he sought firsthand information. The four from Judah stood out as most worthy to stand before the king and therefore were selected.

v. 20. Nebuchadnezzar was a man of wisdom, well educated in the arts and sciences of his day, and could understand various languages (2:4). He was eminently qualified to "inquire of them" and to "commune" with them (v. 19). He examined the candidates himself.

Upon examination of the youths, the king found the four Hebrew youths to be the most outstanding. "In the matter of wisdom": a manner of thinking which seeks for the underlying causes and consequences of principles; "and understanding":—perception, prudence, regard, and discernment—"he found them ten times better than all the magicians and enchanters that were in all his realm." Concerning the expression, "ten times" see comments on verse 14; here it could mean a full or complete idea. The word for "magicians" described "some variety of occultist," and is the word for Egyptian magicians. The word translated "enchanters" (astrologer, KJV) occurs only in Daniel, and likewise describes "some variety of occultist," not always clearly distinguishable (*TWOT* I 86).

v. 21. There is no contradiction between Daniel's continuing "even unto the first year of king Cyrus," and that which said, "In the third year of Cyrus king of Persia a thing was revealed unto Daniel" (10:1). The first indicated the fact that Daniel spanned the entire period of the captivity, from the first to be carried away, even unto the announcement of the decree that the people of Israel could return to their homeland (II Chron. 36:22). The second revealed that Daniel did not return with those who did, but continued in Babylon, and in the third year of Cyrus' reign Jehovah revealed to him the future of the kingdom.

In God's providence, He acts and operates through His natural laws (laws of nature), spiritual laws, and man's respect for these and his moral conduct before Him. When individuals act out of a profound faith in God and respect for His will expressed in His natural and spiritual laws as these men did, God acts for their benefit and His glory.

## Application

As stated in the Preface, our primary objective in writing a brief commentary on the book of Daniel is to consider the incidents in the teaching and events of the prophet that encouraged the people of the captivity, and those that would encourage us in a time of judgment. In my book, *God's Judgments and Punishments*, it was pointed out repeatedly that judgment fell upon Judah and Jerusalem and the people of both, as also upon the heathen nations (e.g. Jer. 25:17-26). The providence of God shines forth in this chapter.

By God's providence the nation was in Babylon rather than Assyria; it was the Lord, who "gave Jehoiakim...into [Nebuchadnezzar's] hand" (v. 2). When a judgment befalls our nation, we can say, It is a judgment from God; we had it coming. He never judges a nation until He has given it ample time to repent.

The same providence that brought them into Babylon, the place of their judgment and captivity, preserved them while they were there. God raised up Daniel and his three friends to represent Him in Nebuchadnezzar's court. At the same time, He prepared and sent Ezekiel to the people that a remnant might be saved.

In whatever manner of judgment God may send upon this, or any nation, the saints can believe that in His providence God will look after His faithful people who may be among those upon whom the judgment is sent. And even to those who have not been faithful, He will seek them and provide for their repentance.

## For Our Encouragement

In every judgment, whether a world judgment, a national judgment, or an individual judgment, one can say that it is a righteous judgment. Each one receives according to his due.

In every national judgment God provides for His own. And though the righteous may suffer for the wickedness of others, it is a price that one pays for the privilege of living in a moral world in which all are free to choose their actions. If men choose to do evil, and I chose to live among them, I must suffer the consequence of my choice. Remember Lot and his wife. He chose to pitch his tent toward Sodom, and came to live in that city. He suffered the loss of all. His wife chose to look back, and she became a pillar of salt (Gen. 19:17, 26).

All judgments in time, even the most severe, eventually come to an end. About God's judgments one can say, "For when thy judgments are in the earth, the inhabitants of the world learn righteousness" (Isa. 26:9). They may not practice it, but they learn that righteousness pays while wickedness leads to destruction. As one of my University professors used to say about Job, "Piety pays; perversity punishes."

# CHAPTER II

# Nebuchadnezzar's First Dream

## NEBUCHADNEZZAR'S DREAM
## AND DEMAND OF THE WISE MEN
## (vv. 1-6)

**Verse 1** *And in the second year of the reign of Nebuchadnezzar, Nebuchadnezzar dreamed dreams; and his spirit was troubled, and his sleep went from him.*
*2 Then the king commanded to call the magicians, and the enchanters, and the sorcerers, and the Chaldeans, to tell the king his dreams. So they came in and stood before the king. 3 And the king said unto them, I have dreamed a dream, and my spirit is troubled to know the dream.*
*4 Then spake the Chaldeans to the king in the Syrian language, O king, live for ever: tell thy servants the dream, and we will show the interpretation. 5 The king answered and said to the Chaldeans, The thing is gone from me: if ye make not known unto me the dream and the interpretation thereof, ye shall be cut in pieces, and your houses shall be made a dunghill. 6 But if ye show the dream and the interpretation thereof, ye shall receive of me gifts and rewards and great honor: therefore show me the dream and the interpretation thereof.*

v. 1. As "And" was a connective between 1:21 and the events preceding the verse, so "And" (2:1) connects the content of chapter two with that of chapter one. This raises the question of the appointment of three years training (1:5, 19) and the second year of the king's reign (2:1) and Daniel's being included among the wise men (2:13). Was there sufficient time for the four Hebrews to complete the period of instruction? In Appendix I of his commentary, Young offered the explanation that in the Palestinian method of numbering the years of a reign, the part of the first year, however short, was numbered as the first year. But, "According to the Babylonian system only the first full year of reign was called the first year of a king's reign." He offered the following table to illustrate the time:

| BABYLONIAN | PALESTINIAN |
|---|---|
| Year of Ascension | First Year |
| First Year | Second Year |
| Second Year | Third Year |
| Third Year | Fourth Year |

This calculation fits the time element in Daniel's three years, chapter one, his "second year" in chapter two, and Jeremiah's "fourth" year of Jehoakim in Jeremiah 46:2.

In the second year of his reign, which would be soon after his return from Judea with the hostages, Nebuchadnezzar had a series of dreams which left him sleepless and his spirit greatly disturbed, deeply agitated. In ancient times great concern was given to dreams; for through these God often revealed His messages to men.

v. 2. Seeking a solution to his problem, and an interpretation to his dreams, for there seems to have been a number of them, one after another, the king sought help from his wise men. He "commanded"—the authority of the monarchs of those ancient kingdoms was absolute—that the wise men be brought in to reveal the dream and give its meaning. These were "magicians...and enchanters," which were introduced and the possible definitions given (1:20). To these officials were added, sorcerers and Chaldeans, and in verse 27 a fifth, soothsayers, is added to the list. Leupold said, "Though we are not absolutely certain in regard to the meaning of any of these terms we know their approximate import" (p. 83).

Sorcerers were a form of witchcraft, members of the occult.

Chaldeans seem to be a special class of wise men, the most important of the group. Probably they were the Babylonian priesthood which occupied a high place in the body classified as wise men. Soothsayers were a class of occultist magicians who predicted the future by cutting livers and by observing cloud formations. Being summoned, these came and stood before the king.

v. 3. When the wise men were assembled, the king told them that he had dreamed a dream which troubled his spirit "to know the dream," and to know its meaning.

v. 4. "The Chaldeans," the most important members of the wise men, seemed to act as spokesman for the group. At this point the language changed from Hebrew to Aramaic. Keil's explanation is offered in the Preface as a possible reason for the change; but actually one does not know the reason for the Bible does not say. The Chaldean speakers requested that the king tell them the dream and they would tell him its interpretation.

v. 5. The king was too smart for this. If they could not tell him the dream, then he could not depend on their interpretation. If they could do the former, he could trust the latter. Barnes took the position that the king had actually forgotten the dream, but Deane, Keil, Leupold, and Young hold the view that the king had not forgotten the dream, but was testing their ability to reveal such things.

"The thing"—literally, "the word"—"is gone from me"; that is the word demanding that they tell him the meaning of the dream and the interpretation. He tested their ability to tell him the meaning by their ability to tell him the dream also. The penalty for failure to do both would be personal destruction by cutting them to pieces and their houses destroyed. The places where they stood would be desecrated by being made a dunghill, a place of refuse.

v. 6. On the other hand, if they could tell him the dream and its interpretation he would reward them with "gifts and rewards and great honor." Therefore prove your claims to such powers, or suffer the consequences. Demonstrate your powers, or admit that you are frauds.

## The Failure of the Wise Men
## (vv. 7-13)

**Verse 7** *They answered the second time and said, Let the king tell his servants the dream, and we will show the interpretation.* **8** *The king answered and said, I know of a certainty that ye would gain time, because ye see the thing is gone from me.* **9** *But if ye make not known unto me the dream, there is but one law for you; for ye have prepared lying and corrupt words to speak before me, till the time be changed: therefore tell me the dream, and I shall know that ye can show me the interpretation thereof.* **10** *The Chaldeans answered before the king, and said, There is not a man upon the earth that can show the king's matter, forasmuch as no king, lord, or ruler, hath asked such a thing of any magician, or enchanter, or Chaldean.* **11** *And it is a rare thing that the king requireth, and there is no other that can show it before the king, except the gods, whose dwelling is not with flesh.* **12** *For this cause the king was angry and very furious, and commanded to destroy all the wise men of Babylon.* **13** *So the decree went forth, and the wise men were to be slain; and they sought Daniel and his companions to be slain.*

v. 7. The wise men in the king's court continued to press him to tell them the dream, and insisted that if he would tell them, then they could tell him its interpretation. The king's response stated an impossibility, even as he demanded an impossibility from them.

v. 8. His statement, "I know for a certainty" that you are stalling for time was false. He could not know this, just as they could not know or interpret the dream. The king's demands and threats were characteristic of the monarchs of that time.

v. 9. The king repeated his threat of their destruction, but expressed a second false charge against the wise men when he said, "For ye have prepared lying and corrupt words to speak before me." He was applying pressure. If he told them the dream this charge may have been true; but under the circumstances it was not correct, only his rashly spoken opinion. "Corrupt words" are companions to "lying words"; they were words intended to deceive and mislead. He concluded that they were stalling for time till the matter was forgotten, or until other matters occupied his mind. The king concluded the matter with a repetition of his point of view: "Therefore tell me the dream, and I shall know that ye can show me the interpretation thereof," which was a smart move on his part. The king was pressing them for an answer; while they stalled for time. If they could get an answer they could improvise an interpretation.

v. 10. The Chaldean's response to the king was true. There was no man among the wise men of Babylon who could do what the king demanded. But there was Daniel to whom God had given the power of "understanding in all visions and dreams" (1:17). They did not know this. On the plea that no man could do what the king commanded, and that "no king, lord, or ruler hath asked such a thing of any magician, or enchanter, or Chaldean," the spokesman made his plea.

v. 11. The request made by the king was so rare that only the gods, not man, "can show it before the king…whose dwelling is not with flesh." This was the point at issue: If the gods can do so, and you represent the gods, then why can you not answer my request? Though not yet apparent, the contest will be between the heathen gods and their representative wise men; and the true God and His representative wise men, Daniel and his three friends.

v. 12. This answer so reflected upon the king's judgment, in demanding that he tell them the dream and they would tell its interpretation, that he went into a rage. Being "angry and very furious," he commanded that all the wise men of Babylon should be destroyed. If they could not do what they were supposed to do, they were frauds worthy of death. Later a similar fit of uncontrolled temper was directed against the three Hebrew children (ch. 3).

v. 13. And so the decree went out that all the wise men of

Babylon should be slain, which included Daniel and his three companions.

## Daniel's Appeal to the King
## (vv. 14-16)

**Verse 14** *Then Daniel returned answer with counsel and prudence to Arioch the captain of the king's guard, who was gone forth to slay the wise men of Babylon;* **15** *he answered and said to Arioch the king's captain, Wherefore is the decree so urgent from the king? then Arioch made the thing known to Daniel.* **16** *And Daniel went in, and desired of the king that he would appoint him a time, and he would show the king the interpretation.*

v. 14. Arioch, the captain of the king's guard, who was responsible for carrying out the king's command to slay all the wise men, conveyed the message to Daniel. In response, "Daniel returned answer with counsel and prudence." Daniel answered judiciously with good taste and judgment, as he had done from the beginning (cf. 1:8, 12).

v. 15. Daniel asked Arioch, "Wherefore is the decree so urgent from the king?" Daniel's word "urgent" in his question to the king was defined by Keil to mean, "**to be hard, sharp,** hence, **to be severe.**" There was no need to be so harsh and hurried in the matter. The king's captain made known unto Daniel what was previously unknown to him.

v. 16. It seems Daniel appeared before the king in person, though he may have been represented by Arioch, the king's captain. Daniel requested a period of time at the end in which he would tell the king the dream and its interpretation. This request and promise showed Daniel's faith that God would give him the answer. The king, although he had accused the other wise men of stalling, granted the request to give the young wise man an opportunity to prove his worth as a "wise man."

# PRAYER–RESPONSE–PRAISE
## (vv. 17-24)

### Prayer (vv. 17-18)

**Verse 17** *Then Daniel went to his house, and made the thing known to Hananiah, Mishael, and Azariah, his companions:* **18** *that they would desire mercies of the God of heaven concerning this secret; that Daniel and his companions should not perish with the rest of the wise men of Babylon.*

v. 17. Although Daniel and his three companions were included in "the **rest** of the wise men of Babylon" (v. 18), apparently the four were not included with the group called before the king at the beginning (v. 2). When the request was granted, Daniel returned to his house and made known the matter to his three companions.

v. 18. The four carried their problem to "the God of heaven," praying for mercy from Him that they should not perish along with "the rest" of the wise men of Babylon. This strongly expressed their faith in the power and protection from the God of their fathers. It is the degree of faith saints need in the time of life-threatening judgments.

### Response (v. 19)

**Verse 19** *Then was the secret revealed unto Daniel in a vision of the night. Then Daniel blessed the God of heaven.*

The secret of the dream and its interpretation was made known to Daniel in a vision. Visions were used extensively by Jehovah in the Old Testament times by which God revealed Himself and His messages to the persons chosen for this purpose. One may see a vision while awake or asleep. The word occurs so often in the book of Daniel, 22 times in the singular and 10 times in the plural, that it must be defined. The word "places the emphasis and primacy on those dimensions which are extra-physical—something seen otherwise than by ordinary sight…a visual sight without corporeal presence" (*ZPEB* V 889). It was by extra-physical sight in Daniel's "vision of the night" that he saw the beasts of Nebuchadnezzar's dream. "Then Daniel blessed the God of heaven," he praised Him for the revelation.

### Praise (vv. 20-24)

**Verse 20** *Daniel answered and said, Blessed be the name of God for ever and ever: for wisdom and might are his.* **21** *And he changeth the times and the seasons: he removeth kings, and setteth up kings; he giveth wisdom unto the wise, and knowledge to them that have understanding:* **22** *he revealeth the deep and secret things; he knoweth what is in the darkness, and the light dwelleth with him.* **23** *I thank thee, and praise thee O thou God of my fathers, who hast given me wisdom and might, and hast now made known unto me what we desired of thee; for thou hast made known unto us the king's matter.* **24** *Therefore Daniel went in unto Arioch, whom the king had appointed to destroy the wise men of Babylon; he went and said thus unto him: Destroy not the wise men of Babylon; bring me in before the king, and I will show unto the king the interpretation.*

v. 20. In response to God's answering his prayer, Daniel offered a prayer of thanksgiving and praised the "name of God for ever and ever." He praised Him for His infinite wisdom and His absolute power by which He always acts in His eternal name. These are His, and His alone: they are the expressions of His Almighty Deity.

v. 21. Although it is said, "For every thing there is a season, and a time for every purpose under heaven" (Eccl. 3:1); it is also said, "He changeth the times and the seasons." God changes these when the need arises; they are under His control to be changed according to His might and wisdom. When His wisdom dictates the need for a change, "He removeth kings, and setteth up kings" (cf. Dan. 4:17). And since wisdom and knowledge are inherent in the nature of Godhood, being with Him in the creation (Prov. 3:19; 8:22- 31), these are His to give to whom He would. They are given to individuals who have the ability and disposition to use them aright. And, it can be said, God who gives these gifts to men, can take them from men.

v. 22. Daniel praised Him because He revealed to men the unknown and unknowable things apart from His revelation. These abide always in the darkness of ignorance and mystery except for His knowledge of them and His ability to reveal them to men. The light which makes these things known dwells only with Him. God's ability to "reveal the deep and secret things" was demonstrated in revealing to Daniel Nebuchadnezzar's dream and its meaning. With Him there is no distinction between the darkness and the light; all things are in the light of His knowledge and understanding, for there is no darkness with God.

v. 23. Daniel continued his prayer of praise and thanksgiving. In this strange land of Babylon there were differences between what he should do and should not do, and the might (power) to overcome whatever temptations he met (cf. 1:8, 20). He was grateful to God for revealing to him the secret of the king's dream. Although the revelation was made known to Daniel only (me), it was what "we" had desired and prayed for. He included the three (us) to share in the honor of the revelation.

v. 24. He could now go to Arioch, armed with the wisdom and might which he had received from his God in revealing the king's secret. He was concerned for the safety of the wise men and made intercession for them, who, in contrast later sought the destruction of Daniel and his companions (chaps. 3 & 6). By God's providence the wise men would now escape death. Daniel used this occasion to honor the power of his God above that of all gods.

## Daniel Honors His God
## (vv. 25-30)

**Verse 25** *Then Arioch brought in Daniel before the king in haste, and said thus unto him I have found a man of the children of the captivity of Judah, that will make known unto the king the interpretation.* **26** *The king answered and said to Daniel, whose name was Belteshazzar, Art thou able to make known unto me the dream which I have seen, and the interpretation thereof?*
**27** *Daniel answered before the king, and said, The secret which the king hath demanded can neither wise men, enchanters, magicians, nor soothsayers, show unto the king;* **28** *but there is a God in heaven that revealeth secrets, and he hath made known to the king Nebuchadnezzar what shall be in the latter days. Thy dream and the visions of thy head upon thy bed, are these:* **29** *as for thee, O king, thy thoughts came into thy mind upon thy bed, what should come to pass hereafter; and he that revealeth secrets hath made known to thee what shall come to pass.* **30** *But as for me, this secret is not revealed to me for any wisdom that I have more than any living, but to the intent that the interpretation may be made known to the king, and that thou mayest know the thoughts of thy heart.*

v. 25. Arioch lost no time in bringing Daniel before the king. He seems to have not relished the responsibility of putting the wise men to death. However, he made it an occasion to put in a word on his own behalf when he said, "I have found...," which stretched the matter somewhat. He was excited at having found a man from among the Hebrew captives who could tell the dream and interpret its meaning, a thing which all the wise men of Babylon could not do.

v. 26. The king seemed a bit suspicious, for he asked if Daniel were able to tell him the dream and its interpretation. Could this young Jew, a captive, do what seasoned Babylonian wise men failed to do?

v. 27. Daniel's response was that the King's demand was beyond the power of any wise men to answer. An attempt to define these various classes of wise men was made already (1:20; 2:2). Among them there were none who could do what was beyond human power.

The gods, figments of man's vain imagination, and fashioned by the skill of human hands from wood, metal, and stone which God had created, were as helpless to reveal the king's dream as the material from which they were made. The wise men upon whom the king depended for answers, were limited in their knowledge to the realms of creation, revelation, experience, and imagination. Creation and experience could not provide them with an answer. They were in no relationship to the source of revelation to receive an answer from Him. Imagination was useless unless the king should provide some basis on which to build, and this the king failed to do.

v. 28. But, there was "a God in heaven" who could reveal secrets; "and He had made known to the king Nebuchadnezzar what shall be in the latter days." The phrase, "the latter days" may not always refer to the period of the Messiah, but in this case it does. It extended into that period, as it was also used by Isaiah (2:2-4) and Micah (4:1- 4). Joel spoke of a period as "afterward," in which God would pour out His Spirit upon all flesh (Joel 2:28), which Peter referred to as "the last days" (Acts 2:17), and these last days as "these days," the present (Acts 3:24). The writer of Hebrews spoke of the termination of the period of the prophets as, "at the end of these days," at which time He has "spoken unto us in his Son" (Heb. 1:2; cf. 9:26). Peter added to his former word, saying that Christ "was manifested at the end of the times" (I Pet. 1:20). And finally, Daniel included in his expression "the latter days," the fourth world empire, the Roman Empire, which definitely was during the Messianic period.

v. 29. In the next two verses, Daniel spoke to the king, saying, "Thy thoughts came into thy mind upon thy bed, what should come to pass hereafter." At some former time God promised that as the maker of the earth and all things upon it, He would give "all these lands [of the nations] into the hand of Nebuchadnezzar the king of Babylon, my servant." These would serve him and his sons, "until the time of his own land come: and then many nations and great kings shall make him their bondman" (Jer. 27:5-7). It is uncertain at what point the king reached in the fulfilling of the promise, but apparently the thoughts of the king were upon future conquests, or upon the establishing of the kingdom's permanency. As God foretold the development of his conquests, he now informed him of the destiny of his empire. What should come to pass hereafter.

v. 30. Daniel hastened to tell the king that it was by no power of his own that he would reveal the dream and its meaning. But his ability was from the God of heaven who made known the interpretation of the dream, "and that thou mayest know the thoughts of thy heart." The king's thoughts were in his mind before he fell asleep. The dream was God's response to his thoughts.

## The Dream
### (vv. 31-35)

**Verse 31** *Thou, O king, sawest, and, behold, a great image. This image, which was mighty, and whose brightness was excellent stood before thee; and the aspect thereof was terrible.* **32** *As for this image, its head was of fine gold, its breast and its arms of silver, its belly and its thighs of brass,* **33** *its legs of iron, its feet part of iron and part of clay.* **34** *Thou sawest till that a stone was cut out without hands, which smote the image upon its feet that were of iron and clay, and brake them in pieces.* **35** *Then was the iron, the clay, the brass, the silver, and the gold, broken in pieces together, and became like the chaff of the summer threshing- floors; and the wind carried them away, so that no place was found for them: and the stone that smote the image became a great mountain, and filled the whole earth.*

v. 31. The great image which the king saw was not an idol, but a statue made of four metals and clay in the form of a mighty human being. It stood before the king in the bright-

# Identification of the Four Kingdoms

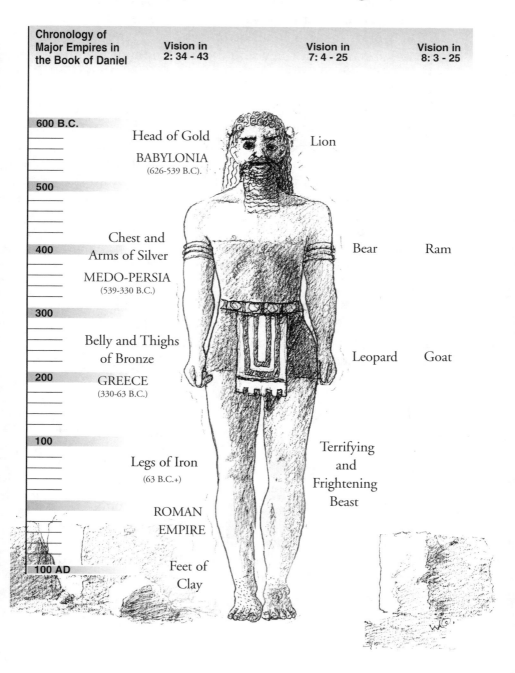

| Chronology of Major Empires in the Book of Daniel | Vision in 2: 34 - 43 | Vision in 7: 4 - 25 | Vision in 8: 3 - 25 |
|---|---|---|---|

**600 B.C.**

Head of Gold

BABYLONIA
(626-539 B.C.).

Lion

**500**

**400**

Chest and Arms of Silver

MEDO-PERSIA
(539-330 B.C.)

Bear

Ram

**300**

**200**

Belly and Thighs of Bronze

GREECE
(330-63 B.C.)

Leopard

Goat

**100**

Legs of Iron
(63 B.C.+)

Terrifying and Frightening Beast

ROMAN EMPIRE

**100 AD**

Feet of Clay

ness of shining metal. Its total appearance was awesome terror. The four metals blended into one human form indicated oneness or unity of some kind. Keil, quoting Kliefoth, said, "The world-power is in all its phases one, therefore all these phases are united in the vision in **one** [emphasis his] image." Keil attributed the following thought to Kliefoth, expressed in Keil's words, "The appearance of the colossal image was terrible, not only on account of its greatness and its metallic splendor, but because it represented the world-power of fearful import to the people of God" (K & D, *Daniel* 102).

vv. 32-33. Most commentators point out that the materials of which the image was composed degenerate from the most precious to the least valuable: from gold to silver to bronze to iron to clay. Young also points out that "only the head constitutes a unified whole." Of the remainder, the order is breast and arms; belly and thighs; legs and feet. The feet are further described as "part of iron, and part of clay."

vv. 34-35. While gazing intently at the gigantic statue, the king's gaze was attracted to a stone being cut out of a mountain without hands. The stone struck the feet of iron and clay, and beginning with their destruction, the image was broken to pieces, crushed, and ground to powder in reverse order: the feet of clay and iron, the brass, the silver, and the gold. And like the chaff of a summer threshing floor, they were carried away by the wind, "so that no place was found for them." They were totally destroyed; never again to exist. On the other hand, the stone that smote the image, "became a great mountain and filled the whole earth."

Nothing is said to indicate whether the stone accomplished the destruction of the image with one catastrophic blow, or whether the destruction was accomplished over a period of time. In a vision or dream sudden destruction would be possible, but in reality the accomplishment of the total destruction was probably by a series of blows over a period of time. Compare the destruction of the golden calf (Ex. 32:20) and Josiah's destruction of altars (II Chron. 34).

## DANIEL'S INTERPRETATION OF THE DREAM
## (vv. 36-45)

### The Head of Gold (vv. 36-38)

**Verse 36** *This is the dream; and we will tell the interpretation thereof before the king.* **37** *Thou, O king, art king of kings, unto whom the God of heaven hath given the kingdom, the power, and the strength, and the glory;* **38** *and wheresoever the children of men dwell, the beasts of the field and the birds of the heavens hath he given into thy hand, and hath made thee to rule over them all: thou art the head of gold.*

v. 36. Having revealed the dream, Daniel began his interpretation with the plural "we," which raises the question, who is included in the "we"? Leupold thinks he included his three friends, though they are not mentioned as being present. Young thinks he used the plural out of a sense of humility. Either is possible. However, when the total context is considered, it appears that Daniel included the three companions. They were included in praying to God on their behalf (v. 18), though the secret was revealed to Daniel (v. 19). When Daniel gave thanks to God for the revelation to Him, it was for what "**we** desired of thee; for thou hast made known unto us the king's matter" (v. 23). And at the conclusion of the matter, he requested that Nebuchadnezzar bestow special favors upon his three companions who played a part in the total picture (v. 49).

v. 37. The title "king of kings" by which Daniel addressed Nebuchadnezzar, was also used by Jehovah in telling Ezekiel how He would use the king (Ezek. 26:7). Though there are other explanations of the phrase suggested by various writers, it seems to me that it is in connection with the promise of Jehovah that He would give Nebuchadnezzar all the nations of the earth to serve him, which would include the subjection of the kings of those nations (Jer. 27:5-7). Daniel emphasized that it was God who gave him the great kingdom of Babylon and all

those subject kingdoms. He gave him the power to take possession, and the supreme power to rule. God gave him the glory,
shining splendor, that belongs to such an exalted position.

v. 38. The promise in Jeremiah 27:5-7 included the beasts of
the field which meant that the whole of any nation—the people, the beasts, and the birds—all that pertained to a nation
were under his kingship. "Thou art the head of gold." Probably the king personified the kingdom which, as the head of
gold, his kingdom would be the greatest of all. It was not the
greatest in territorial extent, but its importance as a kingdom
from the beginning of kingdoms, and from which the others
had originated (Gen. 10:10; 11:1-9), and its importance at the
time, gave it preeminence.

### The Second and Third Kingdoms (v. 39)

**Verse 39** *And after thee shall arise another kingdom
inferior to thee; and another third kingdom of brass,
which shall bear rule over all the earth.*

The second kingdom to appear is "another kingdom,"
which infers the thought that the head of gold signified a
kingdom, rather than the king, though he personified the
entire kingdom. Although these two kingdoms which followed: the Medo-Persian and Macedonian kingdoms were
inferior to the first, as indicated by the descending metallic values, they were world kingdoms. They will be discussed more
fully in chapter 7.

### The Fourth Kingdom—Iron and Clay (vv. 40-43)

**Verse 40** *And the fourth kingdom shall be strong as
iron, forasmuch as iron breaketh in pieces and subdueth
all things; and as iron that crusheth all these, shall it
break in pieces and crush.*

The identity of the fourth kingdom strongly favors the
Roman Empire. However, there are other views defended by

liberal scholars who strive to bring the date of Daniel to the second century B.C. For a rather lengthy list of these see Young's commentary, *The Prophecy of Daniel*, p. 74-75; and for his treatise in defense of the Roman Empire see his Appendix V, 275-294. The Roman Empire was strong as iron to conquer by crushing, breaking in pieces, and bringing the conquered peoples under its power and control. This was demonstrated by its conquest of the world, subduing the nations one by one.

> **Verse 41** *And whereas thou sawest the feet and toes, part of potters' clay and part of iron, it shall be a divided kingdom; but there shall be in it of the strength of the iron, forasmuch as thou sawest the iron mixed with miry clay.*

But there was a weak point in its structure: its feet and toes were part of iron and part of clay. And though it was a divided kingdom it remained strong as iron. But its division was not geographical, it was social and cultural. As iron and clay cannot be fused together, so Rome could not amalgamate its conquered peoples. It tried to do this by the introduction of emperor worship, but this failed.

> **Verse 42** *And as the toes of the feet were part of iron, and part of clay, so the kingdom shall be partly strong, and partly broken.*

The toes of the feet were made of miry clay. If the ten toes symbolized the conquered nations, ten being the symbolical number for fullness of power or rule (see my book, *Revelation an Introduction and Commentary*, p. 46), then here lies the empire's weakness. The empire had the strength of iron, but it was partly strong, or broken because of the miry clay.

> **Verse 43** *And whereas thou sawest the iron mixed with miry clay, they shall mingle themselves with the seed of men; but they shall not cleave one to another, even as iron doth not mingle with clay.*

Regarding the effort to mix the iron and the clay, "they shall mingle themselves with the seed of men; they shall not cleave one to another," just as the two elements, clay and iron, do not cleave one to another. Some have conjectured that this referred to the marriage of kings with princesses of other nations. Others suggest that it meant the intermarriage of the couples of differing nations. Keil commented, "The figure of mixing by seed is derived from the sowing of the field with mingled seed, and denotes all the means employed by the rulers to combine the different nationalities" (p. 109). Their failure to accomplish this goal was their point of weakness.

### The Fifth Kingdom: the Kingdom of God (vv. 44-45)

**Verse 44** *And in the days of those kings shall the God of heaven set up a kingdom which shall never be destroyed, nor shall the sovereignty thereof be left to another people; but it shall break in pieces and consume all these kingdoms, and it shall stand for ever.*

Although "kingdoms," not "kings," was the subject of Daniel's interpretation of the dreams, as said, "In the days of those kings,"—possibly kingdoms, at this point he does not specify which—God would set up His kingdom. These kings would be the rulers or who would rule over the world's kingdoms. The Hebrew word *melek* was used in the Old Testament of degrees of rulers from chieftains of city-states in Phoenicia (Gen. 26:1, 8) to Nebuchadnezzar "king of kings" (Ezek. 26:7) (*TWOT* I 508). This kingdom was "set up" by the "God of heaven" in the days of the rulers of the Roman Empire. In contrast to the earthly kingdoms which were all destroyed, this kingdom would never suffer destruction. This was the kingdom which was being received by the saints in the days of the Messiah (Heb. 12:28). Its sovereignty, the supremacy of the authority and rule of its king and citizens, would be permanent. It would never be left to another people or kingdom as happened to the world-empires of Nebuchadnezzar's dream.

The ruler of the kingdom set up by the God of heaven

would be "from everlasting" (Micah 5:2), as was God (Ps. 90:2), to the end of time when He will deliver the kingdom up to God the Father (I Cor. 15:24-28). And though the weapons of this kingdom would not be carnal weapons (Mic. 5:10; Zech. 9:10), His kingdom would break in pieces and consume the world kingdoms. The king would rule the nations from the throne of God (Rev. 12:5). He would rule them "with a rod of iron"; smiting them with the sharp sword that proceeds "out of his mouth," (Rev. 19:15), the word of God (Heb. 4:12). All the weapons, principles, and human wisdom by which world kingdoms are established, extended, and sustained, must bow in defeat and destruction before the "KING OF KINGS", by the sword of God's eternal truth, and the judgment of the King by that truth.

**Verse 45** *Forasmuch as thou sawest that a stone was cut out of the mountain without hands, and that it brake in pieces the iron, the brass, the clay, the silver, and the gold; the great God hath made known to the king what shall come to pass hereafter: and the dream is certain, and the interpretation thereof sure.*

This is the second time that Daniel mentioned that the stone was cut out without hands, indicating that it was produced by divine power without human agency. He added that it was cut out of a mountain, but does not identify the mountain. Some have identified it as mount Zion, but probably the only significance of its being mentioned is to give the stone's origin. Although early commentators endeavored to identify the stone, it is interesting to note that in explaining the significance of the dream, Daniel gave no interpretation to the stone. The significance of a small stone in comparison to a mountain from which it was cut, and that it grew into a mountain that filled "the whole earth" (v. 35), emphasized the divine origin, (see Psalm 87:1) and small beginning of the kingdom of God, and the ultimate greatness of it. Daniel closed his interpretation with the simple, but positive statement, that he had given a correct and sure explanation of the king's dream.

## The King's Response
## (vv. 46-49)

**Verse 46** *Then the king Nebuchadnezzar fell upon his face, and worshipped Daniel, and commanded that they should offer an oblation and sweet odors unto him.*

That the king was deeply impressed by Daniel's ability to reveal the dream and give the interpretation of it is revealed by his response. Daniel's accepting the worship and sacrifices offered him need not cause one to criticize him as having violated his religious training by accepting or receiving the obeisance as unto himself. For he had twice denied any honor as belonging to him; it all belonged to the God who revealed the dream and its interpretation (vv. 28, 30).

**Verse 47** *The king answered unto Daniel, and said, Of a truth your God is the God of gods, and the Lord of kings, and a revealer of secrets, seeing thou hast been able to reveal this secret.*

Furthermore, the king verified this when he bypassed Daniel and acknowledged God's supremacy to all gods and men, and acknowledged Him as the revealer of secrets. Through Daniel the king was honoring Daniel's God. But he acknowledged Him only as "God of gods," a God among gods; superior to other gods, but one of them. Furthermore, he saw Jehovah as a national god—"your God." The king had a long way yet to go in his learning of the One and only true God.

**Verse 48** *Then the king made Daniel great, and gave him many great gifts, and made him to rule over the whole province of Babylon, and to be chief governor over all the wise men of Babylon.*

The king honored Daniel as God's mediator or agent in revealing the dream and its interpretation. This was done in four ways: 1) by making him great in his kingdom and before its people; 2) by giving him many great gifts, but he does not indicate what they were; 3) by making him ruler over the province of Babylon; 4) and by elevating him to the position of chief governor over all the wise men of Babylon. Daniel demonstrated a mark of greatness by humbly and graciously accepting these without allowing them to affect his spiritual disposition and faithfulness towards his God.

**Verse 49** *And Daniel requested of the king, and he appointed Shadrach, Meshach, and Abed-nego, over the affairs of the province of Babylon; but Daniel was in the gate of the king.*

The honors promised to the seer were followed by another expression of the true greatness of Daniel. His three friends had stood by him when he learned of the king's decree that all wise men of the province should die; they had joined him in praying to God for wisdom in responding to Nebuchadnezzar's demand (vv. 17-18). Daniel wished to share his honors with the three companions by requesting that the king appoint them over affairs of Babylon, which the king granted. However, Daniel retained the more important role of a place at the gate, the seat of government and its administration—the civic center of a city.

## Application

From this dream and Daniel's explanation of its meaning, the people could be assured by two things; 1) God was in control. In His providence the four world empires that would rise in succession would all come to an end by God's mighty providence and power, accomplished by the stone cut out without hands. 2) By His providence and power, the kingdom promised by the prophets before the captivity would be established some time during the sovereignty of those kingdoms. Since that kingdom would grow out of the kingdom of Israel, they would be encouraged to know that the kingdom would not end before God's determination of its time.

In the midst of any judgment of our nation, be assured that its destiny rests in the hands of God. If it is unfit to live longer, He will judge this nation and bring it to an end. But if its people repent and turn to Him, the nation will continue. But whether it repents and continues as a nation, or is destroyed, our consolation is that His kingdom will never be destroyed. What was promised through Daniel is now a reality and we are citizens of it. This assurance should make every saint, in every kind of judgment or national calamity, lift his heart and eyes heavenward in faith. If God fulfilled His promise of such a kingdom, and I am a citizen of it, He will fulfill the promises of the covenant which made me a citizen of that kingdom.

# CHAPTER III

# Nebuchadnezzar's Golden Image: Faith Tested in a Fiery Trial

## The Golden Image and the Kings Command (vv. 1-7)

**Verse 1** *Nebuchadnezzar the king made an image of gold, whose height was threescore cubits, and the breadth thereof six cubits: he set it up in the plain of Dura, in the province of Babylon.*

At what point during the reign of king Nebuchadnezzar he built the golden image is unknown. Though some have guessed, any suggestion is nothing more than a guess. That it was at the height of his conquest of the nations promised to him would be the most plausible. What was the image? a god? himself? or was it a monument to world dominion and his own power as king? as thought by some. This last guess seems the most probable, but we are left without proof. However, the king said to the three, "Is it of purpose,…that you serve not my god, nor worship the golden image which I have set up?" (v. 14). This suggested that it was an image of a god, an object of worship. The image was ninety feet high and nine feet in width; and it was made of gold. But was it solid gold, or made of wood, or a cheaper metal, and overlaid with gold? Again, we are not told, but the latter is probable. The possibility of the latter is indicated by the golden altar in the Jewish tabernacle. It was called the "golden altar" (Heb. 9:4), but it was made of acacia wood and overlaid with gold (Ex. 30:1, 3).

Another unanswered question is where was the plain of Dura located. The name is mentioned three places in the Bible. But since the place nearest to them was in the province of Babylon, it was probably near the city of Babylon.

> **Verse 2** *Then Nebuchadnezzar the king sent to gather together the satraps, the deputies, and the governors, the judges, the treasurers, the counsellors, the sheriffs, and all the rulers of the provinces, to come to the dedication of the image which Nebuchadnezzar the king had set up.*

The dedication of the image and its significance needed to be properly impressed on the people of his kingdom. To insure this the king required representatives from all classes of officials present. Seven specific offices were named, plus "all the rulers of the provinces" were at the gathering. The precise official position of the seven named is so uncertain that any attempt to relate them to our national rulers is omitted. Daniel's naming them indicated his thorough acquaintance with the organization of Nebuchadnezzar's empire and its provinces. The large number and their presence may shed light on the period of his reign indicating the height of his world conquest.

> **Verse 3** *Then the satraps, the deputies, and the governors, the judges, the treasurers, the counsellors, the sheriffs, and all the rulers of the provinces, were gathered together unto the dedication of the image that Nebuchadnezzar the king had set up; and they stood before the image that Nebuchadnezzar had set up.*

When these various officers from the provinces (Daniel names them a second time) gathered for the dedication, "they stood before the image." This probably signified their amazement at its size, and their respect for the king and what the image signified. At least, they stood ready to pay to both whatever homage would be commanded of them.

**Verse 4** *Then the herald cried aloud, To you it is commanded, O peoples, nations, and languages,*

A herald, "an official formerly charged with making royal proclamations," opened the occasion with an announcement of the king's command, addressed to the "peoples, nations, and languages." Inasmuch as this phrase occurs six times in the book of Daniel (3:4, 7; 4:1; 5:19; 6:25; 7:14), each word should be defined. The Aramaic word for "people" is so similar to the Hebrew, that *The Theological Wordbook of the Old Testament* referred to the Hebrew for its definition. The Hebrew "*am* is used largely for a group of people or for people in general." And for "nations," it said, "The term *gôy* is used especially to refer to specifically defined political, ethnic, or territorial groups of people without intending to ascribe a religious or moral connotation" (I 153, 154). "Language" is simply the tongue or speech of the particular people. The combination of the three words seemed to be an expression intended to include all peoples of the earth or the area discussed. It was used also of the Messiah's kingdom (7:14).

**Verse 5** *that at what time ye hear the sound of the cornet, flute, harp, sackbut, psaltery, dulcimer, and all kinds of music, ye fall down and worship the golden image that Nebuchadnezzar the king hath set up;*

Like the officials named in verses 2 and 3, the six kinds of musical instruments named would be so different from ours that any attempt to identify them would be of little value. At the sound of the cornet, flute, harp, sackbut, psaltery, and dulcimer, "all kinds of music" added, all those present were to "fall down and worship the golden image." To the pagans this would be without conscientious objection, for it would be only another god added to those which they already worshipped. But it would be a different matter with the Jews.

**Verse 6** *and whoso falleth not down and worshippeth shall the same hour be cast into the midst of a burning fiery furnace.*

The herald announced next the penalty for not obeying the king's order. They would be "cast into the midst of a burning fiery furnace." Would the furnace have been burning already, as suggested by, "the same hour"; or would it have been prepared, waiting to be ignited? If burning already, this would suggest one of three things: the king expected opposition to his command on the part of some; it was kept burning continuously because of continual use in daily affairs; or it was burning as a determent to disobedience. The second possibility is most likely, if the fiery furnace was a brick kiln which was regularly used in the production of bricks for construction purposes in Babylon.

**Verse 7** *Therefore at that time when all the peoples heard the sound of the cornet, flute, harp, sackbut, psaltery, and all kinds of music, all the peoples, the nations, and the languages, fell down and worshipped the golden image that Nebuchadnezzar the king had set up.*

When the musical instruments began, all are named again, except the dulcimer (bagpipe, KJV), the people fell down and worshipped the image with three exceptions. Daniel's three friends refused to obey the king's command.

## Three Friends Charged With Sedition (vv. 8-12)

**Verse 8** *Wherefore at that time certain Chaldeans came near, and brought accusation against the Jews.*

Whether "the certain Chaldeans" were ethnic or court astrologers (2:2) is uncertain. Keil and Young think the word designates an ethnic relationship; Leupold thinks it refers to court astrologers. The latter quoted the translation of "accusations" as "accuse maliciously" (from Biggs, Driver, Brown) which lends support to his position that they are of the priest-ly caste. Their charge against the three Jews leaves the appearance that they were using a religious charge to accomplish a political end.

> **Verse 9** *They answered and said to Nebuchadnezzar the king, O king, live for ever.* **10** *Thou, O king, hast made a decree, that every man that shall hear the sound of the cornet, flute, harp, sackbut, psaltery, and dulcimer, and all kinds of music, shall fall down and worship the golden image;* **11** *and whoso falleth not down and worshippeth, shall be cast into the midst of a burning fiery furnace.* **12** *There are certain Jews whom thou hast appointed over the affairs of the province of Babylon: Shadrach, Meshach, and Abed-nego; these men, O king have not regarded thee: they serve not thy gods, nor worship the golden image which thou hast set up.*

They reminded the king of his decree and then made their charge. They named Daniel's three friends, and then virtually charged the king with having set these men over the affairs of the province; and charged the three Jews with having refused to obey his command to worship his god. The whole accusation smacks of envy and jealousy on the part of the accusers. These men (probably willfully) had forgotten that through these men and Daniel their lives had been spared (2:24). Indebtedness based on favors is soon forgotten!

## The Faith of the Three is Challenged
## (vv. 13-15)

> **Verse 13** *Then Nebuchadnezzar in his rage and fury commanded to bring Shadrach, Meshach, and Abed-nego. Then they brought these men before the king.*

In an explosive burst of temper, Nebuchadnezzar demanded that Shadrach, Meshach, and Abed-nego be brought in before him.

**Verse 14** *Nebuchadnezzar answered and said unto them, Is it of purpose, O Shadrach, Meshach, and Abednego, that ye serve not my god, nor worship the golden image which I have set up?*

Whether the king's question should be, "Is it true?" (KJV), or, "Is it of purpose? [of evil intent?]" (ASV), is uncertain. Based on a recent archaeological discovery, commentators have returned to the translation of the King James Version. We would say, "Did you do that on purpose?"

As observed earlier, the king's reference to "my god," and of "the golden image," indicates that the golden image was an idol god.

**Verse 15** *Now if ye be ready that at what time ye hear the sound of the cornet, flute, harp, sackbut, psaltery, and dulcimer, and all kinds of music, ye fall down and worship the image which I have made, well: but if ye worship not, ye shall be cast the same hour into the midst of a burning fiery furnace; and who is that god that shall deliver you out of my hands?*

Evidently the king suspected the Chaldeans of ulterior motives in charging the three as they did; therefore he gave them a second chance. By this he manifested a spirit of fairness. Also, by offering them this additional chance he would have his own eyewitness evidence on which to make a judgment. If, when you hear the instruments of music, "ye fall down and worship the image which I have made, well," or, good; you shall escape death. But if not, it is the furnace of fire for you, "And who is that god that can deliver you out of my hands?" Had the king forgotten his experience and declaration concerning the true God? (cf. 2:46-49). Probably it was not an intentional reflection or insult to God, but the expression of his own conviction that even He could not deliver the men from the fiery furnace. This may have been the reason for heating it seven times hotter than was usual (v. 19).

# THEIR FAITH – ONE OF CONVICTION
## (VV. 16-18)

**Verse 16** *Shadrach, Meshach, and Abed-nego answered and said to the king, O Nebuchadnezzar, we have no need to answer thee in this matter.*

A stronger declaration of a faith in Jehovah cannot be found anywhere than that expressed by these three men. Their response should not be interpreted as one of insolence or disrespect for the king, but of determination, based on a firm belief of their faith. Young translates the answer as follows: "We have no need with respect to this matter to make defense before thee" (p. 90). Instead, they were putting their total trust in God.

**Verse 17** *If it be so, our God whom we serve is able to deliver us from the burning fiery furnace; and he will deliver us out of thy hand O king.*

This total trust is further revealed in their answer. If God sees fit, He is able to deliver them from the king's hand; and He will do so.

**Verse 18** *But if not, be it known unto thee, O king, that we will not serve thy gods, nor worship the golden image which thou hast set up.*

However, if, for some reason known only to Himself, He should not deliver them from the fiery furnace, they were completely subject to His will—"But if not"—His will be done; they cannot, under any circumstance in good conscience, worship the image or serve the king's gods. A second chance was not necessary because they stood firm in their decision. There was no need to answer with arguments about their failure to submit to the king's edict. This expression of faith was from themselves apart from Daniel. He was not there to give moral support.

## The Confidence of Faith Tested
## (vv. 19-23)

**Verse 19** *Then was Nebuchadnezzar full of fury, and the form of his visage was changed against Shadrach, Meshach, and Abed-nego: therefore he spake, and commanded that they should heat the furnace seven times more than it was wont to be heated.*

This response of the three men tended further to infuriate the king. "The form of his visage" that is, the image, or "attitude" (*TWOT* II 1065) revealed by the look on his face, changed toward Daniel's three friends. The king's anger led him to speak foolishly in commanding that the furnace be heated seven times hotter than usual. But this was not unusual; men seldom act or speak rationally when angry or in a rage. (Cf. Moses who, when angry, "spake unadvisedly with his lips" Ps. 106:32-33).

**Verse 20** *And he commanded certain mighty men that were in his army to bind Shadrach, Meshach, and Abed-nego and to cast them into the burning fiery furnace.*

There would be no slip-up in carrying out the king's order, he commanded the strongest from among his soldiers to carry out the edict. Oftentimes these mighty, or valiant men were army heroes.

**Verse 21** *Then these men were bound in their hosen, their tunics, and their mantles, and their other garments, and were cast into the midst of the burning fiery furnace.*

Because of the urgency of the king's command, the three men were cast into the fiery furnace in the clothes they had worn to the dedication, a truly royal occasion. The difficulty in identifying the various garments worn by the three men is indicated by the various translations of the commentators and the versions. Translation from two commentators and two versions

will suffice to illustrate my point. Commentators: Leupold—
"boots, leggings, caps, robes"; Young—"mantles, trousers, hats,
their garments." Versions: New King James Version—"coats,
trousers, turbans, other garments"; New International Version—"robes, trousers, turbans, other clothes."

> **Verse 22** *Therefore because the king's commandment*
> *was urgent, and the furnace exceeding hot, the flame of*
> *the fire slew those men that took up Shadrach, Meshach,*
> *and Abed-nego.*

The reader should have the picture of a furnace in his mind.
Probably it was round, probably ten feet or more in diameter,
perpendicular for some eight feet or more, then inclining at
the top until it reaches a circular funnel into which the men
were cast. There would have been a ladder, or steps, leading to
the top, where the condemned were transported by the soldiers. The fire was so fierce that flames were coming out the
top and slew the soldiers. The death of these valiant and faithful servants of the king was the result of his fierce and
uncontrolled temper. In Babylon many brick-kiln or smelting
furnaces were used during that period. Earlier in Bible history
(Genesis 11:3) we find them burning bricks for the tower of
Babel.

> **Verse 23** *And these three men, Shadrach, Meshach, and*
> *Abed-nego, fell down bound into the midst of the*
> *burning fiery furnace.*

Into the midst of such a fierce fire the three men were cast
bound in their clothes. Immediate death was expected by all
spectators.

## Trust—The Conviction of True Faith—Vindicated (vv. 24-27)

> **Verse 24** *Then Nebuchadnezzar the king was*
> *astonished, and rose up in haste: he spake and said unto*

*his counsellors, Did not we cast three men bound into the*
*midst of the fire? They answered and said unto the king.*
*True, O King.*

In our mental picture of the furnace, there would be
an opening at the base through which the draft of air could
flow, thereby intensifying the heat from the burning material.
Also, it would be a means whereby men could look into the
fiery furnace. In his amazement and astonishment, the king
rose—probably he sprang to his feet, for instead of seeing
three bound men being consumed by the fire, he saw four
men walking, though the three had been securely bound. The
fact that they were bound added to their helplessness, and
to the magnitude of the miracle. To be certain that his eyes
were not playing tricks on him, the king asked if they had cast
three men into the furnace. To this they replied, "True, O
king."

**Verse 25** *He answered and said, Lo I see four men loose,*
*walking in the midst of the fire, and they have no hurt;*
*and the aspect of the fourth is like a son of the gods.*

More than being astonished and amazed, the king was star-
tled at what he saw. Instead of seeing three men, he saw four.
Instead of being bound, they were loosed. Instead of lying
helplessly on a bed of hot coals, they were walking about.
Instead of being roasted (cf. Jer. 29:22), they received no
injury. Instead of the fourth having the appearance of ordinary
men, he had the appearance of "a son of the gods." Just how
Nebuchadnezzar would recognize the appearance of "a son of
the gods," we know not. But there was something so striking
about him that it brought forth the exclamation "a son of
Deity" (Young). He spoke from the viewpoint of a pagan and
pagan deities.

The several components of this verse, are so amazing that
they make it exceedingly vulnerable for attacks by liberal theologians and skeptics. But Clarence Macartney said in one of
his sermons, "One's acceptance of miracles depends on

whether he spells his god with a capital 'G'." When one accepts the fact that "God created the heavens and the earth, and all things therein," all miracles within the scope of that reality are believable. If one rejects that premise of God the Creator, then God becomes the proposition for debate, not the miracle.

> **Verse 26** *Then Nebuchadnezzar came near to the mouth of the burning fiery furnace: he spake and said, Shadrach, Meshach, and Abed-nego, ye servants of the Most High God, come forth, and come hither. Then Shadrach, Meshach, and Abed-nego came forth out of the midst of the fire.*

The king came near enough to the opening of the furnace that he could be heard by the three men within it, whom he called by name. Furthermore, he addressed them as "servants of the Most High God," and commanded them to come forth. The three responded by coming "forth out of the midst of the fire" where they had been cast.

> **Verse 27** *And the satraps, the deputies, and the governors, and the king's counsellors, being gathered together, saw these men, that the fire had no power upon their bodies, nor was the hair of their head singed, neither were their hosen changed, nor had the smell of fire passed on them.*

Of the seven official titles named earlier (vv. 2-3), only four of the seven are mentioned among these gathered about the three when they came out of the furnace. But this was a sufficient number to bear ample testimony to the exceeding greatness of this miracle. They could bear witness to the faithfulness of the things named in verse 25, but also they could testify to the fact that: The fire left no mark on their bodies; the hair of their heads were not singed; their clothes suffered no change; and no smell of fire had been left upon them.

## The Effect of the Miracle on Nebuchadnezzar (vv. 28-30)

**Verse 28** *Nebuchadnezzar spake and said, Blessed be the God of Shadrach, Meshach, and Abed-nego, who hath sent his angel, and delivered his servants that trusted in him, and have changed the king's word, and have yielded their bodies, that they might not serve nor worship any god, except their own God.*

Nebuchadnezzar was greatly impressed and deeply moved by the wonderful miracle he beheld, but it failed to do for him what it should have done. To him God was still the tribal deity of the three men. The king praised their faith in Him, and their refusal to worship any other god than their own. Also, he praised them for their willingness and readiness to offer their bodies to the flame in demonstration of their faith. He considered the fourth man in the furnace to have been an angel sent by their God to deliver them. Although the fourth man is not otherwise identified, I have long thought of Him as the pre-incarnate Word of God, the Messiah who came by means of the virgin birth.

**Verse 29** *Therefore I make a decree, that every people, nation, and language, which speak anything amiss against the God of Shadrach, Meshach, and Abed-nego, shall be cut in pieces, and their houses shall be made a dunghill; because there is no other god that is able to deliver after this sort.*

The king found himself in a difficult situation. As Leupold aptly observes, he cannot afford to offend his national gods by acknowledging Jehovah as the only true God. Neither can he afford to offend a God whose power enabled Him to perform the miracle he just witnessed. So, instead of confessing Jehovah as the only true God, he issued a decree that no one should speak a word against the God of the three Jews. To violate the decree would draw the same penalty as announced in 2:5. And although He was considered as the tribal God of the three men, there was no one who could deliver as He had done. He praised the three men for their faithfulness and willingness to offer their bodies as a testimony to their faith.

**Verse 30** *Then the king promoted Shadrach, Meshach, and Abed-nego in the province of Babylon.*

To show his respect for their God, the king promoted Shadrach, Meshach, and Abed-nego to higher positions in the province.

The question may be asked by an inquirer: Where was Daniel throughout the stirring scenes of this chapter? Daniel was not classed as one of these whom the king summoned to come to the dedication of the image. He was not a satrap, deputy, judge, treasurer, counsellor, sheriff, or ruler of a province as were Shadrach, Meshach, and Abed-nego were (cf. 2:49, 3:2).

## For the Encouragement of Saints in Time of Judgment

The faithful saints of God were in captivity because of the wickedness of the people of the nation as a whole which brought on a national judgment. We know not when, nor what will be the nature of God's judgment on our nation; but knowing the nature and character of God, we believe His judgment is inevitable. In the midst of such judgments, saints of God need encouragement, and the book of Daniel provides that encouragement since it was written during such a time. The source of encouragement is the trust of these three men based on genuine faith and conviction.

Consider also a prophecy of Isaiah as a background for our application. In chapter 42 of his book, Jehovah promised to send His Servant, the Savior and Redeemer, into the world whom He would give "for a covenant of the people [the Jews], for a light of the Gentiles" (vv. 1-9). But before that time He would bring a judgment upon the people because of their wickedness (vv. 14-25). However, throughout these trying experiences God made the following promise: "When thou passest through the waters, I will be with thee; and through the rivers, they shall not overflow thee; when thou walkest through the fire, thou shalt not be burned, neither shall the flame kindle upon thee" (43:2). Earlier God promised that when He would bring up the Assyrian army as an overflowing river and it should pass through Judah and threaten Jerusalem, coming "even to the neck" of the city, He would be with the city: "O Immanuel" God be with us (Isa. 8:5-8).

Under the reign of Hezekiah, the son of Ahaz, this promise was put to the test. While the army of the Assyrian King Sennacherib was besieging and taking cities in Judea, this Assyrian King sent a large detachment to besiege Jerusalem. Hezekiah, Isaiah, and others of the city were praying to Jehovah and trusting Him for deliverance. In answer to these prayers, expressions of faith and trust in Him, Jehovah responded by sending his angel, likely the same angel in the fiery furnace, who destroyed 185,000 of the Assyrian army in one night (Isa. 36—37 esp. 37:33-38). God fulfilled His promise concerning the rivers. He was with His faithful people when threatened by the overflowing army of Assyria.

These three men, Shadrach, Meshach, and Abed-nego, now faced the test of fire. It is quite possible, even probable, that they remembered the promise of Jehovah through Isaiah, and His deliverance of Jerusalem when threatened by the Assyrians. If so, this would give them courage when they faced the fiery furnace of Nebuchadnezzar's rage. What Jehovah promised figuratively in Isaiah, He demonstrated literally in the three Hebrew children in the fiery furnace of Daniel.

This is certainly a source of encouragement to saints in any period of judgment or persecution. God fulfilled the promise to the Jews as he was represented by an angel in the threat of Sennacherib, and by a divine messenger in the furnace with the three of His faithful servants. And as the saints of New Testament days faced the fiery trials of life as Christians, He was with them (I Pet. 1:6-9; 4:12), so also He will be with us (Heb. 13:5-6). But this assurance is only for those who face these judgments with the degree of faith and conviction possessed and demonstrated by the three of the captivity.

# CHAPTER IV

# Nebuchadnezzar's Second Dream: A Great Tree Cut Down

## CONCLUSION OR INTRODUCTION?
### (vv. 1-3)

**Verse 1** *Nebuchadnezzar the king, unto all the peoples, nations, and languages, that dwell in all the earth: Peace be multiplied unto you.*

There is a question among commentators whether verses 1-3 should be considered the conclusion to chapter three, or the introduction to chapter four. A definite answer is likely impossible, for it could be either. But evidence at hand indicates that it is an introduction to chapter four. Nebuchadnezzar spoke expressing the wish that peace be multiplied and extended to the peoples of all the earth. The Aramaic word translated "peace" has virtually the same meaning in Aramaic and Hebrew. It may mean "absence of strife," and also it may mean "be complete" in "welfare [and] prosperity" (*TWOT* II 1080). In this instance it probably means welfare and prosperity, for it seems to have been a time in the life of the king that was free from strife.

**Verse 2** *It hath seemed good unto me to show the signs and wonders that the Most High God hath wrought* *toward me. 3 How great are his signs! and how mighty are his wonders! his kingdom is an everlasting kingdom, and his dominion is from generation to generation.*

The king extolled and eulogized "the Most High God" for the signs, wonders, and supernatural acts of God shown toward him, intending to demonstrate His presence and produce faith. These signs and wonders wrought toward the king demonstrated a power beyond that possessed by men or gods, for they were the expression of "the Most High God." Also, he praised the kingdom and dominion of the Most High God as being everlasting. But this fell far short of acknowledging Him as the only true God. In his mind He was the highest of the gods. For he still called Daniel Belteshazzar, bearing the name of his god, in whom was "the spirit of the holy gods" (v. 8). God would give Nebuchadnezzar one more revealed opportunity to reach a higher and more perfect concept of Jehovah's true and only Godhood.

## The King is Troubled by a Dream – Failure of the Wise Men (vv. 4-9)

**Verse 4** *I, Nebuchadnezzar, was at rest in my house, and flourishing in my palace.*

The precise time of this experience in the history of Nebuchadnezzar is not stated, but the words of the king as quoted by Daniel indicates that it was some time after his conquests of the world powers foretold by Jeremiah. He was "at rest," in his house, flourishing (luxuriant, fresh) in his palace. All these expressions indicate a time of peace and tranquillity throughout his empire.

**Verse 5** *I saw a dream which made me afraid; and the thoughts upon my bed and the visions of my head troubled me.*

This peace and tranquillity which he enjoyed was upset by a disturbing dream and visions which left him troubled and afraid. It is difficult to imagine a great warrior, who had gone through the terrible battles of world conquest, being troubled and made afraid by a dream. However, it may have been because of these experience that he had been left with a suspicious and superstitious disposition. Or perhaps he recalled his previous dream and the interpretation by Daniel? This could be another communication for Jehovah.

> **Verse 6** *Therefore made I a decree to bring in all the wise men of Babylon before me, that they might make known unto me the interpretation of the dream.* 7 *Then came in the magicians, the enchanters, the Chaldeans, and the soothsayers; and I told the dream before them; but they did not make known unto me the interpretation thereof.*

In his uneasiness of mind because of the dream, the king issued a decree that "**all** the wise men of Babylon be brought in before" him that they might make known to him the meaning or interpretation of the dream. These came as ordered—four classifications: the magicians, enchanters, Chaldeans, and astrologers. Again Daniel was not included. But these wise men failed to offer an explanation of the dream, although the king made the dream known unto them.

> **Verse 8** *But at the last Daniel came in before me, whose name was Belteshazzar, according to the name of my god, and in whom is the spirit of the holy gods; and I told the dream before him, saying,*

"But at the last Daniel came in before me," which raised the question, Why was he not included with the group of "wise men" who responded to the decree? Was it because he was not included as one among the four classifications? Or, was he otherwise detained or occupied? Since God saw fit to leave the question unanswered, one does not know. However, see comments on verse 18. In addressing Daniel as "Belteshazzar, according to the name of my god," and saying of Daniel, "In whom is the spirit of the holy gods," the king revealed his continued polytheistic faith.

**Verse 9** *O Belteshazzar, master of the magicians, because I know that the spirit of the holy gods is in thee, and no secret troubleth thee, tell me the visions of my dream that I have seen and the interpretation thereof.*

The king stated his continued belief in polytheism by addressing Daniel as Belteshazzar, his god, and as having the "spirit of the holy gods," and, making known unto him the dream (v. 8b). The king stated his confidence in Daniel's ability to tell him the interpretation of the dream. He does not use the word "holy" to describe his gods in the sense of moral perfection, but as set apart from ordinary human beings, as being greater than mortals.

## The Dream
## (vv. 10-18)

### The Tree (vv. 10-12)

**Verse 10** *Thus were the visions of my head upon my bed: I saw, and, behold, a tree in the midst of the earth; and the height thereof was great.* **11** *The tree grew, and was strong, and the height thereof reached unto heaven, and the sight thereof to the end of all the earth.* **12** *The leaves thereof were fair, and the fruit thereof much, and in it was food for all: the beasts of the field had shadow under it, and the birds of the heavens dwelt in the branches thereof, and all flesh was fed from it.*

In the dream Nebuchadnezzar saw a great tree in the midst of the earth, the height of which reached into the heavens. It grew and became strong. Its appearance was visible to the ends of the earth. Its leaves provided protection for the birds within its branches, and shadow under which the beasts of the earth could find shade. Its fruit was plenteous, providing food for all flesh—man, beasts, and birds. A majestic sight!

### The Watcher and His Message (vv. 13-18)

**Verse 13** *I saw in the visions of my head upon my bed, and, behold, a watcher and a holy one came down from heaven.*

As Young observed, "The dream…now takes a new, and sudden turn" indicated by "I saw, [etc.]." The "watcher," "a holy one [that] came down from heaven"—not two but one—identified the "waking, watchful" one as an angel from God. The word indicated a vigilant one who is constant, watchful, keeping a diligent watch over all.

**Verse 14** *He cried aloud, and said thus, Hew down the tree, and cut off its branches, shake off its leaves, and scatter its fruit: let the beasts get away from under it, and the fowls from its branches.*

The command, "Hew down the tree, [etc.]" came from heaven, from the God of heaven, and should have been recognized by the king as a divine message. God spoke and it is done (Ps. 33:9). The command "Hew down the tree," is not addressed to anyone? No particular person is designated, so we accept Keil's statement, "The plural here is to be regarded as impersonal" (151). The branches were to be cut off, the leaves shaken from it, and the fruit scattered. The beasts were to get away from under it, and the fouls to fly from it. It would be stripped of its former glory and the great benefits to man, beasts and birds, which they had looked to for sustaining life ended.

**Verse 15** *Nevertheless leave the stump of its roots in the earth, even with a band of iron and brass, in the tender grass of the field; and let it be wet with the dew of* *heaven: and let his portion be with the beasts in the grass of the earth:*

But the disruption was not permanent. "Leave the stump of its roots in the earth" by which life would be sustained. The tree would grow again. The stump bound with a "band of iron and brass" has produced numerous interpretations. Among them is Keil's suggestion that it referred to the binding as "the withdrawal of free self- determination through the **fetters of madness** [emphasis his]; cf. 'the fetters of affliction,' Ps cvii, 10; Job xxxvi. 8" (p. 152). But this fails to do justice to the symbolic significance of the band of iron and brass.

The band of iron and brass has some symbolic significance, but what? The following is offered as a probable significance. In the king's dream of the great image of four metals (ch. 2), the part of brass symbolized the Macedonian kingdom, which included the military genius of Alexander The Great and the speed of his operation in war. Both of these likewise characterized the Chaldean kingdom and Nebuchadnezzar (cf. Hab. 1:6-11). This was symbolized by the brass. The part of iron in the image symbolized the Roman Empire with its power to conquer and weld a strong, powerful kingdom. This power also characterized Nebuchadnezzar. The two metals of the band symbolized the preservation (the band) of the powers (the metals) of Nebuchadnezzar during the king's illness. They would be restored until the completion of God's use of him. They would be neither lost nor impaired during the "seven times" of his insanity. This does not apply to what might occur later in his life, only to the period of his illness.

The watcher's reference to the tender grass of the field, and being wet with the dew of heaven, probably referred to the interpretation which followed. However, the dew was necessary to provide the tender grass, and it may have contributed to the stump's being kept alive, for the stump symbolized Nebuchadnezzar during the time of his illness. The shift from "it" to "his" indicated the beginning of the interpretation regarding Nebuchadnezzar.

**Verse 16** *let his heart be changed from man's, and let a beast's heart be given unto him; and let seven times pass over him.*

The change of "his" heart from that of a man to that of a beast introduced the nature of the king's madness. His conduct resembled that of an ox dwelling with the cattle, living in the open where he would be wet with the dew of the night, and even eating grass as one of them. "Until seven times pass over him" is not to be interpreted to mean seven years, seven seasons, or seven months. But seven being the number of perfection, or the complete number, it meant until that for which the madness would be sent upon him would be accomplished. It referred to an indefinite time for the complete accomplishment of a divine purpose.

**Verse 17** *The sentence is by the decree of the watchers, and the demand by the word of the holy ones; to the intent that the living may know that the Most High ruleth in the kingdom of men, and giveth it to whomsoever he will, and setteth up over it the lowest of men.*

In the foregoing verse two points are emphasized: First, the certainty of the dream's being fulfilled was assured by the source of the message. It was a decree from heaven, from the Most High God through His messenger. Second, the purpose for which God sent this judgment upon the king was "To the intent that the living may know that the Most High ruleth in the kingdom of men, and giveth it to whomsoever he will, and setteth up over it the lowest of men." In other words, all rulers, whether emperors, kings, or governors, are placed upon thrones, by the sovereign decision of the Almighty. He is the King of the nations. He determines the destiny of men and nations. These are "ministers of God...they are ministers of God's service, attending continually" upon the affairs of government (Rom. 13:4, 6).

**Verse 18** *This dream I, king Nebuchadnezzar, have seen; and thou, O Belteshazzar, declare the interpretation, forasmuch as all the wise men of my kingdom are not able to make known unto me the interpretation; but thou art able; for the spirit of the holy gods is in thee.*

Nebuchadnezzar concluded his words with an appeal to Daniel to give him an interpretation of the dream, "forasmuch as all the wise men of my kingdom are not able to make known unto me the interpretation; but thou art able." This indicated that Daniel was no longer considered a member of the college of wise men, but had been promoted to a higher rank (cf. 2:49); "for the spirit of the holy gods is in thee." All that the king could expect from the spirit of the gods was summed up in Daniel.

## Effect of the Dream Upon Daniel
## (v. 19)

**Verse 19** *Then Daniel, whose name was Belteshazzar, was stricken dumb for a while, and his thoughts troubled him. The king answered and said, Belteshazzar, let not the dream, or the interpretation, trouble thee. Belteshazzar answered and said, My lord, the dream be to them that hate thee, and the interpretation thereof to thine adversaries.*

Belteshazzar was the name given to Daniel by the prince of the eunuchs (1:7), after the name of the king's god (4:8). It was the name by which he was known in the king's court. Upon hearing the monarch's report of the dream, Daniel was dumb—speechless—"for a while" (ASV); "about an hour" (KJV), which would be too long; "as it were an instant, a moment" (Keil, p. 154), which would probably be too short; "quite a time" (Leupold, p. 189). Probably Leupold and the ASV are the most accurate. It is doubtful that Daniel's hesitancy was from fear, for in the following verses, one detects a distinct change in the spirit of the king from that displayed upon former occasions. The tone of Nebuchadnezzar's insistence that Daniel proceed with the interpretation manifested this change. Daniel's response to the king's request manifested a deep concern and seeming affection for him. He would much rather see the dream applied to the king's enemies than to the king himself.

## Interpretation of the Dream
### (vv. 20-27)

**Verse 20** *The tree that thou sawest, which grew, and was strong, whose height reached unto heaven, and the sight thereof to all the earth;* **21** *whose leaves were fair, and the fruit thereof much, and in it was food for all; under which the beasts of the field dwelt, and upon whose branches the birds of the heavens had their habitation:* **22** *it is thou, O king, that art grown and become strong; for thy greatness is grown, and reacheth unto heaven, and thy dominion to the end of the earth.*

Verses 20 and 21 are so nearly identical with verses 10-12 that they need no comment. In verse 22, Daniel comes to the point: The dream pertains to the king Nebuchadnezzar who had grown strong, and whose rule extended to the limits of the known world. He is the tree of the dream.

### The Tree (vv. 23-24)

**Verse 23** *And whereas the king saw a watcher and a holy one coming down from heaven, and saying, Hew down the tree, and destroy it; nevertheless leave the stump of the roots thereof in the earth, even with a band of iron and brass, in the tender grass of the field, and let it be wet with the dew of heaven; and let his portion be with the beasts of the field, till seven times pass over him;*

The watcher the king saw was a heavenly messenger sent from the Most High God with the command, "Hew down the tree, and destroy it." However, the destruction was not permanent, for the roots of the stump were left in the ground, and the stump was with a band of iron and brass. Its life would be preserved, in the midst of the tender grass, and wet with the dew of heaven. At this point the simile changed from a tree and its stump to a man—the king; from "it" to "his." "Let his portion be with the beasts of the field, till seven times pass over him," the time necessary to accomplish the divine purpose for which this judgment came upon him.

**Verse 24** *This is the interpretation, O king, and it is the decree of the Most High, which is come upon my lord the king:*

This was the interpretation of a decree from "the Most High," revealing a judgment which came upon the king. Daniel's deep feeling for Nebuchadnezzar is expressed in two words, "O king." And since it was the decree of "The Most High," it was certain to come to pass. It would be another testimony from "the Most High God" to the king that He alone is God. He is not to be numbered with "the gods".

## The Message to the King (vv. 25-27)

**Verse 25** *that thou shalt be driven from men, and thy dwelling shall be with the beasts of the field, and thou shalt be made to eat grass as oxen, and shalt be wet with the dew of heaven, and seven times shall pass over thee; till thou know that the Most High ruleth in the kingdom of men, and giveth it to whomsoever he will.*

Daniel pointedly directed the interpretation of the dream to the king himself. A state of mental madness or insanity would overcome the king, taking control of his life. He will be "driven from men," from his place of rule over the kingdom. His dwelling will be "with the beasts of the field"; he will be reduced to the level of animals. Instead of eating his meals at the royal table, he will eat grass as oxen of the field depending on God not man to be fed. Instead of the comforts of his royal palace, his body will be wet with the nightly dews that drenched the pasture grass. This will continue until "seven times shall pass over thee." The "seven times" is not seven years, months, or any specific duration of time, but a definite period of indefinite length. This was indicated by the following, "Till thou know that the Most High ruleth in the kingdom of men, and giveth it to whomsoever he will." The king's condition will continue until the objective of the Most High is accomplished, whatever the necessary length of time may be.

> **Verse 26** *And whereas they commanded to leave the stump of the roots of the tree; thy kingdom shall be sure unto thee, after that thou shalt have known that the heavens do rule.*

According to Leupold and Young, the plural "they" does not indicate a plurality of messengers (v. 23), "but it should be noted that the pls. are impersonal" (Young, 107; cf. Leupold, 192). God the Most High does not leave the king in a state of hopeless despair, but left the stump as an assurance that after he has learned the desired lesson, the kingdom will be restored to him. But it will not be restored until he learns who rules the universe.

> **Verse 27** *Wherefore, O king, let my counsel be acceptable unto thee, and break off thy sins by righteousness, and thine iniquities by showing mercy to the poor; if there may be a lengthening of thy tranquillity.*

After delivering the interpretation of the dream to the king, Daniel offered some unrequested advice. The lack of any word of response has led some commentators to think the advise was coolly received. But whatever the king's reaction, the sincere interest of Daniel toward the king seemed evident. He sought the continued extension of the "lengthening of [his] tranquillity," the continued peace and harmony within his kingdom. Daniel's request was that he break with his sins and iniquities, and in their place demonstrate righteousness toward his fel-lowmen, with compassion to the poor. This shows that the king was guilty of unjust treatment and negligence of his sub-jects. This change was not to avert the judgment revealed in the dream, but it was to show God's ability to bring down the proud and debase the arrogant. The change in disposition of the king was to lengthen the period of tranquillity.

## From Dream to Life's Realization
## (vv. 28-33)

In chapter 4, Nebuchadnezzar spoke, telling the dream (vv. 1-18); Daniel spoke, revealing its meaning (vv. 19-27); Daniel, or some other, related its fulfillment (vv. 28-33); the king responded by announcing the result (vv. 34-37).

> **Verse 28** *All this came upon the king Nebuchadnezzar.* **29** *At the end of twelve months he was walking in the royal palace of Babylon.*

At the end of twelve months following Daniel's interpreta-tion of the dream and his advice to the king, all that he had interpreted the dream to mean fell upon Nebuchadnezzar as he was walking upon (margin) the roof of the palace. From this vantage point he commanded a panoramic view of the city in its glory.

> **Verse 30** *The king spake and said, Is not this great Baby-lon, which I have built for the royal dwelling-place, by the might of my power and for the glory of my majesty?*

As he looked upon its grandeur, he spoke within himself, proudly boasting of his building achievements. Filled with pride, he began to boast, This is "great Babylon which I have built...by the might of **my** power...for the glory of **my majesty.** Had he forgotten the dream and its interpreta-tion? Either he forgot for the moment, or it was an intentional defiance of the Most High God. I prefer to think that in beholding the glory of his city, and reveling in his own glory and self-exaltation, he momentarily forgot.

In his article "Babylon" (*ZPEB* I 439-44), D. J. Wiseman described the magnitude and grandeur of the city in Nebuchadnezzar's day. Its palaces, halls, temples built to honor the Babylonian gods, its citadels, and walls surrounding the city, staggers the imagination. Unlike the Assyrian rulers who boasted of their victories and cruelties in wars, although he may have boasted of these, Nebuchadnezzar preferred to boast of his building projects.

> **Verse 31** *While the word was in the king's mouth, there fell a voice from heaven, saying, O king Nebuchadnezzar, to thee it is spoken, The kingdom is departed from thee:* **32** *and thou shalt be driven from men; and thy dwelling shall be with the beasts of the field; thou shalt be made to eat grass as oxen; and seven times shall pass over thee; until thou know that the Most High ruleth in the kingdom of men, and giveth it to whomsoever he will.* **33** *The same hour was the thing fulfilled upon Nebuchadnezzar: and he was driven from men, and did eat grass as oxen, and his body was wet with the dew of heaven, till his hair was grown like eagles' feathers, and his nails like birds' claws.*

Daniel's description of what befell the king is almost word for word parallel to verses 24-26. The king's "kingdom [rule] is departed." He will be driven from men, dwelling with beasts of the field, made to eat grass with the oxen, be wet with the dew of heaven, till seven times pass over; till he shall know that the Most High rules in the kingdoms of men and gives the kingdoms to whom He will. He will eat grass like the oxen about him. Instead of the phrase, "the heavens do rule" (v. 26), the present text (v. 32) has, "the Most High ruleth." The two phrases are synonymous (cf. Matthew's phrase, "kingdom of heaven" and Luke's parallel, "kingdom of God"). In due time the king's hair grew and became matted until it gave the appearance of eagles' feathers; and likewise his nails grew long and sharp till they resembled birds' claws. A pathetic picture for a great monarch, the conqueror of the world.[1]

## The King's Return to Sanity
## (vv. 34-37)

**Verse 34** *And at the end of the days I, Nebuchadnezzar, lifted up mine eyes unto heaven and mine understanding returned unto me, and I blessed the Most High, and I praised and honored him that liveth for ever; for his dominion is an everlasting dominion, and his kingdom from generation to generation;*

v. 34. In his own words the king related his return to sanity, the lesson he learned, and the restoration of his former glory. He made no mention of whether there was a degree of memory restoration that caused him to lift up his eyes to heaven whereby total recovery was realized. In his report, he was concerned only with the fact, not with the process. At the end of the days of the seven times, the period necessary for the achievement of God's purpose, the king lifted his eyes to heaven and was healed. This revealed a universal truth. When one's mind is demented and his reason warped toward self and God by pride and arrogance, these can only be corrected when the individual looks to heaven and realizes the truth concerning himself and God. The upward look brought to his soul an inward conviction of spiritual truth. He now saw God in His true light. His restoration was followed by outward blessings, the return of his former glory.[2]

Upon his recovery from the experience of madness, the king "blessed the Most High," a word that means, to kneel in praising God (p. 991). It is unclear whether he did this by an outward bowing or kneeling, or mentally. "And I **praised** and

---

[1] For a discussion of the nature of the king's malady, the student is referred to E.J. Young's, *The Prophecy of Daniel*, pp. 110-112.

[2] The definitions which follow are taken from *Theological Wordbook of the Old Testament*, vol. II.

~ *84* ~

**honored** him"—to praise is to **laud**, or express devotion to (p. 1079); and to honor is to **glorify God** (p. 1007). "Him that liveth **for ever**," which is equivalent to **everlasting**, and from **generation to generation**, means **perpetually**, for ever; and may be used of the past or future (pp. 1055, 673). His **dominion**: possession of **power, rule** (p. 1080); and **kingdom: royalty, reign**, (sovereignty) (p. 1041) were all restored to him.

> **Verse 35** *and all the inhabitants of the earth are reputed as nothing; and he doeth according to his will in the army of heaven, and among the inhabitants of the earth; and none can stay his hand, or say unto him, What doest thou?*

From this eulogy which praised and extolled Jehovah's greatness, His majestic power, and the eternity of his being, the king spoke of God's relationship to man. He divided his remarks into three sections: 1) The inhabitants of the earth are "reputed," accounted or thought of, "as nothing." Isaiah expressed this thought when he said, "Who hath directed the Spirit of Jehovah, or being his counselor hath taught him?" (40:13). This does not mean that God has no concern for men, but in their relation to Him in power and length of duration they are as nothing. 2) In all matters of purpose and destiny, His will is absolute and final. And the prayer of His saints should be, "Thy will be done, as in heaven, so on earth" (Matt. 6:10). 3) Of the expression, "and none can stay the hand," Keil said, "to strike on the hand, to hinder [is] derived from the custom of striking children on the hand in chastening them" (140). If this is correct, then the king was saying that no one can hinder or restrain God from chastening or punishing individuals where such is necessary. Neither can any one say to God, "What are you doing?" For what He does is not to be questioned by way of correcting Him.

> **Verse 36** *At the same time mine understanding returned unto me; and for the glory of my kingdom, my majesty and brightness returned unto me; and my counselors and*

*my lords sought unto me; and I was established in my*
*kingdom, and excellent greatness was added unto me.*

At the same time he received the spiritual blessings, he also received the external physical blessings of which he was deprived during the seven times which passed over him. These included the glory of his kingdom; his greatness in his kingdom and respect of men; and "brightness," the **splendor of** former days returned to him. His "counselors" and "lords," men of high rank in his cabinet on whom he could depend to assist him by wise counsel and advice sought him. By their seeking him, and his acceptance of them, the king was once more "established," firmly entrenched in his kingdom; "and excellent greatness" was added unto him.

**Verse 37** *Now I, Nebuchadnezzar, praise and extol and*
*honor the King of heaven; for all his works are truth,*
*and his ways justice; and those that walk in pride he*
*is able to abase.*

With this pronouncement of the greatness, power, and majesty of the Most High God, the lesson he has learned, and the restoration of his own glory and royal estate, the king closed his speech with a final word eulogizing and honoring the King of Heaven. He recognized the Heavenly King's works as works of truth, and His ways just; "And those who walk in pride he is able to abase." "Now"—having learned his lesson concerning himself and God—"I...praise and extol [elevate, exalt] and honor the King of heaven."

One may ask, Is there anything lacking in the eulogy, decree, and confession? There seems to be one thing: "He is the **only** God." Unless something in what the king said included this idea, the recognition of the God of Heaven as the only God, thereby rejecting all pagan gods, falls short of the ultimate goal desired by Jehovah

While teaching the Book of Daniel to college students during my career as a teacher of the prophets, I developed a friendship and appreciation for Nebuchadnezzar. Not his cruel pagan despotic characteristics, but in spite of them, his power to change. Parallel to his spiritual growth and appreciation for Jehovah, my respect and admiration grew. This growth in his concept of God is probably the most important factor in the four chapters considered thus far. We must measure him as a pagan, and not by the divine standard of Moses' law or that of Christ, for he lived under neither. But his growth from our first acquaintance with him (ch. 2) to our final sight of him (ch. 4) produced this admiration.

Chapter 2. The king's outburst of temper expressed in anger and fury is inexcusable (v. 12). And we may be critical of the severe penalty pronounced upon the wise men. The severity of it may be criticized, but the imposition of a penalty, even a severe penalty, cannot. The king did not realize that he had asked an absolutely impossible thing of men; but he had asked a service the wise men claimed the ability to do, i.e., to interpret dreams. The king had a standard to be admired: his cabinet must be able to perform within the bounds of their claim and what their office required. But they were phonies. For later when they were told the dream, they could not interpret it (ch. 4). His pagan standard in this incompetency was the death penalty; but competency was the standard that he demanded to be upheld. In our time, standards have dropped so low that, deliver or not, the incompetent person must be kept on the payroll. So, competent or incompetent; from the common laborer, through the fields of education, the student must be passed. In realms of business, government, or to the President of the nation, standards mean little or nothing.

Consider Nebuchadnezzar's attitude toward God. Following Daniel's revealing and interpretation of the dream, the king "fell upon his face, and worshipped Daniel, and commanded that they should offer an oblation and sweet odor unto him" (2:46). This was tantamount to acclaiming Daniel as a god. And of Daniel's God, he said, "Of a truth your God is the God of gods, and the Lord of lords, and a revealer of secrets, seeing thou hast been able to reveal this secret" (v. 47). This reeks with the king's paganistic concept of Daniel, Daniel's God, and the limitation of His power. But it reveals a religious impulse from which God can do His work.

Chapter 3. When Daniel's three friends: Shadrach, Meshach, and Abed-nego, refused to obey the king's order to worship the golden image he had erected, he displayed another explosion of temper. He had not yet learned to control it, but expressed it in a fit of rage and fury, demanding that the three be thrown into the fiery furnace (3:13, 19). Again, neither the temper tantrum nor the extreme penalty can be excused. But the law, though unreasonable from our point of view and that of the three men, must be obeyed. We cannot fault a penalty for the violation of law, but must commend it; however, the penalty should be reasonable. A complete breakdown in a justice system will come if there is too much leniency for the guilty, and too much injustice for the innocent or falsely accused.

Following the deliverance of Daniel's three friends from the fiery furnace by a fourth person who appeared in the furnace with them, the king "blessed" the God of the three men. Furthermore, he advanced a step beyond his former praise: he admitted that their God was greater in power than himself, for He had sustained them in their changing the king's word, by delivering them in their obedience to Him. But he continued to recognize Him as "their God" among the gods being worshipped (v. 28). The king then made a decree that no one should speak anything against the God of the three Hebrews, "Because there is no other god that is able to deliver after this sort" (v. 29). Though He was a God among the gods, He was able to sustain them in the fiery furnace, deliver them from it, and make void the king's order. In these their God exceeded all the gods of the heathen pantheon. Nothing was to be said against Him. This was an advancement over the king's former concept.

Chapter 4. This chapter, which seems to be much later than the events of the former chapters, the king demonstrated a decided change in disposition from that displayed in the earlier two. In this setting he tells the dream, and shows no display of temper when the wise men failed to reveal its meaning. Also, when Daniel revealed the interpretation of the dream and offered his unrequested advice, although the king made no statement of approval, he stated no disapproval. Yet, in spite of his changed disposition in some areas, his proud spirit had to be abased. He must be humbled. The dream which he wanted explained, revealed that humbling experience and what it would accomplish in the king. His advanced and greatly enlarged view of God is to be admired and appreciated.

In the eulogy following his recovery from madness, the king reached the peak of his acknowledgments of Jehovah's greatness. He is now "the Most High"; He "liveth for ever"; His dominion and kingdom are equally perpetual; "all the inhabitants of the earth" are as nothing; "he doeth according to his will"; none can stay His hand, none can question what He does. He is "the King of heaven"; "all his works are truth"; His ways justice; and in His exceeding great power He is able to abase the proud (vv. 34-37).

Would these statements be sufficient for God to accept his faith as acknowledging God's sole deity and the rejection of the idols as gods? If not, did his faith and acknowledgment ever reach that height? We have no means of knowing. The chapter closes the Biblical history of Nebuchadnezzar. D. J. Wisman said in his article, **Nebuchadnezzar**, "Historical sources are lacking for the last years of the reign of Nebuchadnezzar" (*ZPEB* III 396). But inasmuch as Daniel's position at the court of Babylon continued into the third year of the reign of Cyrus (Dan. 10:1), it is wished that his influence on Nebuchadnezzar might have led him to a complete acceptance of Jehovah as the only true God, and to a complete rejection of all false gods.

## A Source of Encouragement

In a time of national judgments against our own nation, what can God's saints find in this chapter that would sustain their faith and give them courage? First and foremost, one can be assured that God rules in the kingdom of men. He gives the position of rule to whomsoever He will. If it serves His purpose, He may give it to the lowest of men (Dan. 4:17, 25).

This may be difficult for one to accept; but be assured in faith that this is so.

God is concerned, not only with accomplishing His purpose, but He is concerned for the welfare of His people. It may be that what He has done, and is doing, is for the good of the nation, and especially for His people within the nation. He may be giving to the nation what it has been asking for and deserves; and it may be His means of turning His people from their love of the materialism to the spiritual life from which they have been led by their own lusts. Yes, God is in control, and for those who love Him and seek to do His will, all things will work out for their good and His glory. The chapter also teaches that one faithful man, a Daniel, at a king's court in such a time might influence his peers to lead to a complete change of history, "For God is able to do exceeding abundantly above all that we ask or think" (Eph. 3:20).

# CHAPTER V

# Belshazzar and the End of Babylonian Rule

## Belshazzar and His Feast
### (vv. 1-4)

**B**elshazzar's name occurs eight times in the book of Daniel and no where else in the Bible, six times in chapter five, and once each in 7:1 and 8:1. Because of this and its being discovered in the monuments only within recent years, the liberal critics have taken occasion to attack the book on this ground.[1] The emphasis given to Belshazzar in Daniel reveals the king's irreverence and contempt for Jehovah the one true God. That he was a ruler in the last days of Babylon is indicated by the following references in Daniel's book: "Belshazzar the king" (Dan. 5:1); "King Belshazzar" (v. 9; 8:1); "Belshazzar the Chaldean king" (v. 5:30); "Belshazzar king of Babylon" (v. 7:1); "Belshazzar" (name only, vv. 2, 22, 29); "the king" and

---

[1] Since it is outside the scope of this work, the objections advanced by the critics is omitted; but the works of several conservative men are suggested: Robert Dick Wilson has written a scholarly, but rather difficult chapter on "Belshazzar" *Studies in the Book of Daniel*, pp. 96-127, Baker Book House, Grand Rapids, 1979 reprint. The same complaint can be made against Wilson's article in the *ISBE*, I, 433. D. J. Wiseman's article, "Belshazzar" (*ZPEB* 515f.) is too brief. Keil does his usual fine job on the subject, but so much has been discovered since his day that his work falls short of being up to date. The two most scholarly, practical, and helpful up to date works at my hand are Leupold's *Exposition of Daniel* (pp. 108-114) and Young's *The Prophecy of Daniel* (pp.115-119).

"O king" (17 times). The frequency of reference to a king by the name of Belshazzar is impressive. It indicates that there was a king, or ruler, by that name though of minor importance, near the end of the Babylonian era. Until strong evidence to the contrary emerges, Daniel must be respected as an authentic historian.

An interesting factor in Daniel's record in chapter five is the phrases of relationship between Belshazzar and Nebuchadnezzar—"my father," "your father," and "his [Belshazzar's] father," which occur six times. Recent evidence has established that Nabonidus was Belshazzar's father, who was not of blood relationship to Nebuchadnezzar. This posed the question, In what sense was Nebuchadnezzar his father? Leupold offered a number of possibilities, but thus far none have been authenticated. The possibility of adoption, marriage, or figurative father as former ruler are not to be ruled out. But whatever answers to questions about his relationship to the kingship of Babylon and Chaldea, it seems that he was never king over the empire as was "his father" Nebuchadnezzar, but served as CO-ruler, or second ruler under Nabonidus his father (vv. 16, 29).

**Verse 1** *Belshazzar the king made a great feast to a thousand of his lords, and drank wine before the thousand.*

The king made a great feast for his lords which was attended by the king, his wives, and his concubines. From the emphasis given to wine in the chapter, it seems that the feast was more a drinking hour or wine-fest than a food festival; although food was probably served. The king's drinking wine "before the thousand" indicates that he was served apart from the lords, probably on an elevated platform where he could be seen by all.

**Verse 2** *Belshazzar, while he tasted the wine, commanded to bring the golden and silver vessels which Nebuchadnezzar his father had taken out of the temple*

*which was in Jerusalem, that the king and his lords, his
wives and his concubines, might drink therefrom.*

"When he tasted the wine," "'When he began to feel the
influence of the wine' (Driver)" (quoted by Young, p. 119), is
probably the correct meaning. Under the influence of wine
men may act irrationally, irreverently, and irresponsibly. So the
king acted in this manner when he ordered the gold and silver
vessels brought by Nebuchadnezzar from the temple of God at
Jerusalem, be brought in that they might drink from them.
Nebuchadnezzar had shown more respect for the vessels taken
from Jehovah's temple in Jerusalem by putting them in the
temple of his god (1:2). In contrast, Belshazzar showed contempt for the God of a conquered people. The consequence of
such a spirit of irreverence should be a warning to all men for
all time.

> **Verse 3** *Then they brought the golden vessels that were
> taken out of the temple of the house of God which was at
> Jerusalem; and the king and his lords, his wives and his
> concubines, drank from them.* **4** *They drank wine, and
> praised the gods of gold, and of silver, of brass, of iron, of
> wood, and of stone.*

When brought in, the semi-intoxicated banqueters desecrated the vessels by using them in drinking to the praise of the
gods of metal, wood, and stone. Truly, "Wine is a mocker,
strong drink a brawler; / And whosoever erreth thereby is not
wise" (Prov. 20:1; cf. 23:29-35). By his actions, Belshazzar
manifested an intemperate disposition and an irreverent attitude toward the true God, even an attitude of contempt for
Him. Yet, he had ample opportunity to have learned better.

## God's Terrifying Message on the Wall
## (vv. 5-9)

**Verse 5** *In the same hour came forth the fingers of a
man's hand, and wrote over against the candlestick upon*

*the plaster of the wall of the king's palace: and the king
saw the part of the hand that wrote.*

While the revelers were drinking wine from the sacred vessels
brought from Jehovah's temple, and riotously praising the heathen gods of their own making, a terrifying sign appeared.
Suddenly the fingers of a man's hand appeared, writing strange
words on the plastered wall behind the candlestick. The candlestick was so situated, and the king seated so that the writing
was clearly visible to him and the group, as the fingers moved
to and fro. Only the fingers were visible as they wrote.

**Verse 6** *Then the king's countenance was changed in him,
and his thoughts troubled him; and the joints of his loins
were loosed, and his knees smote one against another.*

The terror that gripped the king seemed to jolt him into
soberness, for truly it was a sobering scene. The immediate
changes wrought in him were: 1) the expression or color of his
face changed; 2) his thoughts "troubled" (**alarmed, dismayed**
[*TWOT* II 995] him); 3) the firmness and control of his body
failed to function; 4) and his knees shook, or knocked against
each other.

**Verse 7** *The king cried aloud to bring in the enchanters,
the Chaldeans, and the soothsayers. The king spake and
said to the wise men of Babylon, Whosoever shall read this
writing, and show me the interpretation thereof, shall be
clothed with purple, and have a chain of gold about his
neck, and shall be the third ruler in the kingdom.*

The scene caused the king to lose his arrogance and in
terror he cried for the wise men to come immediately; three
classes responded. The kings had not learned the helplessness
of these men, or that they were deceivers. Even now in an
"enlightened age," people seek the guidance of astrologers,
fortune tellers, and false prognosticators, when only God can
declare the future.

The king promised that whoever could read and reveal the interpretation of the writing would receive royal clothes, a gold chain about his neck, "and be the third ruler in the kingdom." The offer of third ruler was not understood until it was discovered from the monuments that Nabonidus his father was king, and he was second, therefore the highest position in the kingdom that he could offer was third place. However, that position was not made clear.

**Verse 8** *Then came in all the king's wise men; but they could not read the writing, nor make known to the king the interpretation.*

Why all the wise men did not come in with the three classes named is not revealed. "All" were now present, but the wisdom of the entire body could not read the writing nor make known its message. This should not be surprising. For in describing the fall of Babylon at the hands of Cyrus (Isa. 47), Isaiah foretold the failure of the Babylonian king's wise men to be able to help. They would be unable to deliver themselves from the destruction (vv. 12-14). To attempt an explanation of the language in which the message was written is folly; and to decide on the ground of Daniel's reading of the message and its interpretation that it was some form of early Hebrew is likewise without foundation. We do not, and cannot know what language it was, for God did not reveal it.

**Verse 9** *Then was king Belshazzar greatly troubled, and his countenance was changed in him, and his lords were perplexed.*

The failure of all the wise men to read and explain the writing left the group in a state of utter confusion and suspension. The king was greatly agitated and disturbed, and his assembled lords "were upset and tumultuous" (Young). Having been sheltered and enjoying a general peace in our nation, how much of the extraordinary would it require to throw our people into a state of total confusion?

## The Queen's Appearance and Recommendation
## (vv. 10-12)

**Verse 10** *Now the queen by reason of the words of the king and his lords came into the banquet house: the queen spake and said, O king, live for ever; let not thy thoughts trouble thee, nor let thy countenance be changed.* **11** *There is a man in thy kingdom, in whom is the spirit of the holy gods; and in the days of thy father light and understanding and wisdom, like the wisdom of the gods, were found in him; and the king Nebuchadnezzar thy father, the king, I say, thy father made him master of the magicians enchanters, Chaldeans, and soothsayers;*

The queen, who had not been present at the banquet where the writing on the wall occurred (Dan. 5:1-9), was attracted by the words of the king, by the confusion of the group and by their loud speaking. She is not identified specifically, but from her knowledge of Nebuchadnezzar and Daniel, and the service rendered by Daniel to that king, leads to the conclusion that she was a widow of the former king. If so, she was the "queen-mother" in the palace. Her advice to Belshazzar was that he be not over agitated by the situation, for she was there to offer a solution.

There was a man who had served Nebuchadnezzar, his father, by resolving and explaining dreams. She used the expression "thy father" three times. The great king was not his paternal father, for it has been clearly established that Nabonidus held that relationship. The specific relationship indicated by her language is uncertain. It could have been by adoption somewhere in the line; or by marriage at some point; or it could have been in the line of occupation of the throne. Whatever the relationship, the queen revealed a thorough knowledge of Daniel's powers and service to the former king. Also, she told Belshazzar of the appointment of Daniel to the rank of "master" of the wise men, which raised the question of why he was not among them?

**Verse 12** *forasmuch as an excellent spirit, and knowledge, and understanding, interpreting of dreams, and showing of dark sentences, and dissolving of doubts, were found in the same Daniel, whom the king named Belteshazzar. Now let Daniel be called, and he will show the interpretation.*

Nebuchadnezzar found in Daniel the spirit of the holy gods, i.e., the spirit of wisdom and understanding, the power to understand and interpret dreams, power and wisdom that pertained only to deity and the supernatural. Because of these qualities, he changed his name to Belteshazzar, **Protect the King!** (4:8). Considering all this, the queen advised Belshazzar to call for Daniel, "he will show the interpretation." Her confidence in Daniel's ability was complete. Such confidence and respect were earned.

The queen came to play a woman's role in the great drama of Biblical history. She could not reveal the words or their meaning, but she could direct the king to one who could. From the beginning women have played an important part in the destiny of humanity, both for bad and for good.

The world has had its Eves who, being beguiled, have led their husbands into sin (I Tim. 2:13-14; Gen. 3:1-6). It has had its Delilahs on whose laps many of her victims heads have been rolled (Judg. 16:19); and its queens who turned the hearts of their kings away from God to idolatry (I Kings 11:1-6); and its Jezebels whose influence led a nation into idolatry and ultimate ruin (I Kings 16:30-34).

On the other hand, there were the great women of the Bible and their wonderful influence for good. There were its Jochebeds who gave the world its Moses (Ex. 6:20); its Deborahs and its Jaels, who inspired armies and contributed to their victories (Judg. 4); and forget not the Huldahs who revealed God's will in trying times (II Kings 22:14-22). Included in this list is the virgin Mary who produced the human body in which the fullness of deity dwelt (Matt. 1:21); and Joannas and Susannas who minister unto Jesus of their substance (Lk. 8:3). Then there were the Mary Magdalenes who heralded the resurrection of the Savior to disheartened disciples (John 20:1f.); and there were the Euodias and the Syntyches who labored with the Lord's preachers in proclaiming the gospel (Phil. 4:2-3). Do not overlook the Loises and the Eunices who have given unnumbered Timothys to the Lord as evangelists of His glorious gospel (II Tim. 1:5). These are to mention only a few. Alongside of these there are the thousands who work, and have worked, quietly behind the scenes, whose names are known only to God. May their number be multiplied in this wicked and perverse world.

## Failure of the Wise Men–The King's Last Hope (vv. 13-16)

**Verse 13** *Then was Daniel brought in before the king. The king spake and said unto Daniel, Art thou that Daniel, who art of the children of the captivity of Judah, whom the king my father brought out of Judah?*
**14** *I have heard of thee, that the spirit of the gods is in thee, and that light and understanding and excellent wisdom are found in thee.*

Following the queen's recommendation, Daniel was brought before the king. Young saw in the king's questions a condescending air of egoism and haughtiness, which seems to show through. Do the questions reflect a knowledge derived from the queen's visit? or, Do they express a knowledge derived from the background of his life? If the latter, there would be a cover, an attempted cover-up for what he had done and not done. For of the history related by Daniel in his speech that follows, he said, "Thou knewest all this" (v. 22). The verse that follows leaves the question unanswered. His knowledge could have been from either source.

**Verse 15** *And now the wise men, the enchanters, have been brought in before me, that they should read this writing, and make known unto me the interpretation thereof; but they could not show the interpretation of the thing.*

Belshazzar related the purpose for which the wise men were brought in and repeated their failure to explain the meaning of the written words. But the wise men should not be censored for their failure, for the writing was from God, and only one given divine power could read and interpret the message. If they should be censored at all, it was for their working under the delusion that they had such power.

> **Verse 16** *But I have heard of thee, that thou canst give interpretations, and dissolve doubts: now if thou canst read the writing, and make known to me the interpretation thereof, thou shalt be clothed with purple, and have a chain of gold about thy neck, and shalt be the third ruler in the kingdom.*

It appeared that Belshazzar gave the impression that his knowledge of Daniel was hearsay. But in Daniel's response it seemed that his knowledge of the prophet went beyond that. Daniel's power to read and interpret such messages was from God, which source the king failed to acknowledge. If Daniel could do what the wise men failed to do, he would bestow upon him the same honors he promised the wise men."[2]

## Daniel's Speech: God and Nebuchadnezzar (vv. 17-21)

> **Verse 17** *Then Daniel answered and said before the king, Let thy gifts be to thyself, and give thy rewards to another; nevertheless I will read the writing unto the king, and make known to him the interpretation.*

---

[2] **Interpretation.** "The most obvious significance of the word *hawa* in Daniel is thus to denote the ability to do something which the great intellectuals of the Babylonian empire were incapable of doing. Daniel could explain current and coming events as well as their political and theological implications. The Babylonian soothsayers, magicians, and other professionals could not. But Daniel does not emerge as merely a human hero because of this. Rather, the God of Daniel emerges as the only deity through whose revelation history makes sense. This distinction is plainly made both in chapter two (vv. 26-28) and in chapter five (vv. 9, 18)." *TWOT* II 1019 (2722a).

Daniel began his speech with a dignified, firm rejection of the rewards for translating and explaining the writing. Keil described the refusal as not being out of fear for himself, or for the king, or of the king, but "to avoid, as a divinely enlightened seer, every appearance of self- interest in the presence of such a king,…and would unhesitatingly declare the truth, whether it might be pleasing or displeasing to the king" (p. 187). Daniel had previously refused such gifts. He impressed the fact that power from God cannot be bought. God's power is not for sale.

**Verse 18** *O thou king, the Most High God gave Nebuchadnezzar thy father the kingdom, and greatness, and glory, and majesty;*

From his brief introduction and declaration of purpose, Daniel proceeded to magnify and glorify the God of heaven as "the Most High God" and His relation to Nebuchadnezzar. In so doing, he revealed the contrast between Nebuchadnezzar and Belshazzar. There was Nebuchadnezzar's respect for God (as expressed in 4:34-37), and Belshazzar's utter contempt for Him as demonstrated by his acts at the feasts (vv. 2-4).

**Verse 19** *and because of the greatness that he gave him, all the peoples, nations, and languages trembled and feared before him: whom he would he slew, and whom he would he kept alive; and whom he would he raised up, and whom he would he put down.*

It was the same Most High God that gave to the king, his father, the kingdom, greatness, glory, and majesty (cf. 2:37-38).It was because of these gifts from God that the peoples of the earth "trembled and feared before him." Furthermore, the power given him from the Most High God as ruler, was absolute and final, but it was from God. Whom the king willed, he raised up, and whom he willed he cast down.

**Verse 20** *But when his heart was lifted up, and his spirit was hardened so that he dealt proudly, he was deposed from his kingly throne, and they took his glory from him:*

But when he failed to recognize the source of this power, and "his heart was lifted up, and his spirit was hardened" (the two seem to be used synonymously, Young), he proudly boasted of his achievements as accomplished by himself. His lifted up heart and his hardened spirit is the "they" that took his glory from him (see Prov. 16:18). When he did this, the power given him to raise and cast down was now used against him; he was "deposed from his kingly throne." Primarily, the word "deposed" means "to descend"; he was caused to descend from a king on his throne to an animal in the field.

**Verse 21** *and he was driven from the sons of men, and his heart was made like the beasts', and his dwelling was with the wild asses; he was fed with grass like oxen, and his body was wet with the dew of heaven; until he knew that the Most High God ruleth in the kingdom of men, and that he setteth up over it whomsoever he will.*

"The sons of men" were all of mankind, all human beings from whose presence he was driven. No longer was he the wise and powerful monarch who controlled the kingdoms of the world, but he was a man with a beast's heart. As such he was compelled to dwell among the wild asses, undomesticated donkeys, that eat grass as the oxen of the field, and be wet with the dew of heaven. This state of Nebuchadnezzar continued until he knew and acknowledged that the Most High ruled in the kingdom of men, and gave it to whomsoever He would. This explains the "seven times" mentioned before. The phrase does not designate a specific period of time, but a sufficient length of time to accomplish a specific purpose of God. With this review of Nebuchadnezzar's sin of pride, God's judgment of it, and the execution of His judgment, Daniel closed this phase of his speech.

## Daniel's Speech Continued: God and Belteshazzar (vv. 22-24)

**Verse 22** *And thou his son, O Belshazzar, hast not humbled thy heart, though thou knewest all this,*

Daniel introduced his speech to Belshazzar by charging him with knowing the things relating to his father, Nebuchadnezzar, and was fully responsible for his irreverent and blasphemous conduct. He acted presumptuously in what he had done.

**Verse 23** *but hast lifted up thyself against the Lord of heaven; and they have brought the vessels of his house before thee, and thou and thy lords, thy wives and thy concubines, have drunk wine from them; and thou hast praised the gods, of silver and gold, of brass, iron, wood, and stone, which see not, nor hear, nor know; and the God in whose hand thy breath is, and whose are all thy ways, hast thou not glorified.*

He exalted himself in his own eyes, and attempted to do the same in the eyes of those present. He demonstrated an arrogant contempt for the Most High God: 1) He elevated himself against Him, "the Lord of heaven"; 2) he called for the sacred vessels which the former great king had brought from the house of God in Jerusalem, to be brought into the banquet hall; 3) from these they drank wine in praise to the gods of metal, wood, and stone, gods which can neither hear, see, nor know anything; 4) the God in whose hand was the king's breath of life which determined the destiny of life, he mocked instead of honored. The king's life was in the hand that wrote the message.

**Verse 24** *Then was the part of the hand sent from before him, and this writing was inscribed.*

It was because of the king's disdain for God and all that is holy that the fingers of the hand had appeared. The fingers and writing came from God with a message from Him. Daniel was now ready to discuss the writing and its message.

## The Inscription and Its Message
## (vv. 25-28)

**Verse 25** *And this is the writing, that was inscribed: MENE, MENE, TEKEL, UPHARSIN.*

With this severe rebuke to the king, Daniel proceeded to translate the inscription, which apparently remained visible upon the wall.

**Verse 26** *This is the interpretation of the thing: MENE; God hath numbered thy kingdom, and brought it to an end.*

Daniel followed the translation by revealing the interpretation. Keil said, "In all the three words there lies a double sense, which is brought out in the interpretation" (p. 189). Of this double meaning, Leupold said of **Mene**. "to number," "There is a kind of double meaning in the verb 'to number.' It means not only, 'to count' but 'to fix the limit of'" (p. 234). Young said of the word, "MENE numbered, God has numbered (MENE) the days (i.e., the length of duration) of the kingdom and finished it," and it is now being brought to an end (p. 126f.). Leupold thinks "that the repetition of the word is an indication of the double meaning to be sought in the term" (p. 234). However, Young thinks "the repeated MENE is probably for the sake of emphasis" (p. 125).

**Verse 27** *TEKEL; thou art weighed in the balances, and art found wanting.*

"TEKEL, thou art weighed in the balances, and art found wanting." "**Wanting**—lacking, deficient in moral worth" (Young, p. 127). Weighed in God's balances, he fell far short of the divine demand for a ruler acceptable to

Him. He and his kingdom would be brought to an end.

**Verse 28** *PERES; thy kingdom is divided, and given to the Medes and Persians.*

"PERES: thy kingdom is divided," or, broken up; "it will be given to the Medes and Persians." It is noted in the first reading, the word **upharsin** occurs (v. 25), and in the second, the word **peres** is substituted. The following clarified the double usage: "The word 'upharsin' is the conjunction [U] 'and' plus the plural [**pharsin**] of peres" (*TWOT*, II, 1060). Daniel used the word **parsin** or **pharsin** in its double sense, meaning "Persians"; giving the empire to the Medes and Persians (Leupold 235); see also Young 127. In summary, God determined a fixed time limit of the king and the kingdom and was bringing both to an end. The moral character of the king fell short of that which God will endure. The kingdom was broken, separated from the king and given to the Medes and Persians.

## The End of an Era: The Beginning of Another (vv. 29-31)

**Verse 29** *Then commanded Belshazzar and they clothed Daniel with purple, and put a chain of gold about his neck, and made proclamation concerning him, that he should be the third ruler in the kingdom.*

From whatever motive Belshazzar acted, he carried out his promise of reward for reading and interpreting the miraculous message. By some influence Daniel changed his former declaration of indifference and accepted the reward. It has been pointed out that Nabonidus was king and Belshazzar his son ruled under him; therefore third place was the highest position the king could offer. The king's order seems to have been carried out immediately. Could Daniel have accepted it to honor his God? Could it have been that Belshazzar believed the message on the wall, and in the absence of his father he wanted to leave the position secured, therefore he acted without delay.

Since Daniel did not answer these questions we raised, we must leave it there and not speculate.

**Verse 30** *In that night Belshazzar the Chaldean king was slain.*

In that night Belshazzar was slain, whose death brought to an end the great Babylonian empire and the era of its world domination. The battle was not described. A monument quoted Cyrus as saying that he took the city without a battle. But however fierce or light the fighting may have been, or sporadic, it seems that the city was not destroyed.

**Verse 31** *And Darius the Mede received the kingdom, being about threescore and two years old.*

"And Darius the Mede received the kingdom, being about threescore and two years old." The identity of Darius the Mede has for a long time occasioned debate among Bible students. Because his name has not been found among the inscriptions of the monuments of ancient days, or among the letters of that period, liberal theologians have argued that the writer of the book of Daniel, who wrote during the second century B.C., was ignorant of the history of the sixth century B.C. and confused Darius the Mede with Darius Hystaspes (521-486 B.C.). This theory was thoroughly refuted by Robert Dick Wilson in his classic defense of the Book of Daniel: *Studies in the Book of Daniel,* originally printed in 1917, in two volumes, but reprinted in 1979 by Baker Book House, Grand Rapids, in one volume. He devoted six chapters (VII-XII, pp. 128-263) to some aspect of Darius the Mede. This was before many modern discoveries and translations from the monuments, and he mistook Gobryas, a governor under Cyrus, for Darius instead of Gubaru, discussed below. (See also Wilson's article, "Darius the Mede," *ISBE,* II, 788).

Leupold, in his commentary, accepted Wilson's conclusion that Gobryas of the monuments is Darius the Mede of Daniel (p. 238). Young says simply, "The identification of this king is as yet unknown, since secular historical sources are silent concerning him" (p. 131); this statement was made in 1949. However, when the manuscript for Whitcomb's book, discussed below, was received and read, Young wrote to Whitcomb, saying, "I personally incline toward your solution," footnote to Whitcomb's book, p. 26.

The most convincing book that I have read is the one mentioned above, *Darius the Mede* by John C. Whitcomb, Jr., (published by Wm. B. Eerdman's Pub. Co., Grand Rapids, Michigan, 1959.) Whitcomb began by quoting every passage in the Bible that pertained to Darius the Mede. He followed by quoting the letters and monument inscriptions in which a governor, Gubaru was named. Whitcomb paralleled likeness between Darius and what is said about Gubaru. The writer proceeded by meeting objections to his view that Gubaru was the most likely historical character for the Biblical Darius the Mede of Biblical fame. Like Young, only stronger, I lean towards Whitcomb's solution of the problem.

## What We Can Learn From the Chapter

The purpose in writing this commentary on Daniel is to learn lessons that will encourage us while suffering the judgment on a nation for its sins. One lesson learned is that national sins bring national judgment; but that judgment will end, and judgment will come upon that nation which God used as the instrument of His judgment. The seventy years captivity came to an end with the fall of Babylon.

A second lesson observed is that faithfulness of God's saints under the pains of judgment serves for good to those through whom the judgment is executed. Consider the growth and development of Nebuchadnezzar's faith and comprehension of God's greatness through the faithfulness of Daniel and his three friends; and of the queen mother who remembered Daniel's power through his God and recommended calling for him in time of need. One can never realize fully the leavening influence faithful lives can have on the world.

A third lesson learned is that living in a nation where citizens have a voice in the selection of a ruler it is important to exercise that power of choice wisely. What are our priorities, economy or moral values? One learns by experience the truth of the following: "It is an abomination to kings to commit wickedness; / For the throne is established by righteousness" (Prov. 16:12). And we need neither fret nor worry over a wicked ruler, for there is a divine law that will prevail: "Fret not thyself because of evil doers; / Neither be thou envious at the wicked: / For there shall be no reward to the evil man; / The lamp of the wicked shall be put out" (Prov. 24:19-20). Trust God, and leave the judgment to Him. It will be from Him we will be suffering the judgment coming upon us. God took care of His faithful saints in Babylon and He will take care of His faithful in our nation. Amen!

# CHAPTER VI

# Daniel in the Lion's Den

The most casual Bible students observe the likeness between chapters three and six, but seldom give serious consideration to the differences between the two. As Leupold observed, the first was not a matter of persecution; but the second was, which observation seems to be correct.

In the case of the three men (ch. 3), their being cast into the fiery furnace was prompted by the wrath of an angry king whose stubborn arrogance had been offended by the equally stubborn faith of three servants of God. They refused to bow in worship to the image which the king made. In the case of Daniel (ch. 6), the faithful man of God refused to honor the edict of the king who had been duped into signing a decree ordering all prayers offered to any god be offered through the king. This law was prompted by envious men in offices under Daniel who could find fault with him only in his relation to his God.

In the first test (ch. 3), for some unrevealed (but probably providential) reason, Daniel was absent. They proved they could stand on their own faith. Now in his old age, Daniel's faithfulness to his God would be tested as was that of the three earlier. And in each instance, the first under the Babylonian rule when three men's faith was tried in a fiery furnace, and the second, under the rule of a different kingdom, one man's faith was tested in a den of lions. Both the three and the one stood firm. And in both instances God proved faithful to His covenant promises. He stood firmly with His faithful servants.

## Daniel Under Darius the New King
## (vv. 1-3)

**Verse 1** *It pleased Darius to set over the kingdom a hundred and twenty satraps, who should be throughout the whole kingdom;*

The extent of the kingdom received by Darius the Mede seems somewhat uncertain. That it included the "realm of the Chaldeans" over which Belshazzar ruled is clear (5:31; 9:1, cf. Esther 1:1). It was not the entire Medo-Persian Empire is equally clear, for Nabonidus, the father of Belshazzar, ruled over the Babylonian Empire until the night that Babylon fell to the Medes and Persians. From that time Cyrus ruled over the great Medo-Persian Empire which included the former Babylonian lands and peoples. Leupold said that some writers extend his rule to include Chaldea, Babylon, Accad, and Susiana (246); whereas Robert Dick Wilson limited it to "the kingdom of Belshazzar the Chaldean," which he "received from Cyrus his overlord" (op. cit. 143f.).

This raised the question: Did Darius appoint 120 satraps over the entire Medo-Persian Empire? or, Did the appointment relate to Babylonia (Chaldea) only? Although the answer may remain unclear, we quote Wilson's observation: "The monumental evidence shows the possibility of 120 satraps being installed in the province of Babylonia, alone" (*idem.*). The **satrap** is from a Hebrew and Greek word translated "**viceroy, lieutenant, prince**: prob. derived from a Pers. word meaning **protector of the realm**" (*ZPEB* 5 286). The extent of a satrap's authority and power seems not to have been definite, but varied with the location and disposition of the one doing the appointing.

**Verse 2** *and over them three presidents, of whom Daniel was one; that these satraps might give account unto them, and that the king should have no damage.*

Over the satraps Darius appointed three **presidents**, of whom Daniel was one. To these presidents the satraps gave account of their stewardship, "that the king should have no damage." **Damage**, "suffer wrong" (*TWOT* II 1045), which probably included financial, political, or be wronged in any way by his enemies.

**Verse 3** *Then this Daniel was distinguished above the presidents and the satraps, because an excellent spirit was in him; and the king thought to set him over the whole realm.*

Apparently the king realized early the special character and political qualities of Daniel, "for he was distinguished—be pre-eminent" (*Ibid.*, 1046), above the other two presidents or the satraps. This was not because of his physical appearance or charming personality, but because of "an excellent spirit" that was in him; i.e., "preeminent, surpassing" (*Ibid.*, 1030) spirit that shone forth through his personality. Because of this special spirit developed through his many years of association with and subjection to Jehovah, the king thought to set him over all the realm. Whether there was any connection between Belshazzar's fulfilled promise (5:29), and the prominence given to Daniel by Darius, is not revealed. It is possible that he only certified the former king's appointment.

## The Plot Against Daniel
## (vv. 4-9)

### The Conference (vv. 4-6)

**Verse 4** *Then the presidents and the satraps sought to find occasion against Daniel as touching the kingdom; but they could find no occasion nor fault, forasmuch as*

*he was faithful, neither was there any error or fault
found in him.*

The time is not designated, but it seems that envy and jealousy arose soon after Daniel's appointment over the joint presidents and the satraps residing in Babylon. Although other causes may be revealed later, it seemed that these two, envy and jealousy, sparked the immediate reaction and opposition to Daniel. The body of these men wanted to formulate charges against God's aging servant and present them to the king. They began the search by investigating his handling of kingdom affairs, probably those in the realm of finance and business. But in the realm investigated they found no fault or error, "forasmuch as he was faithful" to God's standard and the demands of the king.

**Verse 5** *Then said these men, We shall not find any
occasion against this Daniel, except we find it against
him concerning the law of his God.*

The close and binding relation between heathen kingdoms and pagan gods has been revealed already; therefore if they were to find fault it would have to be in this realm. They must find some point of contradiction between the law of Daniel's God, or the keeping of that law by Daniel, and the religious laws of their nation.

**Verse 6** *Then these presidents and satraps assembled
together to the king, and said thus unto him, King
Darius, live for ever.*

When they devised their scheme, or plan of attack, the two presidents and the satraps dwelling in Babylon, for there is no indication that the satraps from over the entire empire, or even in all Chaldea were invited—"assembled together to the king." The word "assembled" is a strong word which means, "to be in tumult" (*TWOT* II 1071), and is translated by Keil, "to assail one in a tumultuous manner" (p. 208). Leupold said, "'Came thronging' is a very acceptable rendering" (p. 254). Young writes that after discussing the word at length, James Allan Montgomery commented, "They acted in concert, harmoniously" (p. 133). Knowing the character of those kings of that day, this interpretation by Montgomery appears to be more properly what we would expect.

## Presentation of the Deceptive Plot (vv. 7-9)

**Verse 7** *All the presidents of the kingdom, the deputies and the satraps, the counselors and the governors, have consulted together to establish a royal statute, and to make a strong interdict, that whosoever shall ask a petition of any god or man for thirty days, save of thee, O king, he shall be cast into the den of lions.* **8** *Now, O king, establish the interdict, and sign the writing, that it be not changed, according to the law of the Medes and Persians, which altereth not.*

After the salutation to the king according to the custom of that day (v. 6), the plotters introduced their request with a lie intended to deceive, when they said, "**All** the presidents," for Daniel was not present or included. And unless the addition of "deputies, counselors, and governors" is covered by the word "satrap," then these were falsely added to impress the king, which added weight to their request. "Have consulted together" seems to be false, for the members of the conference named above included only the two presidents and the satraps. The request was stated: That the king establish and sign an interdict (a decree of retraction, restriction; *TWOT* II 990) enforced by the law of the Medes and the Persians, that all petitions or prayers to man or God be offered through the king as mediator. The penalty for violating the interdict was most extreme, to be cast into the lions' den.

**Verse 9** *Wherefore king Darius signed the writing and the interdict.*

Having no ground for suspicion of deceit or duplicity on the part of his government employees, the king signed the edict into law. A law that could be neither retracted nor violated without paying the penalty. The question should be asked: Why did Darius allow himself to be so readily deceived? Many answers have been offered. Some think it was because of his vanity; he was flattered. But at the risk of being charged with adding speculation to speculations, this writer offers his explanation. As a newly appointed king over the province, and with full confidence in his officials surrounding him, he saw this as an opportunity to become acquainted with the religious views and concerns of his subjects. With this newly gained information gleaned over a thirty day period he would be in a better position to govern as their king. Remember, all life of that time was based upon religion, they were subject to their gods.

## Faith Tested
## (vv. 10-18)

### The Trap Sprung (vv. 10-12)

**Verse 10** *And when Daniel knew that the writing was signed, he went into his house (now his windows were open in his chamber toward Jerusalem); and he kneeled upon his knees three times a day, and prayed, and gave thanks before his God, as he did aforetime.*

Such a law affected the whole population of the city and would soon be known to all. And though not present at the assembly of the governors and satraps, nor when it was signed, Daniel soon learned of the signing of the law by the king. And being informed, Daniel went to his house, and as was his custom kneeled before an open window and prayed toward Jerusalem. Now an old man, from his youth Daniel never wavered in his faith and service to his God. For him to have ceased from his custom, or to pray in secret, or to have acted in any way other than what he did would have been to manifest a heart of unbelief, so he followed his custom. His posture in prayer, kneeling "upon his knees," indicated a spirit of humility and deep reverence toward God, emulated by Paul (Eph. 3:14), and a worthy example for saints to follow.

> **Verse 11** *Then these men assembled together, and found Daniel making petition and supplication before his God.* **12** *Then they came near, and spake before the king concerning the king's interdict: Hast thou not signed an interdict, that every man that shall make petition unto any god or man within thirty days, save unto thee, O king, shall be cast into the den of lions? The king answered and said, The thing is true, according to the law of the Medes and Persians, which altereth not.*

The men assembled (same word occurring in v. 6, 15), with sufficient evidence to spring their trap. Daniel was offering petitions and supplications to his God in violation of the interdict, not having gone through the king.

The body of officials lost no time in going to the king with the information about Daniel's action. However, they began with the question: Have you not signed such an edict? His admission to the question put him under the necessity of putting Daniel to death according to the strict law of the Medes and the Persians. The king admitted that such was true. The king was caught in their trap.

### The King's Reaction (vv. 13-15)

> **Verse 13** *Then answered they and said before the king, That Daniel, who is of the children of the captivity of Judah, regardeth not thee, O king, nor the interdict that thou hast signed, but maketh his petition three times a day.*

Their charge breathed contempt—"**That** Daniel" a captive, a Jew (therefore of a foreign religion), has shown contempt for your interdict. Such contempt of a foreigner, showing such respect for a foreign God, inferred contempt for you and the gods we serve.

> **Verse 14** *Then the king, when he heard these words, was sore displeased, and set his heart on Daniel to deliver him; and he labored till the going down of the sun to rescue him.*

When he heard the charge, the reaction of the King was summed up in four words, [He] "was sore displeased" ("vexed," Young). With whom was he displeased? Not with Daniel who had disregarded the interdict, as is seen in his action that followed. Probably with himself for so thoughtlessly signing such an interdict; but especially he was displeased with the men who spawned and hatched the law and its consequence by deceiving him. This was indicated by what followed. The manner in which they introduced the charge with a question; and the wording and tone of the charge indicated the character and spirit of the men involved. All this combined to produce his sore displeasure. The king realized that he had been duped, deceived by his own officials. Though futile, he "set his heart" on delivering Daniel, and spent the remainder of the day in an effort to rescue the man whom he respected. But the law of the Medes and the Persians was against his effort.

> **Verse 15** *Then these men assembled together unto the king, and said unto the king, Know, O king, that it is a law of the Medes and Persians, that no interdict nor statute which the king establisheth may be changed.*

The enemies of Daniel knew they had the king "in a corner," and were determined that he should not get out of it. And so, once more they assembled (same word, v. 6) with the king, and in an arrogant, condescending manner, reminded him that according to the law of the Medes and Persians, he had signed an interdict that could not be changed. He knew the unchangeable character of the law, but their attitude would cost them heavily.

### The Faith of Daniel and Darius Tested (vv. 16-18)

**Verse 16** *Then the king commanded, and they brought Daniel, and cast him into the den of lions. Now the king spake and said unto Daniel, Thy God whom thou servest continually, he will deliver thee.*

Although the law signed by the king was a regrettable law, the king had no alternative but to enforce it. As Daniel was cast into the den of lions, two factors were observable: The Babylonians executed their arch criminals by casting them into a furnace of fire (ch. 2); and the Medo-Persians dispensed with their criminals by casting them into a den of lions. Daniel's continued faith and service to his God so impressed Darius the Mede that his faith in Daniel's faith and service were able to save Daniel. Both the faith of Daniel and the faith of Darius in Daniel's faith were being tested. The king confessed his faith when he said, "Thy God whom thou servest continually, he will deliver thee."

The type and shape of the den is unknown. But what is said in verse 24 of the lion's mastery over the plotters against Daniel who were cast to the lions, "before they came to the bottom of the den," indicated that it sloped from the top to the bottom. This being true, it may have been a cavern in the earth, modified for this purpose. It also had a top, for Daniel was taken "up out of the den" (v. 23).

**Verse 17** *And a stone was brought, and laid upon the mouth of the den; and the king sealed it with his own signet, and with the signet of his lords; that nothing might be changed concerning Daniel.*

However the den was constructed, a stone was laid upon the "mouth" of the den and it was sealed "with his own signet, and with the signets of his lords." This guaranteed that there would be no foul play by anyone. The king could not open the den and deliver Daniel, neither could the satraps kill him and the other party not know it.

**Verse 18** *Then the king went to his palace, and passed the night fasting; neither were instruments of music brought before him; and his sleep fled from him.*

How did Daniel pass the night? Did he spend it in prayer? Or, in the security of his faith, did he find a place as comfortable as possible, stretch out, and sleep as soundly as if in his bed at home? This is unknown. But the king spent a sleepless night, refusing any kind of entertainment, spending the night fasting. Such concern for his faithful servant gives a favorable view of what some pagan rulers may have been like.

## Faith Rewarded and Evil Recompensed
## (vv. 19-24)

### Faith Vindicated: Daniel's Deliverance (vv. 19-23)

**Verse 19** *Then the king arose very early in the morning, and went in haste unto the den of lions.* **20** *And when he came near unto the den to Daniel he cried with a lamentable voice; the king spake and said to Daniel, O Daniel, servant of the living God, is thy God, whom thou servest continually able to deliver thee from the lions?*

The favorable impression made by the king's concern for Daniel in trying to deliver him from the Lion's den, and his expression of faith in God's deliverance, is further enhanced by the king's continued concern. After spending a sleepless night, the king arose early in the morning and hastened to the lions' den. And in a pained voice that expressed grief, he inquired if the God whom Daniel trusted and served had been able to deliver him. Was his question an expression of doubt? or, did it express a desire for a positive confirmation of his faith expressed the night before? I prefer to believe it was the latter; his desire was to hear Daniel's voice which would vindicate the faith he expressed as he left the den the previous night (cf. v. 16). God sent his angel who shut the mouths of the lions; it was not the lack of hunger (Heb. 11:33).

> **Verse 21** *Then said Daniel unto the king, O king, live for ever.* **22** *My God hath sent his angel, and hath shut the lions' mouths, and they have not hurt me; forasmuch as before him innocency was found in me; and also before thee, O king, have I done no hurt.*

Daniel's response confirmed the validity of his faith in God, as well as the king's faith in Daniel's faith, and the king's own faith in God and His power. God responded to the need by sending His angel to close the mouths of the lions. But it should be observed that God's response was to one who was faithful in both his responsibility to God and his obligation to the king. Faith in God's response to man's need rests on man's faithfulness to God's requirement of man's trust in Him.

> **Verse 23** *Then was the king exceeding glad, and commanded that they should take Daniel up out of the den. So Daniel was taken up out of the den, and no manner of hurt was found upon him, because he had trusted in his God.*

The sound of Daniel's voice made the king "exceeding glad," which tells much about the king's concern for his faithful servant. It tells much about the character of Darius the Mede; he manifested a compassionate spirit. When the servants lifted Daniel out of the den at the command of Darius, there was found no hurt on him. Like the three friends of Daniel who came out of the fire unscathed, not even the smell of smoke on them; so Daniel came out of the lions' den without a scratch on him.

### Evil Recompensed (v. 24)

**Verse 24** *And the king commanded, and they brought those men that had accused Daniel, and they cast them into the den of lions, them, their children, and their wives; and the lions had the mastery of them, and brake all their bones in pieces, before they came to the bottom of the den.*

Not all the governors and satraps in the empire, and possibly not all in Babylon were destroyed; only "those men that accused Daniel" met death. They, their wives and children were cast into the den of lions. And before they had reached the bottom of the den, the lions had mastered them, breaking all their bones. This is a graphic and impressive illustration of two Biblical truths: God's faithfulness in keeping His promise as the avenger of wrongs committed by men (cf. Deut. 32:35; Rom. 12:19); the far-reaching influence of sin as it affects the family of the guilty party (cf. Achan and his family and possessions, Josh. 7:24). This illustrates the principle of how the innocent may suffer the consequential judgments of the wicked.

## Darius' Decree and Daniel's Extended Service
## (vv. 25-28)

### The Decree (vv. 25-27)

**Verse 25** *Then king Darius wrote unto all the peoples, nations, and languages, that dwell in all the earth: Peace be multiplied unto you.*

Did the decree extend throughout the entire Medo-Persian Empire, or was it limited to the region ruled over by Darius the Mede? Leupold said the words translated, "peoples...that dwell in all the earth," could "just as correctly be translated by the words 'That dwell in all the **land**'" (p. 273).

**Verse 26** *I make a decree, that in all the dominion of my kingdom men tremble and fear before the God of Daniel; for he is the living God, and stedfast for ever, and his kingdom that which shall not be destroyed; and his dominion shall be even unto the end.*

And inasmuch as it has been fairly well established that Darius' kingdom included only Chaldea, and possibly two or three small provinces, this is all he included when he said, "I make a decree, that in all the dominion of my kingdom...." And though he honored Daniel's God as "the living God," whose kingdom and dominion would be to the end, and decreed that the people would so honor Him—he did not recognize Him as the Only God; to Darius the Living God was but a national God among all the national gods.

**Verse 27** *He delivereth and rescueth, and he worketh signs and wonders in heaven and in earth, who hath delivered Daniel from the power of the lions.*

He can deliver and rescue, as demonstrated; and also, "he worketh signs and wonders in heaven and in earth, who hath delivered Daniel from the power of the lions." How could he admit this, and not recognize a divine power beyond that of all the gods, the only God of such concern for His servant with the power to shut the mouth of the lions? But such unbelief is characteristic of the human race. In the light of a similar miracle centuries later, after the deliverance of the apostles from prison by an angel, His own people stumbled at believing (Acts 5:19-29; cf. Acts 12:7ff.).

## Daniel's Extended Service (v. 28)

**Verse 28** *So this Daniel prospered in the reign of Darius, and in the reign of Cyrus the Persian.*

This same Daniel whom they sought to destroy by the lions, not only lived long enough into the reign of Cyrus the Persian to see the long train of his brethren leave for home, but he prospered during the time. One wonders, did Daniel point out to Cyrus Isaiah's prophecy which said he would be raised to power and allow them to return? (Isa. 44:28—45:7). At any rate, both Darius and Cyrus recognized the worth of this faithful servant of God to the welfare of their kingdom and retained his services.

## Encouragement For A Time of Judgment

Consequential judgments for wickedness in time are inevitable. How they come, when they come, these are in the hand of God. But come they will, for God changes not. In such times the saints needs encouragement. Are there principles in this chapter of Daniel on which to ponder? Remember, the people of Israel were in Babylon because of judgment against their sins. When God brings judgment upon the world of the ungodly, the saints will suffer also. Here are a few suggestions to follow:

1. Continue constant in prayer; Daniel sets the example. The time to learn to pray is now. Prayer provides and maintains a constant relationship and fellowship with God. When the evil day comes, that relationship is already established. Daniel did not allow opposition to his faith to hinder him in his prayer life.

2. Maintain a state of constant righteousness before God and man by faithfulness to God in serving him as did Daniel. And maintain the same toward man by fulfilling whatever responsibility one has toward him in social relationships— "Dare to be a Daniel" (v. 22).

3. Daniel was delivered from the lions' den, "Because he had trusted in his God" (v. 23b). "There is no other way, but to trust and obey." Trust in God will ultimately bring deliverance; it may be in physical death, but it will come.

4. In the midst of the trial of Daniel's faith, God "sent his angel and shut the lions' mouths" (v. 22). Also, there were four in the fiery furnace, the three Hebrew children plus God's divine representative (ch. 3). The Holy Spirit said of the angels,

"Are they not all ministering spirits, sent forth to do service for the sake of them that shall inherit salvation?" (Heb. 1:14). Is our faith and trust sufficiently strong to accept the passage in Hebrews, or must we explain it away by applying it only to the apostolic period? Consider this incident that happened to a rancher in Texas who is well-known to me. He was underneath his dump truck greasing it, when he felt something scaly touch his arm. Scrambling out from beneath the truck he saw that it was a rattlesnake. He had touched it, but it did not strike. Had God sent an angel that closed its mouth? God sent one to close the mouths of lions; could he not send one to close the mouth of a snake? This man is a Christian who prays each morning for God's protection during the day. Prayers are answered.

5. We will have enemies when we stand strong in trust of God, for the world hates God and those who faithfully serve Him. But from this chapter learn that vengeance belongs to God, not man. Therefore leave the recompence to Him.

6. The judgment will come to an end, either as we are allowed to return home as the captives did, or in our call to the heavenly home at the end of our captivity in this life. And so, keep the faith, rejoice in the Lord always, and again, rejoice in Him. "The righteous is delivered out of trouble; / And the wicked cometh in his stead" (Prov. 11:8).

7. And finally, so live and trust God in the midst of adversity and suffering that your life of faith will impress those of the world as did Daniel who impressed Nebuchadnezzar and Darius, and Cyrus.

8. Daniel's faith, hope, and courage should inspire the same in the hearts of God's people to meet the trials and judgment in every age. Daniel's example should motivate us to be stedfast in the struggles of life.

# The Nation's Future:
# Dreams and Visions of Daniel

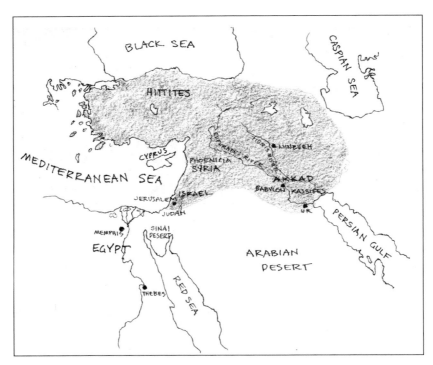

*Babylonian Empire (7:4)*

# CHAPTER VII

# The Four Beasts and the Kingdom of God

**In** a short exposition of *Daniel, His Life and Times*, H. Deane divided the book of Daniel into two sections, placing the end of section A at the conclusion of chapter six, and the beginning of section B with chapter seven. However, H. C. Leupold who also divided the book into two sections, included chapter seven as the conclusion of section A, and begins section B with chapter eight. His basic argument rested on Daniel's use of the Aramaic language from 2:4 through 7:28. His second argument rested on the claim that chapter seven rounds out section A very neatly. He made other points, but these suffice to get his argument. No doubt every commentator has a preference, depending on his approach to the book.

When one considers section A as historical, interspersed with prophecy in the form of Daniel's interpretation of the dreams of others, and section B as almost, if not entirely, prophetically of Daniel's visions, with historical interpretations, then the division of chapters 1-6, and 7-12 is preferable. The parallel between chapters two and seven make each of these chapters the beginning of the section. Nebuchadnezzar's dream (ch. 2) emphasized the external or human aspect of the world kingdoms and their relation to the kingdom of God;

whereas Daniel's dream of the same kingdoms (ch. 7) emphasized the internal or moral character in their relation to the
kingdom of God.

Before an exposition is made of each dream and its vi- sions,
it might be helpful to make a brief summary of Daniel's
dreams showing the progressive development of these in
revealing the future of the world kingdoms and the kingdom
of God. Modern movies and video cassettes present an illustration of Daniel's method. Each series of visions is an episode
of the total picture. The series of dreams and visions in chapter seven reveal a parallel to Nebuchadnezzar's dreams and
visions in chapter two. Daniel's dreams and visions began with
the breaking forth of four winds upon the sea of society or
humanity, out of which four great and terrible beasts emerge.
The vision of these melted into the background, and another
came into view which likewise receded into the background.
The judgment and destruction of these followed, which likewise faded out of the picture. This was followed by a third
vision in which a man came to the ancient of days where he
received an indestructible eternal kingdom. This vision likewise faded into the background. Daniel was affected mightily
by the vision of the fourth beast, and asked for help in understanding it. In a fourth phase of the first episode, the meaning
of the fourth beast was made known to him. And it also faded
into the background (ch. 7).

Two years later Daniel saw in another vision a ram standing
by the river Ulai; the ram had two horns which stood high, but
one was higher than the other. While he beheld the ram, a he-
goat, with a notable horn between its eyes, came bounding out
of the west. The he-goat broke the two horns of the ram, leaving the ram powerless and defeated. In his power and anger,
the horn between the eyes of the he goat was also broken, and
four conspicuous horns came up in its stead. Out of one of the
four horns there came a little horn. This little horn sought the
destruction of God's people. Again Daniel sought help in
understanding the vision; wherefore God sent Gabriel to reveal
certain aspects of the vision to him (ch. 8).

In a third dated scene, Daniel was introduced as reading

Jeremiah's prophecy in which he realized that the seventy year period of the prophet was drawing to a close. He prayed fervently to Jehovah for help, who responded by sending Gabriel to him with another vision, that of the seventy weeks. This vision dealt with the future of the kingdom of God and its coming (ch. 9).

In a fourth dated scene, a fourth vision was brought before the prophet depicting a "great warfare." This vision terrified the prophet. Again God sent an angel to comfort and instruct him, an angel of unusual appearance. He was sent to make known to Daniel what would be the lot of his people in later days. Strengthened by the angel's words, Daniel was ready to hear his explanation of the vision (ch. 10). This was followed by the angel's explanation of the warfare that would come, which is probably the most difficult and controversial chapter in the book of Daniel, if not in the entire Bible (ch. 11).

In the final vision he was made to realize that there would be terrible times, trying days, and painful experiences before the final and permanent establishment of the kingdom of God. But victory would ultimately be realized by God's faithful people, His saints (ch. 12).

## The Background of the Dreams
## (vv. 1-3)

**Verse 1** *In the first year of Belshazzar king of Babylon Daniel had a dream and visions of his head upon his bed: then he wrote the dream and told the sum of the matters.*

According to D. J. Wiseman, the third year (8:1) of Belshazzar was ca. 547 B.C., which would place the first year ca. 549 B.C. (*ZPEB* I 516). Visions may be seen while awake or asleep, and may take a more definite form than dreams, which may be more vague than their counterpart. (For a fuller definition see note, 2:19.) Both occurred to Daniel while upon his bed. "The sum of the matters" meant to bring under one head the complete total of the essential parts, presenting a total picture.

**Verse 2** *Daniel spake and said, I saw in my vision by night, and, behold, the four winds of heaven brake forth upon the great sea.*

In this scene the four winds of heaven symbolized the strong forces which produce upheavals in society, out of which develop nations or various forms of government within nations. Beside these winds of upheaval, there were winds that scatter (Jer. 18:17; 49:32), and there are "destroying winds" (Jer. 51:1). The "great sea" was not the Mediterranean sea, but the sea of society or humanity (cf. Isa. 57:20; Rev. 13:1; 20:13; 21:1). Out of the winds of upheaval, whether they be political, ethnic, social, or economic, various nations and forms of government develop.

**Verse 3** *And four great beasts came up from the sea, diverse one from another.*

From the turbulent sea of society Daniel beheld four great beasts emerge, "diverse one from another." As the people who make up the various nations differ in characteristics, so the nations comprised of these individuals are diverse one from another. Each had characteristics peculiar to its self. Each of these kingdoms, or empires, would be used to serve Jehovah's purpose according to its diverse characteristics.

## The Four Beasts
## (vv. 4-8)

### Like a Lion (v. 4)

**Verse 4** *The first was like a lion, and had eagle's wings: I beheld till the wings thereof were plucked, and it was lifted up from the earth, and made to stand upon two feet as a man; and a man's heart was given to it.*

In Nebuchadnezzar's dream of the great statue the head was the most important, for it was the ruling member of the body.

The gold head, the most precious of the metals, symbolized Nebuchadnezzar, "king of kings," to whom God gave the kingdoms of earth (2:37-38). And now, in Daniel's dream, the lion, the king of beasts, and the eagle, king of the birds, symbolized the Babylonian kingdom which, under Nebuchadnezzar, became the ruling kingdom of earth. Nebuchadnezzar has been referred to already as a lion (Jer. 4:7; 50:17) and an eagle (Hab. 1:8; Ezek. 17:3, 12). The kingdom and its king were inseparable; they were as one. Therefore what one did was shared by the other.

As "king of kings" (2:37; Ezek. 26:7), Nebuchadnezzar ruled over the kings and the kingdoms of earth. By God's "great power" these kings and kingdoms were given to Nebuchadnezzar, which God promised, and fulfilled the promise. "…And now have I given all these lands into the hand of Nebuchadnezzar the king of Babylon, my servant; and the beasts of the field also have I given him to serve him. And all the nations shall serve him, and his son, and his son's son, until the time of his own land come: and then many nations and great kings shall make him their bondman. And it shall come to pass that the nation and the kingdom which will not serve the same Nebuchadnezzar king of Babylon, and that will not put their neck under the yoke of the king of Babylon, that nation will I punish, saith Jehovah, with the sword, and with the famine, and with the pestilence, until I have consumed them by his hand" (Jer. 27:6-8). The sword of conquest was Jehovah's sword in the hand of Nebuchadnezzar; it was Jehovah's power by which he conquered the kingdoms (Ezek. 30:24-25).

Daniel beheld until the wings were plucked, the beast stood up on two feet like a man, and a man's heart was given to it. This seems to indicate that when the nations were conquered by the power of God through the Babylonian king, his special power from God ceased. His rule of the empire of which very little was known following the conquest, was like other kings who ruled their subjects, with ordinary human wisdom.

## Like to a Bear (v. 5)

**Verse 5** *And, behold, another beast, a second, like to a bear; and it was raised up on one side, and three ribs were in its mouth between its teeth: and they said thus unto it, Arise, devour much flesh.*

The bear was less regal in appearance than the lion, being more lumbering and awkward appearing in its movements. However, it was strong and ferocious, second only to the lion. Whether the extensive area of the bear's habitat, being found in large sections of the world, had any significance in selecting the bear to represent the Medo-Persian empire is uncertain. But it is possible, since that kingdom was the largest ever until the Roman Empire reached its full extent (5a).

Instead of discussing the various interpretations offered by

*Medo-Persian Empire (7:5)*

commentators on the phrase, "raised up on one side," it seems preferable to interpret it in the light of Daniel's vision in which he saw a ram with two high horns, "but one was higher than the other" (8:3). The higher symbolized the Persian preeminence over Medea. And so, the being raised up on one side seems to indicate the same thing, the Persian preeminence of the two (5b).

The "three ribs...in its mouth" likewise have given occasion for many interpretations, the most generally accepted view is that they represented Babylon, Lydia, and Egypt. But since the empire included so many former kingdoms and provinces, and it occurs in a figurative and symbolic context, this seems unlikely. If three is the divine number, not simply the trinity, then could not the three represent the total provinces allotted by divine providence to Cyrus and the empire? About one hundred years before his birth, God named Cyrus and promised that He would hold his hand and through him He would subdue nations and for him He would open gates (Isa. 45:1-2. cf. vv. 3-8). The Medo-Persians arose and devoured much flesh, the complete conquest of the divine allotment. Compare with verse 20.

## "Like a Leopard" (v. 6)

**Verse 6** *After this I beheld, and, lo, another, like a leopard, which had upon its back four wings of a bird; the beast had also four heads; and dominion was given to it.*

This is the most controversial of the four beasts. Does it symbolize the Syrian kingdom of Antiochus Epiphanes, or the conquest and kingdom of Alexander the Great? The larger commentaries discuss this question at lengths, refuting the arguments of liberal scholars who seek to establish the late date for Daniel. Without arguing the matter, I accept the conservative view that the leopard symbolizes Alexander and his Macedonian conquest and kingdom. To be discussed in chapter 8.

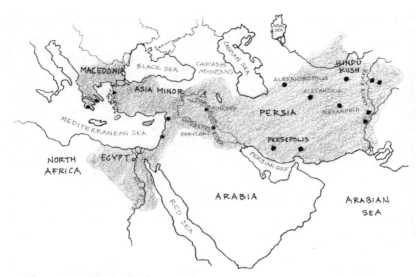

*The Grecian Empire (7:7)*

The leopard, a member of the lion family, was fiercer than the tiger, and often attacked man without provocation. The word "back," on which were the four wings, can be translated, **"back or sides**...The Kethib [the original of the MT of the OT (*ZPEB* 3 785)] takes it as plural, 'sides'" (*TWOT* II 999).

If we accept "sides" instead of "back" as the translation, which some scholars do, then the wings symbolized speed, the speed with which Alexander led his army and with which he conquered nations. The four heads represent the four kingdoms into which it was divided at the death of Alexander.

## An "Unearthly Beast" (vv. 7-8)

**Verse 7** *After this I saw in the night visions, and, behold, a fourth beast terrible and powerful, and strong exceedingly; and it had great iron teeth; it devoured and*

*brake in pieces, and stamped the residue with its feet;*
*and it was diverse from all the beasts that were before it:*
*and it had ten horns.*

This beast has no counterpart in the realm of nature; in all the animal kingdom there was no creature with which to compare it. It "was diverse from all the beasts that were before it." Daniel exhausted his vocabulary in describing its distinct and terrifying appearance. It was "terrible…powerful…strong exceedingly; it had great iron teeth; [these had great crushing power with which] it devoured." What it could not devour it "stamped" under its feet, leaving its victim crushed and ruined; a mark of wanton brutality. The point in which it was diverse from the others was that, "it had ten horns," which will be discussed below.

**Verse 8** *I considered the horns, and, behold there came up among them another horn, a little one, before which three of the first horns were plucked up by the roots: and, behold, in this horn were eyes like the eyes of a man, and a mouth speaking great things.*

Daniel continued to look intently at the horns; he beheld a "little horn" that came up "among" the ten, before which three of the ten horns were plucked up "by the roots." And, marvel of marvels, this little horn had eyes like a man, and a mouth speaking great things. No wonder Daniel was fascinated, and later asked for an explanation of the fourth beast.

Although the four beasts, which symbolized four great empires, were diverse one from another (v. 3), they had three things in common: 1) each sought to conquer, control, and rule the world by military force; 2) each was an idolatrous

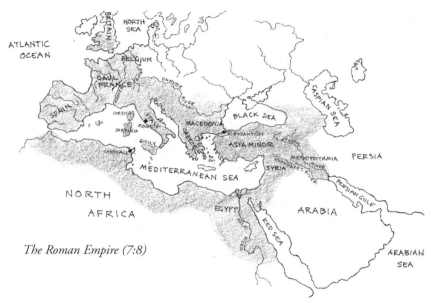

*The Roman Empire (7:8)*

nation, worshipping its pantheon of idol gods of its own creation; 3) each strongly opposed Jehovah God and His
kingdom; each was an enemy of God. Almost two centuries
earlier, Jehovah challenged the idols to prove their godhood by
declaring the future at the present; or, do something good or
evil. He then rested His claim to be the only God on the
ground of His ability to declare future events, the end from the
beginning (Isa. 41:21-29). The chapters that followed set forth
aspects of the conflict (43—48). Jehovah now declared the
judgment of the four beasts and the establishment of His own
indestructible kingdom during the domination of the fourth
beast. This proved the impotence of the idols, and established
His claim to be the only true God.

## Judgment of the Four Beasts
## (vv. 9-12)

**Verse 9** *I beheld till thrones were placed and one that
was ancient of days did sit: his raiment was white as
snow, and the hair of his head like pure wool; his throne
was fiery flames, and the wheels thereof burning fire.*

As the vision of the beasts faded, into the background, Daniel continued to look until a second vision appeared, one of majestic grandeur. It was a courtroom scene befitting the majesty of the God of heaven. Thrones were set in place, but who would occupy them? Were the occupants the seraphim of Isaiah 6? or the cherubim of Ezekiel 10? or a special group of angels? Or, were they for the prophets who warned the nations when God sent them to the people of Israel, but who had prophesied to the nations as well? Were they the faithful remnant who was persecuted by the cruel nations of the world? Were they Jehovah and the pre-incarnate Christ? We are not told, therefore each is left to make his own guess. An "ancient of days" sat upon one of the thrones of special design and beauty. It was of "fiery flames, and the wheels thereof burning fire." The fire was symbolic of the finality of the judgment; the ones judged would never again exist. And the wheels symbolized the universality of God the Judge, He could be everywhere, His judgments were not limited to Zion-Jerusalem.

Daniel does not say that he saw God; but that God was represented by a very aged and honorable One, arrayed in a snow-white robe, whose hair was like pure wool. Each of these, the white robe and hair, probably symbolized absolute purity, as well as age that extended back to the beginning of nations and empires which would be judged. The "fiery flames" and "burning fire" impressed the fact that Jehovah is a "devouring fire" (Deut. 4:24; Heb. 12:29); and that a fire goes before Him, "And burneth up his adversaries round about" (Ps. 97:3).

**Verse 10** *A fiery stream issued and came forth from before him: thousands of thousands ministered unto him, and ten thousand times ten thousand stood before him: the judgment was set, and the books were opened.*

"A fiery stream issued and came forth from before him," adding to the awesome picture of Jehovah's court. It was the figure of an active volcano with its stream of flowing lava, destroying every thing in its path. Describing His righteousness and justice, an unnamed psalmist said, "A fire goeth before him, / And burneth up his adversaries round about" (Ps. 97:3). This fiery stream may be synonymous with the great innumerable host that minister unto Him, since He makes "winds [angels, Heb. 1:7] his messengers; / Flames of fire his ministers" (Ps. 104:4; Heb. 1:14).

When the court was called to order, "the books were opened." "The books" symbolized the charges brought against the ones being judged and their penalties executed. Also, the books included God's moral law, the violation of which had condemned the nations in the world judgment revealed by Isaiah (Isa. 24:5-6). Also, they contained the prophecies addressed by Jehovah to the heathen nations via the prophets sent to Israel.

> **Verse 11** *I beheld at that time because of the voice of the great words which the horn spake; I beheld even till the beast was slain, and its body destroyed, and it was given to be burned with fire.*

Daniel was especially concerned about the great words of the little horn that grew up from among the ten horns. He continued his intense gaze until the beast was slain and burned, which included the little horn. It was reserved for John the apostle to reveal the destruction of the beast which would be destroyed by the Messiah and His army (Rev. 19:19-20). The beast's being burned with fire symbolized the completeness of its destruction. It would never exist again.

> **Verse 12** *And as for the rest of the beasts, their dominion was taken away: yet their lives were prolonged for a season and a time.*

The fate of the first three beasts was not so important as that of the fourth, therefore their fate was passed over until the fate of the fourth beast and the little horn was determined. And though "their dominion [to '**dominate, have mastery**' over, *TWOT* II 928] was taken away," each life of a pagan nature and character lived by one empire that continued living in the beast that followed, "until a season and a time." Of this last phrase, Paul's statement to the philosophers at Athens offered a correct interpretation, when he said of the nations, God "having determined their appointed seasons, and the bounds of their habitation" (Acts 17:26). Each continued until the God of heaven determined the time of its end.

## The Heavenly Kingdom Bestowed
## (vv. 13-14)

**Verse 13** *I saw in the night-visions, and, behold, there came with the clouds of heaven one like unto a son of man, and he came even to the ancient of days, and they brought him near before him.*

Daniel saw in this third night-vision one "like unto a son of man" coming unto the "ancient of days." Though He was "like unto" a man, He was more than a man. Daniel spoke from heaven's point of view, for he came "unto the ancient of days"—unto God, represented in the vision as an aged man who for long ages had promised the establishment of His spiritual kingdom. This one was brought near before "the ancient of days" who had sat in judgment of the four beasts. His judgment and the destruction of the heathen kingdoms must be executed before the establishment of His own kingdom; for it must be demonstrated that He is the only God, and that His kingdom is the only permanent one.

**Verse 14** *And there was given him dominion, and glory, and a kingdom, that all the peoples, nations, and languages should serve him: his dominion is an everlasting dominion, which shall not pass away, and his kingdom that which shall not be destroyed.*

What was given to Nebuchadnezzar whereby he was recognized as "king of kings," namely, "dominion, glory, and a kingdom" was now given unto this one who came before the ancient of days. These were a permanent, everlasting possession which would never be destroyed or pass away. Furthermore, "All the peoples, nations, and languages" would serve Him, recognizing His absolute sovereignty.

There should be no argument as to who or what this scene referred. Daniel spoke from heaven's point of view. He was describing the return of God's Son, as the Son of man and the Son of God, when He received the promised kingdom from His Father. And Luke, speaking from earth's point of view, described the same event in the first two chapters of Acts.

Following His resurrection and prior to His ascension, Jesus declared that all authority in heaven and on earth had been given to Him (Matt. 28:18). In his introduction of Acts, Luke told of "all that Jesus began both to do and to teach, until the day in which he was received up" (1:1-2); therefore, the one who was received up was the one who had done and taught marvelous things, the Son of man, the Son of God. After giving His charge to the apostles (1:8), "As they were looking, he was taken up; and a **cloud** received him out of their sight. And while they were looking stedfastly into heaven as he went," two angels stood by them. These angels testified as follows: "This Jesus, who was received up from you **into heaven**, shall so come in like manner as ye beheld him **going into heaven**" (1:9-11). So, when He left the earth He ascended into heaven to the "ancient of days."

On the Pentecost following the resurrection of Jesus, when the Holy Spirit came upon the apostles, Peter preached concerning Jesus of Nazareth, that He was "**a man** approved of God unto you," whom they had crucified, whom God had raised from the dead. He was at that time, "by the right hand of God exalted" (2:22, 33), whom "God had made both Lord and Christ, this Jesus whom ye crucified" (v. 36). And the writer of Hebrews said that God testified of Him as His Son: "But of the Son he saith, Thy **throne**, O God, is forever and ever; / And thy **sceptre**...is the sceptre of thy **kingdom**" (Heb. 1:8). So, He has a throne, a sceptre, and a kingdom. These He received when He returned to heaven.

John the apostle testified that Jesus was caught up unto the throne of God from which He rules the nations with a rod of iron (Rev. 12:5; cf. Ps. 2:7-9). In this position He is the true "King of kings" (Rev. 17:14; 19:16). The kingdom over which He rules is the kingdom that would never be destroyed or pass away (Dan. 2:44; 7:14), for it shall endure to the end of time, and then be delivered back to God the Father (I Cor. 15:24-28). It is the eternal kingdom of present day saints (II Pet. 1:11). In summary, there would be four great kingdoms of the world, symbolized by four great beasts. These would be judged by Jehovah and destroyed; and then the kingdom of God (that is, the rein of God) would be established and delivered to the Messiah.

## Daniel's Perplexity
## (vv. 15-16)

**Verse 15** *As for me, Daniel, my spirit was grieved in the midst of my body, and the visions of my head troubled me.*

Daniel's reaction to the vision was twofold: he was grieved in spirit and troubled in mind. It is doubtful that the terrible appearance of the beasts caused this reaction; but the realization of what lay ahead for his people. There was the terrible period of the Babylonian captivity which was nearing its end, but according to the vision, there were three world kingdoms yet to be endured by God's people.

**Verse 16** *I came near unto one of them that stood by, and asked him the truth concerning all this. So he told me, and made me know the interpretation of the things.*

In this state of perplexity Daniel sought the help of one of the attendants who stood by. He desired to know the truth concerning the things he had just seen in the vision. The attendant's ready response indicated that he was one of the heavenly beings present.

## The Explanation
## (vv. 17-22)

(vv. 17-19)

**Verse 17** *These great beasts, which are four, are four kings, that shall arise out of the earth.*

The four beasts are four kings, probably four kingdoms (v. 23) rather than individual kings. That they came out of the earth, of which the sea is a part (v. 2), from which they emerged (v. 3), indicated their worldly character in contrast to the kingdom received by the one who came before the ancient of days. These were world empires, all of the same origin and spirit.

**Verse 18** *But the saints of the Most High shall receive the kingdom, and possess the kingdom for ever, even for ever and ever.*

Sensing the perplexity of the prophet, the attendant quickly spoke a word of encouragement: "The saints of the Most High" would receive and possess the kingdom. The Aramaic word for "possess" means, "**Take possession**. The related Hebrew words emphasized strength and riches" (*TWOT* II 1020). Jesus said to His disciples, "Fear not, little flock; for it is your Father's good pleasure to give you the kingdom" (Luke 12:32; see verse 22 below). Their possession of the kingdom would be for eternity. In every dark cloud revealed by the prophets pertaining to the children of God, there was a break through which a beam of light shined, which encouraged the hearts of the saints.

**Verse 19** *Then I desired to know the truth concerning the fourth beast, which was diverse from all of them, exceeding terrible, whose teeth were of iron, and its nails of brass; which devoured, brake in pieces, and stamped the residue with its feet;*

The seer's special interest was focused on the fourth beast and the horns, its being diverse, different from the others. This distinction was made three times. Its exceeding terrible aspect was repeated, probably for emphasis (cf. vv. 7-8). To its "teeth of iron" to crush and grind, was added "nails of brass," which would tear, lacerate, and destroy. This repetition of ferocious destroying power gave emphasis to the exceedingly oppressive and troublous times faced by the people of God in coming days. This described the Roman Empire.

### The Ten Horns and the Little Horn, (cf. vv. 7b-8a) (vv. 20-22)

**Verse 20** *And concerning the ten horns that were on its head, and the other horn which came up, and before which three fell, even that horn that had eyes, and a mouth that spake great things, whose look was more stout than its fellows.*

In these highly figurative visions of beasts, horns, and a horn, there is no reason for interpreting numerals one, three, and ten as literal; but like the other aspects of the visions, these must be considered as symbolic also. Inasmuch as the conflict between the kingdom of God and the Roman Empire was set forth in Revelation, and many of the same symbols are used by John, much of this interpretation of these verses is based on John's visions and use of the same symbolism.

A mark of the fourth beast's diversity was its ten horns (v. 7). Daniel desired to know the meaning of these ten horns and "the other horn," which is the "little one," "another horn" (v. 8). In further explanation of the fourth beast by the one explaining the vision to Daniel, he said, "The ten horns" are "ten kings" (v. 24). By comparing this vision of Daniel with John's vision of the beast out of the sea, having seven heads and ten horns, it appears evident that both visions symbolize the Roman Empire, a composite of the first three beasts of Daniel's vision (Rev. 13:1-2). This beast (the Roman Empire) support-ed the harlot (Rome, the harlot of Rev. 17—18). This harlot was "the great city, which reigneth over the kings of the earth" (Rev. 17:18). "And the ten horns that thou sawest are ten kings, who have received no kingdom as yet" (17:12). So, horns symbolize kings or kingdoms in both visions.

The question asked is: Are the numbers 1, 3, and 10 symbolic, or literal numbers? Everything in the context is symbolic, even "kings" may refer to kingdoms. Why should numbers be considered literal and not symbolical? "One" may signify a "unity," e.g. as "The Lord is one" (Deut. 6:4; Mark 12:29, 32), but the "one" is composed of three persons. God said of the husband-wife, two persons, they "shall be one flesh" (Gen. 2:24). The Spirit said the ten kings, would receive authority as kings for "one hour" (Rev. 17:12), that is, for a short period. No ten kings ever ruled for one literal hour. The author of "Numbers" (*ISBE* IV 2162) listed more than a dozen Bible instances where ten is used, then said, "[These] show plainly that 10 was a favorite symbolic number, suggestive of a rounded total, large or small." These considerations show that these numbers are used symbolically.

In the light of this evidence, the ten horns of Daniel (v. 20) which are ten kings (v. 24) would be the total number of emperors (kings) in the Roman Empire from Augustus to Constantine (some 45). And the Spirit said to John, "The ten horns that thou sawest are ten kings, who have received no kingdom as yet" (Rev. 17:12); These would be the kings of the empire beyond the period of Domitian, the period in which John wrote, some 36 in number.[1] Also, "the three" which fell before "the other horn," the "little horn" of verse 8, was a symbolic number representing those whom God suffered to be taken out of the way, not any three definite rulers. This horn with the eyes, mouth, and a stout look (v. 20) is discussed in the following verse.

---

[1] these two numbers of emperors before and after Constantine are taken from *Rome, History of,* Microsoft Corporation 1993-1996.

**Verse 21** *I beheld, and the same horn made war with the saints, and prevailed against them;*

Daniel said that the horn of verse 20, "made war with the saints, and prevailed against them." Again, we ask, Does the prophet have one individual ruler in mind? or, is he using the number symbolically of a small number of rulers who led in persecution of the saints? It should be remembered that not all rulers, but only a small number of Roman rulers led in intensive efforts to destroy the kingdom of God, although all were anti-God and opposed "the faith." Coleman-Norton listed ten rulers who led the Roman nation in the most severe persecutions (P. R. Coleman-Norton, *Roman State and the Christian Church*, vol. III, London. S. P. C. K., 1911. p. 1179). Compare this horn with the beast of ten horns that came up out of the sea (Rev. 13:5-7); this horn of Daniel's vision seemed to represent the persecuting element of the rulers of John's vision. Compare also the "time, times, and half a time"—three and a half years—of Daniel's vision (7:25) with that of John's vision of the persecution that continued for forty-two months, also three and a half years (Rev. 13:5); the same time lapse.

**Verse 22** *until the ancient of days came, and judgment was given to the saints of the Most High, and the time came that the saints possessed the kingdom.*

This persecution by the little horn would continue "until the ancient of days came and judgment was given to [**for**, margin, or **on behalf of**, Young, p. 159] the saints of the Most High." This time when judgment was given on behalf of the saints, seems to be when Constantine was made ruler. It is God who makes such decisions of rulers of nations (cf. 4:17; 2:37). It was God who put it in the minds of these to do His will, "until the words of God should be accomplished" (Rev. 17:17), which word of God is the word of the prophets and apostles.

## Further Explanation of the Visions
## (vv. 23-28)

Inasmuch as the three visions which appeared to Daniel presented in brief the future history of the heathen empires and the kingdom of God, the speaker felt the need for further explanation to the seer. Therefore he continued with a fuller explanation of the beast, the horns, and the ultimate destiny of the kingdom of God and the saints.

### The Fourth Beast (v. 23)

**Verse 23** *Thus he said, The fourth beast shall be a fourth kingdom upon earth, which shall be diverse from all the kingdoms, and shall devour the whole earth, and shall tread it down, and break it in pieces.*

The speaker introduced the four beasts as four kings (v. 17) and explained that the fourth beast was a fourth kingdom, "which shall be diverse from all the kingdoms," different from the other three. This was the fourth time the speaker used the word "diverse": The four beasts were diverse "one from another" (v. 3); the fourth was diverse in that it had ten horns (v. 7); the fourth beast was diverse from the others in its exceeding ferociousness (v. 19); and the fourth was diverse in that it devoured the known powers of earth, treading the earth under foot, and breaking it in pieces as one would a potter's vessel.

### The Ten Horns and the One Horn (vv. 24-25)

**Verse 24** *And as for the ten horns, out of this kingdom shall ten kings arise; and another shall arise after them; and he shall be diverse from the former, and he shall put down three kings.*

The ten horns were ten kings which symbolized the total number of the beast's kings. The "another" king that shall arise after the ten was the "little horn" (v. 8), "diverse" from these ten. This was the fifth time that "diverse" appears, It was a "diverse" king, different from others, in a diverse kingdom. "After them," the ten, does not mean following the reign of the symbolic ten kings, for he "shall put down three kings." It was pointed out that this horn symbolized the persecuting element of the kings. Therefore, it would be after the kingdom was established as an empire and an unspecified number had been ruling. The "three" should not be thought of as three individuals, but as the divine number taken out of the way by the Lord, for it was He who put in their hearts what they were doing (Rev. 17:17).

> **Verse 25** *And he shall speak words against the Most High, and shall wear out the saints of the Most High; and he shall think to change the times and the law; and they shall be given into his hand until a time and times and half a time.*

The words this horn spoke were "against the Most High." The horn "had eyes, and a mouth that spake great things" (v. 20). It seemed that the "mouth speaking great things and blasphemies," was the "mouth" given to the beast out of the sea, i.e., the Roman Empire (Rev. 13:5). Daniel saw the persecuting element as a horn, John saw the group as "a mouth" given to the empire to blaspheme God. And though the little horn would "wear out the saints…and think to change the times and the law" toward emperor worship, there would always be a faithful remnant who would refuse to comply. Further evidence for this interpretation is the equal time of persecutions in Daniel and John. The "horn" of Daniel was for "a time and times and half a time," and that of the "mouth" of John was "forty and two months" (Rev. 13:5). Each period was three and a half years.

One should note that three and a half years in Daniel and the same length of time in Revelation was a time of adversity, opposition, and persecution. Compare the five occurrences of equal length in Revelation: the Holy city trodden under foot forty and two months (11:2); the two witnesses clothed in sackcloth twelve hundred sixty days (11:3); the radiant woman in the wilderness, fleeing from the dragon, twelve hundred sixty days (12:6); the same woman in the wilderness where she was nourished for "a time, times, and half a time" (12:14); the beast who warred against God and the saints was given forty and two months (13:4-5). The use of this time period, a broken seven, further confirm this position.

## (v. 26-28)

**Verse 26** *But the judgment shall be set, and they shall take away his dominion, to consume and to destroy it unto the end.*

"But the judgment shall be set, the judgment of verses 9-12, in which "they," the "ancient of days" and the occupants of the "thrones" of the court are "set" and dominion of the beast is taken away and he shall be destroyed "unto the end," that is, for all time. This end time destruction was portrayed by John in Revelation as a great warfare between the victorious Christ, the "KING OF KINGS AND LORD OF LORDS" and His spiritual followers, and the beast. In this decisive war, the beast out of the sea, the Roman Empire and his helper, the beast out of the earth, false religion, were "cast alive into the lake of fire" (Rev. 19:11-21).

**Verse 27** *And the kingdom and the dominion, and the greatness of the kingdoms under the whole heaven, shall be given to the people of the saints of the Most High: his kingdom is an everlasting kingdom, and all dominions shall serve and obey him.*

Chapter two closed with the assurance that in the days of those kings (kingdoms), the God of heaven would set up His kingdom which would never be destroyed (2:44). In like manner, this chapter which parallels chapter two, closed on a similar upbeat note. The prophet was shown in the third night vision that upon the return to heaven of one "like unto a son of man" there had been given Him (the Messiah), dominion, glory, and a kingdom. This kingdom would consist of people from all the nations of earth (vv. 13-14). The prophet said that all these things "shall be given to the people of the saints of the Most High." It shall be an everlasting kingdom, the one promised in chapter two. In spite of the opposition of four mighty kingdoms of earth, God's purpose would be achieved. His kingdom would be established and all nations would "flow unto it" (Isa 2:2). These would be His subjects (cf. Ps. 2; 110; Rev. 12:5; et al.).

> **Verse 28** *Here is the end of the matter. As for me, Daniel, my thoughts much troubled me, and my countenance was changed in me: but I kept the matter in my heart.*

In spite of the explanation of the visions given by the attendant to Daniel, visions which troubled him, he concluded by saying, "my thoughts much troubled me," which probably manifested concern in the expression on his face. But he kept the matter in his heart to ponder in the days to come. One can now look at the visions from this side of their appearance to Daniel, judgment of the nations, and the Book of Revelation, but Daniel looked at it from the other side.

## Summary and Encouragement

In Daniel, three night visions and the explanation of them by one of the throng before Jehovah, God provided for His people and the world a capsule history of the future of His kingdom and the four great world-empires. The captives were on the threshold of emerging from a seventy year captivity of the first beast. But there would be three beasts to follow which would rule over His people and the remnant. During the fourth empire, the third one yet to come, the most fierce and terrible of the group, God would set up His kingdom amidst terrible persecutions. In His judgment and destruction of the four beasts (the world empires), and the establishment of His kingdom that would never be destroyed, He would prove that He is the only God, the Most High. Daniel's future visions revealed some features of the lot of His people in the midst of these kingdoms until victory over Satan's effort to overthrow God's purpose and prevent the establishment of His kingdom during the time of the fourth beast.

In time of national calamity, looked upon as judgment from God because of national sins, the Christian finds encouragement in the fact that it is a righteous judgment that is well deserved.

Likewise he finds comfort in the confidence that while wearing the name, "Lord of lords and King of kings" (Rev. 17:14; or vice versa, 19:16) in His war against Satan the Christ never lost a skirmish, much less a battle. And in the passage, 17:14, the promise to His faithful followers, they, too, will overcome. Now seated on the throne of the universe, He rules the nations with a "rod of iron" (Rev. 12:5), and His own kingdom with the "sceptre of uprightness" (Heb. 1:8), neither of which can fail.

The everlasting kingdom of Daniel 7:13-14 has been set up, and the saints of the Most High possess it (7:18, 27), and the believer has been translated into it (Col. 1:13). This fact affords great comfort, hope, and power to hold fast under all trials and opposition.

# CHAPTER VIII

# The Ram and the He-Goat

## THE VISION (vv. 1-14)

### Introduction (v. 1-2)

**Verse 1** *In the third year of the reign of king Belshazzar a vision appeared unto me, even unto me, Daniel, after that which appeared unto me at the first.*

The third year of Belshazzar would be 547 BC (*ZPEB* 1 516), which may have been the last year of his reign. "A vision appeared to me, even unto me Daniel," emphasized the fact that the vision was to the seer personally. The "one at the first" was the vision of chapter seven in which the four beasts were introduced. But only the fourth was discussed; for it challenged Daniel's interest and concern more than the second and the third beasts. These two were revealed in greater detail because they would play an important role in the future history of God's people. The events of this chapter and chapter eleven through verse thirty five symbolized the events of the sixty two weeks of the seventy weeks (Dan. 9:24-27). These were passed over in favor of the first and last periods. The significance of this period must not be minimized. But the events were not so important to the answer of Daniel's desire to know the future of the kingdom: its people, city, and temple, as the other two. The events following the return of the people from Babylon: the building of the city, the temple, and wall about the city (the first seven weeks), and the end under the fourth empire (the last week) were of special interest to him. The reader should keep in mind that this is a vision of the distant future; not a history of the past.

> **Verse 2** *And I saw in the vision; now it was so, that when I saw, I was in Shushan the palace, which is in the province of Elam; and I saw in the vision, and I was by the river Ulai.*

All commentators consulted, except Barnes, thought Daniel was in Shushan (Susa) the palace only in the vision, not in person. Barnes thought he was there in person. Susa was between two hundred and three hundred miles east of Babylon, it is probable he was in Shushan in vision. Two other instances are recorded of one being in a place named in a vision. Ezekiel was transported from Babylon to Jerusalem in such a vision (Ezek. 8:1-5); and John was transported into a wilderness (Rev. 17:3). Susa was the ancient capital of the Elamite empire, but was also the capital of Medo-Persia at the time of Daniel. The river Ulai, a wide man-made irrigation canal near Susa, is found only here and in verse 16.

## The Ram (A Male Sheep) (vv. 3-4)

> **Verse 3** *Then I lifted up mine eyes, and saw, and, behold, there stood before the river a ram which had two horns: and the two horns were high; but one was higher than the other, and the higher came up last.*

To "lift up his eyes" was to give attention to what was in view; and what he saw was a ram standing before the river. The unique feature that attracted his attention was the ram's two high horns with one higher than the other. Daniel was impressed that the higher horn came up after the other. One should realize that a matter can be presented in a vision which cannot be manifested in reality. Each horn came up while the viewer watched.

**Verse 4** *I saw the ram pushing westward, and northward, and southward; and no beasts could stand before him, neither was there any that could deliver out of his hand; but he did according to his will, and magnified himself.*

The ram was pushing in three directions: westward, northward, and southward. He was invincible; no beast could stop him, or hinder his progress; he was destined to rule the world. In the eyes of men he magnified himself. He symbolized the Medo-Persian Empire. The greatness of this beast began with Cyrus whom God raised up as His "shepherd" and "anointed," before whom He was removing all barriers (Isa. 44:18 - 45:7). It was probable, that through this vision and the prophet's knowledge of Isaiah's writings, he began to realize that the time of deliverance from bondage and return of the captives to their homeland was drawing near.

## The He-goat (Lit. "buck-goat" Leupold) (vv. 5-8)

**Verse 5** *And as I was considering, behold, a he-goat came from the west over the face of the whole earth, and touched not the ground: and the goat had a notable horn between his eyes.*

While Daniel pondered the vision just seen, a he-goat came bounding out of the west with such speed that his feet were not touching the ground. The speed of Alexander and the Macedonian Empire was symbolized by the leopard with four wings on its sides (7:6). Another special feature of the he-goat was the notable horn, a horn of distinction "between his eyes." The horn symbolized Alexander, the son of Philip of Macedon, a genius in his own right and a military leader of renown.

**Verse 6** *And he came to the ram that had the two horns, which I saw standing before the river, and ran upon him in the fury of his power.*

Daniel beheld the rough he-goat rushing upon the ram in "the fury of his power." This fury of Alexander's fury and that of his army was the pent up rage from years of smarting under the invasions of Persian emperors. At the age of twenty, upon the death of his father Philip, Alexander inherited a kingdom. The attempts of the Persians to conquer the Greeks was thwarted by two decisive battles: Darius the Great was defeated at the battle of Marathon (490 BC), and Xerxes was defeated in a sea battle off the coast of Salamis ten years later. These invasions of the Persians account for the fury of the he-goat. The power of Alexander's well trained army was motivated by that explosive fury.

> **Verse 7** *And I saw him come close unto the ram, and he was moved with anger against him, and smote the ram, and brake his two horns; and there was no power in the ram to stand before him; but he cast him down to the ground, and trampled upon him; and there was none that could deliver the ram out of his hand.*

The implacable hatred and intense fury of the he-goat, the Macedonian army, led by Alexander (the horn), was poured upon the ram, breaking his two horns. This left the ram shorn of his power to resist, whereupon the goat cast him down to the ground, trampled him and left him totally defeated. The two horns indicate the composite character of the Medo-Persian Empire? Alexander and his army completely routed the Persians in two major contests, the battle at the river Granicus, and a later battle at Issus. There were others, but these two left the ram at the goat's feet, crushed to rise no more.

> **Verse 8** *And the he-goat magnified himself exceedingly; and when he was strong the great horn was broken; and instead of it there came up four notable horns toward the four winds of heaven.*

The conquest of the ram by the he-goat led the goat to "magnify himself exceedingly." "In the last year of his life [Alexander] appeared to ask Greek states to treat him as divine" (*ZPEB* I 98). Whether providential or otherwise, in such a state of affairs, and in his own outrageous conduct, "the great horn was broken; and in its place came up four notable horns toward the four winds of heaven," which were four smaller kingdoms.

## The Little Horn (vv. 9-14)

> **Verse 9** *And out of one of them came forth a little horn, which waxed exceeding great, toward the south, and toward the east, and toward the glorious land.*

Daniel beheld four horns come up where the one had been, and out of one of those horns came forth "a little horn." This "little horn" should not be confused with the little horn of 7:8, for it came up among the ten horns which symbolized the rulers of the Roman Empire. This one came out of one of the four that followed Alexander's death. From a state of littleness it waxed great from Syria eastward, to Babylon and Persia, southward into Egypt, and to the glorious land, Judah.

> **Verse 10** *And it waxed great, even to the host of heaven; and some of the host and of the stars it cast down to the ground, and trampled upon them.*

Daniel's interest was in its "greatness" in opposition to God and that which pertained to Him, the state of the "glorious land," Judea. It waxed great against "the host of heaven," the people of God. Some of these, "the stars," were the leaders among the host who were cast down and trampled under foot. This use of "stars," to symbolize great leaders was first used by Joel (Joel 2:10; 3:15) and later by Isaiah (Isaiah 13:10). These leaders were especially oppressed by the little horn because of their religious commitment to Jehovah.

**Verse 11** *Yea, it magnified itself, even to the prince of the host; and it took away from him the continual burnt-offering, and the place of his sanctuary was cast down.*

"The prince of the host" was "the God of heaven" (*TWOT* II 885); Keil made the same observation (297). This application of the term was indicated by the use of **him** and **his** in the following sentence: "and it [the horn] took away from **him** [the prince] the continual burnt-offering, and the place of **his** [the prince's] sanctuary was cast down." These two, the burnt-offerings and the place of the sanctuary, belonged to God, the Prince, or King, of His people, and of the nations (Jer. 10:7).

**Verse 12** *And the host was given over to it together with the continual burnt-offering through transgression; and it cast down truth to the ground, and it did its pleasure and prospered.*

The host, i.e. the people, together with the sacrifices and the sanctuary were given over to the horn by God because of transgression. Also "truth," the law, was despised and cast down. This foretold their calamity with the little horn "through [because of (*TWOT* II 1067)] transgression," transgression of the host, the people of the Lord, should have forewarned them when the situation came. But it failed to do so. They followed the pattern developed before the Babylonian captivity. And the little horn "did its pleasure and prospered" until God intervened. The horn exalted itself against God, the Prince of

Heaven; against the host, His people; against the burnt-offerings, the sacrifices of worship; against His sanctuary, the
temple; and against the truth, His law.

> **Verse 13** *Then I heard a holy one speaking; and another*
> *holy one said unto that certain one who spake, How*
> *long shall be the vision concerning the continual burnt-*
> *offering, and the transgression that maketh desolate,*
> *to give both the sanctuary and the host to be trodden*
> *under foot?*

The "holy one" who asked the question and the "holy
one" that responded, were angels, for none other than
messengers from God could have answered the question. On
the one hand, this was probably asked for the benefit of
Daniel; and on the other hand it may have been that the
angel did not know, and desiring to know asked the question
for his own information. Angels had a special interest in the
development of God's purpose and work for human redemption (I Pet. 1:12). The question was, "How long?" which
seems to involve phases of the following: the withholding
of the sacrifices?; the desecration of the sanctuary, the
temple?; and, the host and the sanctuary to be "trodden
under foot"?

> **Verse 14** *And he said unto me, Unto two thousand and*
> *three hundred evenings and mornings; then shall the*
> *sanctuary be cleansed.*

The question may be simple, or it may be difficult. But the
answer is difficult. Is it 2300 literal days? or is 2300 evening
and morning the times of sacrifices, therefore, 1150 days? Or,
is it symbolical? and if so, how shall we reckon the symbolical
use of the 2300 days? Keil devoted seven pages to discussing
various explanations, arriving at this answer. "The 2300 cannot, it is true, be directly a symbolical number as 7, 10, 40, 70,
and other numbers are, but yet it can stand in such a relation
to the number seven as to receive a symbolical meaning"
(p. 306). "Thus the answer of the angel has this meaning:

The time of the predicted oppression of Israel, and of the desolation of the sanctuary by Antiochus Epiphanes, the little horn, shall not reach the full duration of a period of divine judgment" (p. 307). This seems to be the best answer to the question.

## GABRIEL'S INTERPRETATION OF THE DREAM
## (vv. 15-27)

### Daniel's Perplexity Seeks Understanding: Gabriel's Response (vv. 15-18)

**Verse 15** *and it came to pass, when I, even I Daniel, had seen the vision, that I sought to understand it; and, behold, there stood before me as the appearance of a man.*

As in verse one, Daniel emphasized that the vision was made to him, making it clear that the vision did not appear to another who received it and related it to him. The dream was so unusual and vivid that he sought help in understanding it. In response to this desire, there stood one before him whose form was "as the appearance of a man." He was not a man, but an angel who appeared as a man, speaking as a man.

**Verse 16** *And I heard a man's voice between the banks of the Ulai, which called, and said, Gabriel, make this man to understand the vision.*

"A man's voice," understandable by Daniel, spoke from between the banks of the Ulai river, addressing the one who appeared "as a man," saying, "Gabriel, make this man to understand the vision." The one who spoke was not identified, but from what was said about Gabriel in other Scriptures, it must have come from Jehovah God. Later, Gabriel was "caused to fly swiftly" unto Daniel (9:21). And when he appeared before Zacharias to announce the birth of John the Baptist, he introduced himself as, "Gabriel, that stand[s] in the presence of God" (Luke 1:19). And six months later, "Gabriel was sent from God" with a message to Mary in Nazareth (v. 26). The instructor who made the vision understandable to Daniel was a special messenger, Gabriel, an angel sent from God to reveal the meaning to him.

> **Verse 17** *So he came near where I stood; and when he came, I was affrighted, and fell upon my face: but he said unto me, Understand, O son of man; for the vision belongeth to the time of the end.*

When the angel approached him, Daniel was afraid and fell upon his face. Such a reaction in the presence of God is not unusual; for in His presence, Isaiah cried, "Woe is me! for I am undone" (Isa. 6:5). Ezekiel responded to such experiences by falling "upon his face" (Ezek. 1:28; 3:23). And in a vision, the apostle John saw the glorified Christ, and "fell at his feet as one dead" (Rev. 1:17). The angel comforted the prophet by assuring him that the vision was not for immediate fulfillment, but pertained "to the time of the end."

> **Verse 18** *Now as he was speaking with me, I fell into a deep sleep with my face toward the ground; but he touched me, and set me upright.*

As the angel continued to speak, Daniel was more intensely affected, for he "swooned" (Young), falling upon his face. But a touch from the angel aroused him, and set him upon his feet; or, "Where I had been" (margin).

### Gabriel's Explanation: the Ram and the He-goat (vv. 19-22)

> **Verse 19** *And he said, Behold, I will make thee know what shall be in the latter time of the indignation; for it belongeth to the appointed time of the end.*

Gabriel's explanation to Daniel was: "The vision belongeth to the time of the end" (v. 17). He now revealed that "the time of the end" was "the latter time of the indignation." "The basic idea" of the Hebrew word translated **indignation** "is expressing or experiencing intense anger" (*TWOT* I 247). When the word was used of God's indignation, most often it expresses His wrath against heathen nations. But the word was also used to express His anger against His own people (e.g. Isa. 10:5; 26:20). In this instance it was the indignation of God against His people because of their transgression following the invasion of Alexander (v. 12).

Alexander was a devoted advocate of Greek philosophy and religion. As a result of his time spent conquering Tyre in Palestine en route to Egypt, he greatly influenced the Jews, especially the young priests. These accepted many of the Greek customs, much of their life styles, and their religious influences. This led to increased corruption of morals and transgressions of the law. "The time of the end" is not the "end of time." But, according to the context, it would be the end of the judgment of God against the transgression of the law by the Jews, as expressed in the 2300 days of verse 14.

**Verse 20** *The ram which thou sawest, that had the two horns, they are the kings of Media and Persia.*

The ram symbolized the kingdom of Medo-Persia, and the two horns "are the kings of Media and Persia" - not two kingdoms, but the one kingdom of the two peoples, Medes and Persians combined under Cyrus into one. The distinction between "kings" and "kingdom" is not always clearly delineated (compare 7:17 with 7:23). The higher horn that came up last, symbolized the kings of Persia (8:3).

**Verse 21** *And the rough he-goat is the king of Greece: and the great horn that is between his eyes is the first king.*

The he-goat was interpreted to be "the king" (the kingdom) of Greece, and "the great horn" is "the first king." That is, it is Alexander the Great, not first in point of time, but "primacy," first in importance.

**Verse 22** *And as for that which was broken, in the place whereof four stood up, four kingdoms shall stand up out of the nation, but not with his power.*

After conquering the Persian empire, Alexander pressed on eastward until he came within the realm of India; there his army refused to go farther. He turned his way back to Babylon where he died at the early age of 33 years. This was symbolized by the breaking of "the great horn," and the raising up of the four notable horns toward the four winds (v. 8). At his death there was none with the leadership ability of Alexander, so ultimately his empire was divided among the following four generals: "These are 1) Macedonia under Cassander, 2) Thrace and Asia Minor under Lysimachus, 3) Syria under Seleucous, and 4) Egypt under Ptolemy" (Young, 169). The "Four winds" refer to the four directions of the compass. Their power would be inferior to that of Alexander.

## "The King of Fierce Countenance" (vv. 23-26)

**Verse 23** *And in the latter time of their kingdom, when the transgressors are come to the full, a king of fierce countenance, and understanding dark sentences, shall stand up.*

This one is the "little horn" that came out of one of the four horns that grew up in the place of the special horn (vv. 9-12). Antiochus became king of Syria in 175 B.C. His ambition was to Hellenize his subject provinces; but Judea stood in his way. The nation and its culture had to be destroyed, and this he determined to do. (See comments, 9- 14.) It was when the transgressions of the Jews came to the full end. God never executed His judgments of a nation until the cup of its people's iniquity reached a point beyond which God could no longer tolerate them (cf. Gen. 15:16). "Of fierce countenance," that is, an impudent or belligerent appearance, "bold and crafty" (Leupold). "And understanding dark sayings," probably refers to his crafty and cunning, skillful and clever ability in the use of deceptive language. In our modern speech, he knew how to speak with a "forked tongue."

> **Verse 24** *And his power shall be mighty, but not by his own power; and he shall destroy wonderfully, and shall prosper and do his pleasure; and he shall destroy the mighty ones and the holy people.*

Though his power was "mighty," it would not be of himself; it would be of God, for God used him as the executor of His judgment, as He had used other nations before him. This "king of fierce countenance" did destroy the worthy, and buy the services of the wicked who would serve his purpose. He was a master at deception using cunning, and craftiness to achieve his goal.

> **Verse 25** *And through his policy he shall cause craft to prosper in his hand; and he shall magnify himself in his heart, and in their security shall he destroy many: he shall also stand up against the prince of princes; but he shall be broken without hand.*

In following his policy of craft, cunning, and cruelty toward God's people and others, and by exalting himself in his own heart, Antiochus was able to exert his efforts toward achieving his goal for a while. But when he stood up against God, the "Prince of princes," he was "broken without hand." He was rewarded with destruction. In their false sense of security, in their false view that even in their faithlessness, God would fight for them, many were destroyed.

> **Verse 26** *And the vision of the evenings and mornings which hath been told is true: but shut thou up the vision; for it belongeth to many days to come.*

The judgment of God through Antiochus and the heathen kingdoms, would come to an end with the termination of the

2300 "evenings and mornings." The judgment at this time would not continue until the full destruction of the Jews.

### Effect of the Vision on Daniel (v. 27)

**Verse 27** *And I, Daniel, fainted, and was sick certain days; then I rose up, and did the king's business: and I wondered at the vision, but none understood it.*

Although full comprehension of what lay ahead for the people of God may not have been understood by Daniel, yet certain matters were clear. There would be three world empires beyond the Babylonian kingdom under whose domination the people of God would live. In the days of the third empire, the "king of fierce countenance" would set his mind and hand to destroy the concept of Jehovah, of His people, of His temple and the divine system of worship, and of His law. And though the judgment would not be full with complete destruction, it meant terrible sufferings for the people of whom Daniel was a part. Add this vision and its suffering to that of the fourth empire of the earlier vision, the realization of the terrible days that lay ahead left him faint and sick. Afterward he recovered and arose to attend the king's business. He could do this in spite of not understanding all he wanted to know. One can be grateful that now, this side of the fulfillment, he can understand the vision and profit from it.

# Daniel's Prayer and Gabriel's Second Visit

## The Books and Their Message
## (vv. 1-2)

**Verse 1** *In the first year of Darius the son of Ahasuerus, of the seed of the Medes, who was made king over the realm of the Chaldeans,*

The first year of Darius the Mede would be 539 B.C. For a discussion of his identity see comments under 5:31. He was appointed king by Cyrus the conqueror of Babylon. The extent of his reign as king has been discussed earlier (see comments, 5:31; 6:1).

**Verse 2** *in the first year of his reign I, Daniel, understood by the books the number of the years whereof the word of Jehovah came to Jeremiah the prophet, for the accomplishing of the desolations of Jerusalem, even seventy years.*

It appears that Daniel was a diligent student of the Scriptures, for he understood "by the books," which were books already written and in circulation. How many, or which ones, were in his library was not divulged. But from the things mentioned in his prayer there must have been a goodly number. He mentioned "thy precepts" and "thine ordinances" "from which

Israel had turned away"; and because of these departures, "the curse" was poured out upon them (v. 11; the curse of Lev. 26 and Deut. 28). There were "his servants the prophets" by whom God set His laws before them (v. 10). He dealt with things written in the law of Moses as if thoroughly familiar with them (v. 13). But "the books" to which he made special mention were the books of Isaiah and Jeremiah. Reference to Isaiah because he had said so much about the coming of Cyrus and his relation to the fall of Babylon and return of the Jews. He referred to Jeremiah because the prophet specifically told the duration of the captivity. Having been brought to Babylon as a youth it was improbable that he knew these things at the time.

In his prophecy of judgment against Babylon (Isa. 13-14), Isaiah named the Medes as the instrument of God's judgment (13:17). Later he called Cyrus by name as the conqueror of Babylon who would let the Jews return to Jerusalem and rebuild their temple (44:28). Jehovah addressed Cyrus directly, telling him what He would do for Cyrus in giving him the nations of the world (45:1-7). Jehovah raised him up for the special purpose of letting "my exiles go free" (v. 13). God rested His claim to being the sole Deity on His ability to declare the end from the beginning (46:8-11; 48:3-11, 14-15). And since Daniel served into the third year of the rule of Cyrus, there can be little doubt that he pointed out these prophecies to him and the fact that God's word addressed him in particular (45:1).

It was the reading of Jeremiah in particular, and Isaiah probably, that led Daniel to realize that the time of their return to the homeland was drawing near. Jeremiah said that the conquered nations would serve the king of Babylon seventy years (25:11); "And...when seventy years are accomplished...I will punish the king of Babylon, and that nation" over which he had ruled (v. 12). Later he said, "After seventy years are accomplished for Babylon, I will visit you [Israel], and perform my good word toward you, in causing you to return to this place" Jerusalem (29:10). This seventy year period was fast drawing to a close; and the prophecy of Isaiah concerning Babylon's fall to Cyrus was fulfilled already.

# DANIEL'S PRAYER
## (vv. 3-19)

## The Set of His face
### (vv. 3-4)

**Verse 3** *And I set my face unto the Lord God, to seek by prayer and supplications, with fasting and sackcloth and ashes.*

"To set his face" means that he turned his face toward the Lord, looking to Him for an answer to two possible questions. One was in the form of a question and the other a problem. When would the seventy years end and the return begin? The problem was that the people were in no spiritual condition to return to their homeland. Regarding the question, would the seventy years begin when he and his three friends were carried to Babylon as hostages (606/605 B.C.)? or, when Jerusalem was destroyed and the people were brought to Babylon (587 B.C.)? This problem was the primary substance of his prayer.

Prayer to God means to talk to Him, to "seek by entreaty, spiritual communion, a devout petition." Supplication emphasized the humble attitude or humility of the petitioner; "to make humble petition, entreaty, or petition" (*New Century Dictionary*). To these Daniel added "fasting," abstaining from food that the body and spirit could be given wholly to his communion with God. The "sackcloth," was a coarse hair garment worn next to the body in time of grief or distress, and "ashes" which were cast into the air upon one's head. Both indicated a humble penitent spirit.

**Verse 4** *And I prayed unto Jehovah my God, and made confession, and said, Oh, Lord, the great and dreadful God, who keepeth covenant and lovingkindness with them that love him and keep his commandments.*

The address of his prayer was "unto Jehovah my God." Concerning which Keil made the observation: "If we wish our prayers to be heard, the God, to whom we pray, **must** become our God" (emphasis his, p. 330). The prayers and supplications of Daniel were deeply spiritual and emotional, lofty and dignified, fervent and intense. From this prayer James could well have deduced his conclusion: "The supplication [effectual fervent prayer, KJV] of a righteous man availeth much in its working" (James 5:16). Before Daniel finished, an angel was there in response to his prayers and supplications (Dan. 9:20-21). He began by addressing Jehovah as, "Oh, Lord," a term that occurred eight times in the prayer, besides "O our God" once, and "O my God" twice. These emotional expressions revealed the fervor and intensity with which he prayed.

The two attributes of God with which Daniel continued were "The great and dreadful God"; and, "Who keepeth covenant and lovingkindness with them that love him and keep his commandments," were also used by Moses in Deuteronomy 7. The latter occurred in verse 9, "Know therefore that Jehovah thy God, he is God, the faithful God, who keepeth covenant and lovingkindness with them that love him and keep his commandments to a thousand generations." The former occurred in verse 21, "Thou shalt not be affrighted at them; for Jehovah thy God is in the midst of thee, a great God and a terrible." "A great and **terrible**," God who was terrible to the enemies of faithful Israel. Daniel's word translated **dreadful**, and Moses' word translated **terrible** are from the same root word *yārē* which is subject to a number of uses (*TWOT* I 399-401). Since the two words came from the same root word, and Moses' use of the word was in reference to Israel's enemies and God's, it appears that Daniel used **dreadful** of the sinful and rebellious Jews as enemies of God and His law of truth. It was for the sins of these that he confessed to "the great and dreadful God." The nation experienced both the faithfulness with which He kept His part of the covenant, and the dreadfulness of His wrath and judgment culminating in seventy years in Babylon.

# CONFESSION OF A NATION'S SINS
## (vv. 5-10)

### "We Have Sinned" (vv. 5-6)

**Verse 5** *we have sinned, and have dealt perversely, and have done wickedly, and have rebelled, even turning aside from thy precepts and from thine ordinances;* **6** *neither have we hearkened unto thy servants the prophets, that spake in thy name to our kings, our princes, and our fathers, and to all the people of the land.*

Daniel spoke for the nation, and although he spoke for the nation, sin is a personal, individual matter. Each is responsible for his own conduct. However, each is influenced by the conduct of others, and it seems that the influence of evil moves the multitude instead of that which is right. Daniel named five specific realms in which they erred. The first is general: 1) "We have sinned" - missed the mark. The target in God's field of spiritual archery is holiness; "Ye shall be holy; for I Jehovah your God am holy" (Lev. 19:2). It was the target then; and it remains the target forever (I Pet. 1:16). 2) They had acted "perversely," which comes from a word meaning "to bend, twist, to act crookedly"; to influence in the wrong direction (*TWOT* II 650). 3) "Have done wickedly," they acted contrary to righteousness; a negative behavior that grows out of evil thoughts. Life and actions contrary to God's character (*TWOT* II 863). 4) Daniel defined their rebellion as "turning aside from thy precepts," that is, from God's commandments; and from His ordinances referring to His rule of government and standards of life. 5) Neither did they listen to God's laws through His servants the prophets, whom God sent to point the way. These were mentioned some twelve times. They addressed their message to kings, nobles, fathers of families, and to all the people of the land. The sins were positive and negative in kind, willful and indifferent.

## Jehovah's Righteousness - Israel's Shame (vv. 7-10)

**Verse 7** *O Lord, righteousness belongeth unto thee, but unto us confusion of face, as at this day; to the men of Judah, and to the inhabitants of Jerusalem, and unto all Israel, that are near, and that are far off, through all the countries whither thou has driven them, because of their trespass that they have trespassed against thee.*

Jehovah's revelation of Himself to Israel has always been in absolute righteousness, a characteristic of His Godhood. This righteousness "became the ultimate standard to human conduct" (*TWOT* II 754). But Israel's response was the shame of sin, rebellion, and idolatry, which had led to captivity and the "confusion of face" (shame) of that time. This state of shame covered the whole people: those remaining in Judah and Jerusalem, those near and those scattered throughout the world. The reason was they had trespassed against their God. Using Numbers 5:12-13 where a woman committed a trespass against her husband by committing adultery with another man, V. P. Hamilton said "It is obvious, then, that to 'commit a trespass' means to act unfaithfully, to break a contract" (*TWOT* I 520). This is what Israel did repeatedly.

**Verse 8** *O Lord, to us belongeth confusion of face, to our kings, to our princes, and to our fathers, because we have sinned against thee.*

Daniel repeated the state of shame that covered the whole people, but brought into focus those primarily responsible, the "kings," "princes," and "fathers." These should have led them in the right way. The nation was scattered near and far, in captivity because of sin; but it seemed that their punishment had not achieved much in changing their character and practices.

**Verse 9** *To the Lord our God belong mercies and forgiveness; for we have rebelled against him;*

To the righteousness mentioned in verse 7, that belongs to God, Daniel added "mercies and forgiveness." His "tender mercy" was His compassion for His scattered people, lost and without a shepherd, bewildered and confused. In this state of rebellion against God, it required divine and infinite mercy to forgive such people, even when genuine repentance was manifested. But, "God's tender mercy" was sufficient to procure forgiveness, for, it "is rooted in his free love and grace" (*TWOT* II 843). And since all sin ultimately is against God (cf. Ps. 51:4), only God can forgive it, which He does (cf. Ps. 32:5). The particular sin of this verse is that of rebellion: "For we have rebelled against him," which was described in verse 5 as, "turning aside from thy precepts and from thine ordinances," which were a part of the covenant which their fathers agreed to keep (Ex. 24:3, 5-8). It seems that their rebellion was an attempt to nullify or abdicate the covenant made with Jehovah.

**Verse 10** *neither have we obeyed the voice of Jehovah our God, to walk in his laws, which he set before us by his servants the prophets.*

By not walking in His laws, they refused to obey His voice, for the law (apparently the Pentateuch) was His word, the voice of Jehovah. For, "His servants the prophets" neither preached nor gave new laws, but endeavored to turn the people back to the law of Moses, which was the law of God.

## Confession of Sins Continued -
## CONSCIOUSNESS OF SINS INTENSIFIED
## (vv. 11-14)

### National Transgression (vv. 11-12)

**Verse 11** *Yea, all Israel have transgressed thy law, even turning aside, that they should not obey thy voice: therefore hath the curse been poured out upon us, and the* *oath that is written in the law of Moses the servant of God; for we have sinned against him.*

The nation (all Israel) was guilty of transgressing God's law. "To transgress" is from a word that means to "move outside," or apart from the law. They turned from it, ignoring it by giving no heed to God's voice addressing them in the law. Because of this, "the curse" was poured out upon them. "The curse" was clearly stated in Leviticus 26:14-45, and in Deuteronomy 28:15-68. The oath mentioned was the oath of the covenant which included the curse and the blessings (29:9, 12). "Poured out" indicated the fullness or intensity of the execution of the curse (cf. "wrath like fire," Lam. 2:4; Isa. 42:25, et al.).

**Verse 12** *And he hath confirmed his words, which he spake against us, and against our judges that judged us, by bringing upon us a great evil; for under the whole heaven hath not been done as hath been done upon Jerusalem.*

The word "confirmed" or "established" (Gen. 17:19) is from a word meaning to "stand." God made His word to stand firm; He fulfilled His part of the covenant, the good and the evil. He fulfilled the covenant by delivering the nation into Canaan, driving out the inhabitants of the land, and pouring out the blessing as promised (Lev. 26:3-13; Deut. 28:1-14). And now He made the word of the curse to "stand," as He made the good to stand. God made the heavens and the earth, and "when I call unto them, they stand up together" (Isa. 48:13).

The primary sense of "judges that judged us" referred to rulers who exercised the processes of government. In this instance, they were the men who exercised that responsibility according to the law of God by Moses. But instead, they judged and led the people so as to bring upon the nation "this great evil" of destruction and seventy years of captivity. In the statement, "For under the whole heaven hath not been done as hath been done upon Jerusalem," was revealed a principle stressed throughout the Bible. The more God does for an individual or a people, the more He expects of them. He chose Israel as His people, He made a special covenant with them. He gave them His laws, set His sanctuary in the midst of them, and blessed them above all peoples of the earth. And what did He receive in return? They rejected Him for lifeless idols (Ezek. 8:17). It is no wonder why He judged Jerusalem as He did. Here is a solemn warning for everyone. The greater the blessings, the greater the responsibilities that go with the blessings. Conversely, the greater the abuse of these, the greater the punishment.

## The Law of Evil (vv. 13-14)

**Verse 13** *As it is written in the law of Moses, all this evil is come upon us: yet have we not entreated the favor of Jehovah our God, that we should turn from our iniquities, and have discernment in thy truth.*

Although the evil of the curse written in the law of Moses (Lev. 26; Deut. 28) came upon Israel, "yet have we not entreated [sought] the favor of Jehovah." They did not seek his grace by turning "from their iniquities." A concerted effort to obtain His favor demanded this. "Iniquities" came from a root word meaning, "bend, twist, distort," expressing itself in "crooked behavior, perversion" (*TWOT* II 650). Isaiah's charge against the crucifiers of the Messiah well illustrated its meaning: "All we like sheep **have gone astray**; we have turned every one **to his own way**; and Jehovah hath laid on him **the iniquity** of us all" (Isa. 53:6). The word **iniquity** summed up the condition of being **astray** by turning to one's **own way**. When turning from iniquities, one's own way to God's way, one will "have discernment" in God's truth. Discernment means "insight or comprehension" in wise behavior which, in its turn, means "conforming one's life to the Character of God" (*TWOT* II 877).

**Verse 14** *Therefore hath Jehovah watched over the evil, and brought it upon us; for Jehovah our God is righteous in all his works which he doeth, and we have not obeyed his voice.*

Because of this lack of conformity to the character and law of God, Jehovah "watched over the evil, and brought it upon us." A characteristic of Jehovah is His watchfulness over the whole of His creation (II Chron. 16:9; Zech. 4:10); and of His word, He said, "I watch over my word to perform it" (Jer. 1:12); and also, He watches over His people for good and for evil (Jer. 31:28; 44:27). Whatever He does as a result of what He sees will be a righteous work. And since the people had not obeyed Him, this evil came upon them.

This raises a question, How can one harmonize this statement with that of Amos who quoted Jehovah as saying, "shall evil befall a city, and Jehovah hath not done it" (Amos 3:6)? And "I make peace, and create evil" (Isa. 45:7)? The evil of these passages is the evil of divine judgments that inevitably follow the rejection of God's laws for good. From the study of sins and judgment made thus far, one can deduce the following conclusion. Within every law and work of God for the good of man, there is inherent in that law a counter law; for the violation or rejection of that law for good, there is a judgmental law of evil consequences within the law for good. Therefore, the God of creation is the creator of the evil consequences that follow the rejection of the good.

## Conclusion of the Confession
## (v. 15)

**Verse 15** *And now, O Lord our God, that hast brought thy people forth out of the land of Egypt with a mighty hand, and hast gotten thee renown, as at this day; we have sinned, we have done wickedly.*

Throughout his prayer of confession of sins, Daniel identified himself with the people as a sinner: "we" "us" "our." Being of "the seed royal" (1:3), he identified himself with the kings and nobles also, who led the people into sin. However, no specific sin was confessed and none was charged against him. This does not mean that he never transgressed a law of God for no man can make such a claim (cf. Eccl. 7:20).

Daniel closed the confession of sins with the introduction of his appeal to Jehovah for mercy. In bringing His people out of Egypt Jehovah gained renown among all the nations, and in the history of the human race since that time. The mightiness of His hand has revealed in the mighty miraculous works throughout their history, including the captivity. He closed the confession with a final statement, "We have sinned and done wickedly." In spite of all that God did in their redemption and keeping the covenant made with their fathers, they have done wickedly. Daniel made an appeal for mercy and lovingkindness equal to the demonstrated mighty works in their redemption.

## A Plea for Forgiveness on the Ground of God's Righteousness and Mercy ( vv. 16-19)

### Jehovah Versus His People (v. 16)

**Verse 16** *O Lord, according to all thy righteousness, let thine anger and thy wrath, I pray thee, be turned away from thy city Jerusalem, thy holy mountain; because for our sins, and for the iniquities of our fathers, Jerusalem and thy people are become a reproach to all that are round about us.*

God's righteousness was His righteous deeds and actions, all had been in righteousness. His "anger" was righteous indignation; His "wrath" was a judicial wrath; and all His "judgments" had ever been "righteous judgments" (Rom. 2:5). The judgment against Jerusalem and mount Zion left Jerusalem in ruins as it was at that day. Judgment came because of the sins of the people which Daniel freely confessed. These became a reproach, a disgrace or dishonor, a scorn to all those about them. The most inclusive and severe expressions of God's provocation is recorded in Jeremiah 32:31-36.

> **Verse 17** *Now therefore, O our God, hearken unto the prayer of thy servant, and to his supplications, and cause thy face to shine upon thy sanctuary that is desolate, for the Lord's sake.*

The prophet identified himself with the people in the sins confessed (vv. 3, 12, et al.). Now he identified the people with himself in their relationship to God "O our God." He implored God's attention to "hearken," that is, to give heed to His confession and to respond favorably to his plea. To make His "face to shine" upon the desolate temple in the city of ruins would be to reversing the conditions from desolation to life and honor and glory. His petition was, Do this for the Lord's own glory and honor.

> **Verse 18** *O my God, incline thine ear, and hear; open thine eyes, and behold our desolations, and the city which is called by thy name: for we do not present our supplications before thee for our righteousnesses, but for thy great mercies' sake.*

Daniel again addressed Jehovah, "O my God" (cf. v. 4 and comments), identifying a relationship between him and the Lord that provided a ground on which he made the petition. "Incline thine ear," was a request that God bring His ear into a position to hear Daniel's plea and respond by acting favorably upon it. "Open thine eyes and behold," like the inclined ear Daniel meant that His eyes let Jehovah look intently on the condition of the sanctuary and respond favorably. For both the sanctuary and the city were called by the name of Jehovah, and were recognized by the nations and God's own people as His. For the sake of thy own name and mercy, act. The plea is not made on the ground of merit, their own righteousness. "For," as Isaiah said long before, "We are all become as one that is unclean, and all our righteousnesses are as a polluted garment [filthy rags, KJV]" (Isa 64:6). Jehovah said of the fruit of His vineyard Israel, "He looked for justice, but, behold, oppression; and for righteousness, but, behold, a cry [from the oppressed]" (Isa. 5:7).[1]

**Verse 19** *O Lord, hear; O Lord, forgive; O Lord, hearken and do; defer not, for thine own sake, O my God, because thy city and thy people are called by thy name.*

The fervency of this threefold plea needs no explanation; it could be no more intense than the words expressed. Again, the plea is on the ground of God's honor, to reveal the greatness of His mercies, and on the ground of the prophet's relation to Jehovah, "O my God." "Defer not," do not postpone action or put off responding. This request is neither irreverent nor a display of impatience by Daniel, but the expression of an earnest desire. The people experienced the dreadful judgment of Jehovah; let them now experience the loving kindness of our covenant-keeping God (cf. v. 4).

---

[1] One of the most inclusive condemnations of the children of Israel and of Judah, and the classifications individually and Jehovah's condemnation of them is spoken by Him through Jeremiah. In order to emphasize their respective classifications, these are set forth in bold letters. "For this city hath been to me a provocation of mine anger and of my wrath from the day that they built it even unto this day; that I should remove it from before my face, because of all the evil of the **children** of Israel and of the **children** of Judah, which they have done to provoke me to anger, they, their **kings**, their **princes**, their **priests**, and their **prophets**, and the **men of Judah**, and the **inhabitants of Jerusalem**. And they have turned unto me the back, and not the face: and though I taught them, rising up early and teaching them, yet they have not hearkened to receive instruction. But they set their abominations in the house which is called by my name, to defile it" (Jer. 32:31-34).

# PRAYER ANSWERED
## (vv. 20-23)

## Gabriel's Second Visit to Daniel (vv. 20-23)

### The Time (vv. 20-21)

**Verse 20** *And while I was speaking, and praying, and confessing my sin and the sin of my people Israel, and presenting my supplication before Jehovah my God for the holy mountain of my God;*

Daniel was "speaking" to the Lord when Gabriel appeared to him. The most simple definition of prayer is "talking with the Lord." It took the form of petitions, intercession, thanksgiving, or confession of sins as with Daniel at this time; he discussed and presented supplications concerning the city of Jerusalem/Zion, now in ruins.

**Verse 21** *yea, while I was speaking in prayer, the man Gabriel, whom I had seen in the vision at the beginning being caused to fly swiftly, touched me about the time of the evening oblation.*

In the midst of his petition concerning the city and mount, "the man Gabriel" appeared with the appearance of and speaking as a man (8:16). It was "about the time of the evening oblation"; probably between three and four o'clock in the afternoon. It was the time when many engaged in prayer. The phrase, "caused to fly swiftly" presents a difficulty. The two Hebrew words are "*yāēp*, **weary**," and *yéāp* **weariness**" (*TWOT* I 390). Young translated the phrase, "**to fly in weariness**," but admitted that it could be translated, "**to be weary in weariness**" (p. 190). Keil translated the Hebrew word, "**weariness**—wearied in weariness, i.e. very wearied or tired...The words perfectly agree with the condition of Daniel described in chapter viii. 17f, 27." From the context of this quotation, it was easily recognized that Keil applied the expression to Daniel, not to the angel. Leupold translated verse 21 as follows, applying the phrase to Daniel: "While I [Daniel] was yet speaking in prayer, the man Gabriel, whom I, in a state of utter exhaustion, saw in the vision at the beginning, touched me, at the time of the evening oblation" (p. 399). This interpretation by the two writers, Keil and Leupold seemed to make the best sense of any commentators consulted. What evidence exists that shows angels become "weary in (or, with) weariness?"

## Gabriel's Mission (vv. 22-23)

**Verse 22** *And he instructed me, and talked with me, and said, O Daniel, I am now come forth to give thee wisdom and understanding.*

The angel's mission was to instruct Daniel, that he might understand the future of the city, the mountain (center of divine judgment), and people of God (cf. vv. 19, 20). He gave him wisdom and understanding, i.e., insight and comprehension of what lay before him and the people of God.

**Verse 23** *At the beginning of thy supplications the commandment went forth, and I am come to tell thee; for thou art greatly beloved: therefore consider the matter, and understand the vision.*

The message of understanding and insight came from heaven, from whence the angel was sent. Therefore his comprehension would be divine in its origin and certainty. The vision revealed to Daniel understanding, knowledge, and wisdom. Daniel was a saint, precious in the sight of the Lord and beloved by Him. The great love was the reward bestowed on the servant of God because he had been faithful to Him under every circumstance of trial that he faced for nearly seventy years.

## For Our Encouragement

When life becomes a puzzle, and we are concerned about both present and future, What is it all about? Do as Daniel did. Take it to the Lord in fervent and believing prayer, for only from Him can we find the answer. In response to his prayer, the angel said, "I have come to give thee understanding." Solomon prayed for wisdom and understanding, and God gave him both (I Kings 3:9-12). And Paul said to Timothy, "Consider what I say; for the Lord shall give thee understanding in all things" (II Tim. 2:7). Understanding begins with the human part. "Consider," comes from the Greek "*noeō*, to perceive with the mind (*nous*), think about, ponder" (Vine I 230). Consider the problem and ponder it. Consider what God said relative to it; then pray about it. God's promise to Timothy was, and other Christians is, "For the Lord will give thee understanding in all things." If, after understanding the problem one needs wisdom to handle it, James said, "But if any of you lacketh wisdom, let him ask of God, who giveth to all liberally and upbraideth not; and it shall be given him" (Jas. 1:5). When one follows the word of God He can handle the matter.

# The Seventy Weeks

## Foundation Stones

"The Seventy Weeks" is a vital and important part of the book of Daniel. Before discussing the text, several background elements and passages should be considered. These serve as an introduction to the exposition to the four verses.

**The Time Period.** The setting of chapter 9 is "the first year of Darius the Mede" and of his reign (9:1-2; 5:31). It is also the year in which Cyrus issued the proclamation that the Jews could return to their homeland 539/38 B.C. (II Chron. 36:22-23; Ezra 1:1-2). The word was Jehovah's through Jeremiah the prophet (Jer. 25:11-12; 29:10). The proclamation came through Cyrus.

**Visions.** The messages of Jehovah to Daniel came through visions, vivid supernatural scenes viewed while either awake or asleep.

**Symbols,** or symbolic figures. In the visions revealed to Daniel, the figures were symbolical: the sea, the winds, the beasts that came up out of the sea, and the numbers (ch. 7); also the ram, the he-goat, the two horns, the one horn, the four horns were symbolic (ch. 8). Since symbols abound in Daniel's visions, one should not attempt to make literal the numbers, weeks, etc., in the vision of the seventy weeks (ch. 9), but seek the correct symbolic meaning.

**The Prayer.** The burden of Daniel's prayer was a confession of the sins, transgressions, and iniquities of the people; and he closed with a special interest in the honor and reputation of Jehovah. These were now dimmed in the eyes of the heathen nations because of Israel's sins, just confessed, by the condition of the city, the temple in ruins, and by His people now in captivity. What would be the end of these; ultimate destruction, or victory? The answer to these questions is the thrust of the vision of the seventy weeks.[1]

## Daniel's Perplexity: Question Raised – Answer Sought

As Daniel was drawing his confession of the sins of the people to a close, he made a fervent and moving petition to Jehovah. The plea was on behalf of "**the city** Jerusalem, **thy holy mountain…thy people**…thy sanctuary"—all of these were desolate, in a state of ruin (9:16-18). The seventy years of Jeremiah's prophecy were drawing to a close. The people had not shown repentance by turning away from sin and turning to God.

The prophet made his plea on the ground of God's righteousness, mercies, and for His name's sake. His question was: What would be the end of these—the city and mountain of God, His sanctuary, and His people? The vision of the seventy weeks was God's answer to his question. It contained both bad and good.

## The Only Truly Reliable Sources of Help in Exegesis

The many varied interpretations of commentators through the years attest to the difficulty of the vision. I shall neither present them nor attempt to refute their conclusions. Rather, I will state my view drawn from the following facts: the **angels** who were sent to Daniel from Jehovah; the **prophets** who wrote on various phases of subjects relative to Daniel's visions; the **Messiah** on whom I depend almost entirely for interpret-

---

[1] See Appendix A on the numbers seven, seventy, etc. by Phil Roberts.

ing the latter part of verse 27; and the **apostles** whose writings throw light on various aspects of Daniel's vision.

**Angels.** Consider the two missions of Gabriel to Daniel (chapters 8, 9), and include the words of the unnamed messenger of chapter 10. The mission of each of the three visits was to give Daniel understanding of his visions that extended to the end of the nation, even into the Messianic age. Gabriel was sent by God to Daniel to make him know what would be in the last days, and it was Gabriel whom God sent to announce to Zacharias the birth of John the Baptist (Luke 1:5-23). The angel introduced himself as "Gabriel, who stands in the presence of God," was sent to tell him the good tidings of John's birth (v. 19). Gabriel was also sent from God six months later to announce to Mary the birth of Jesus, the Son of God, the Son of David, and the coming of the long expected kingdom over which He should rule (Luke 1:26-38).

In the vision of the ram and the he-goat, Gabriel was instructed, "Make this man [Daniel] to understand the vision" (8:16); wherefore Gabriel said, "Understand, O son of man: for the vision belongeth to the time of the end...And he said, Behold, I will make thee know what shall be in the latter time of the indignation; for it belongeth to the appointed time of the end" (vv. 17, 19).

The second appearance of Gabriel to Daniel happened prior to the vision of the seventy weeks, at which time Daniel reported the angel as saying, "O Daniel, I am now come forth to give thee wisdom and understanding,...therefore consider the matter, and understand the vision," the vision of the seventy weeks (9:22-23), which extended to the destruction of Jerusalem (v. 27).

The third appearance of a heavenly being to visit the seer was one of special grandeur and glory, who came to give Daniel understanding. He came to tell Daniel of a "great warfare" (10:1), and to make him "understand the words" that he would speak unto him (v. 11), which words were quite significant. The angel said, "Now I am come to make thee understand what shall befall thy people in the latter days; [which was what Daniel wanted to hear] for the vision was yet for many days" (v. 14). The person and the understanding of this angel will be explored in the following chapters.

By the understanding and wisdom given by God's messengers Daniel would understand visions that extended into the latter days, the time of the Messiah. The details involved the city, the people, the sanctuary, and their end. By considering facts thus far presented, one can appeal to the prophets, angels, the Messiah, and the apostles of His generation for help in understanding the vision of the seventy weeks, even unto its termination.

**Prophets.** In the fourth Servant Song, Isaiah related the Servant (the Messiah) with the following three terms: transgressions, sins, and iniquities (ch. 53). The prophet began the chapter with a question, "Who hath believed **our** message?" (v. 1), which raised the question, Who does he include in the word "our"? The apostles John and Paul answered the question. John quoted the verse (John 12:37-38), and then said, "These things said Isaiah, because he saw his [Jesus'] glory; and he [Isaiah] spake of him [Jesus]" (v. 41). And so, Isaiah referred to the Messiah. Paul included the other apostles, the heralds of the good tidings, when he quoted Isaiah 52:7 concerning the bringers of glad tidings, and added: "But they did not all hearken to the glad tidings, For Isaiah saith, Lord, who hath believed our report?" (Rom. 10:15-17). Isaiah included prophets (represented by himself). The Servant-Messiah, and the apostles were the heralds of the gospel.

Consider Isaiah 53 also, where one finds help on verse 24. "He [the Servant] was wounded for our **transgressions**" (v. 5), "cut off out of the land of the living for the transgressions of my people to whom the stroke was due" (v. 8). It was for no transgressions of His own, but for those of humanity that He was cut off. He "was numbered with the transgressors:…, and made intercession for the transgressors" (v. 12).

"He [the Servant] was bruised [**crushed**]" (*TWOT* I 188) "for our **iniquities**;…and with his stripes we are healed" (v. 5). In the following verse the prophet clarified what "iniquity" is from God's viewpoint: "All we like sheep have gone astray; we have turned every one to his own way; and Jehovah hath laid on him the iniquity of us all" (v. 6). Therefore, iniquity is to leave God's way and go our own, in rebellion against Him. "By the knowledge of himself" referred to knowledge that comes through teaching: "And all thy children shall be taught of Jehovah; and great shall be the peace of thy children" (54:13); "shall my righteous servant justify many; and he shall bear their iniquities" (53:11).

Of **sin** (or sins) Isaiah said, Jehovah would "make his [the servant's] soul an offering for sin...he shall prolong his days [by the resurrection, HH], and the pleasure of Jehovah shall prosper in his hand" (v. 10). All of this, "because he poured out his soul unto death:...he bare the sin of many" (v. 12). It was by the sacrifice of Himself that those of Isaiah's day, and people this side of the cross, would be saved: "And for this cause he is the mediator of a new covenant, that a death having taken place for the redemption of the transgressions that were under the first covenant, they that have been called may receive the promise of the eternal inheritance" (Heb. 9:15). This understanding helps in dealing with the three terms, transgression, iniquity, and sin in Daniel 9:24.

**Jesus the Messiah.** In His personal earthly life, Jesus claimed that he was equal with God in deity, "I and the Father are one" (John 10:30), that "Before Abraham was born, I am," CO-eternal with God (8:58); and that "before the world was," He had equal divine glory with the Father, and that He was loved by Him (17:5, 24). He claimed that scripture was fulfilled in Him (Luke 4:21), and that Moses, the Jews' greatest prophet, wrote of Him (John 5:46). In Him one could find no better commentator to interpret Daniel.

**Apostles.** In his second recorded sermon, after telling of Moses' prophecy from the mouth of God concerning the Christ (Acts 3:21-23), Peter said, "All the prophets,...as many as have spoken, **they also told of these days**" (v. 24). But what did they say that pertained to "these days," the days of the apostles? They included "the days of Christ's ministry" (Isa. 49:1-13; 50:4-9; 52:13 - 53:11), His crucifixion (Ps. 22), resurrection (Ps. 16:8-10); His return to heaven and receiving the kingdom (Dan. 7:13-14); His receiving the throne and ruling the nations with the rod of iron (Ps. 2). All of these were preached from the prophets by the apostles. They were the last days - the days of the Holy Spirit and His guidance of the apostles (Joel 2:28-32; Acts 2:1-4, 16-21). The prophets spoke by the Holy Spirit (II Peter 1:20-21); and likewise the apostles spoke by the same Spirit (John 14:26; 16:13-14; Acts 1:5, 8). Inasmuch as both prophets and apostles spoke by the Holy Spirit, the Spirit of Truth, the message of the two groups harmonized. When appeal is made to the apostles for an interpretation of a prophecy, the ground is safe and sure. "These days" included the days of the gospel message; the word that would go forth from Jerusalem, included all nations as its hearers (Isa. 2:2-4; Matt. 28:18-19; Mark 16:15-16; Acts 1:8), the "good tidings of peace" and "salvation" (Isa. 52:7; Rom. 10:15). This evidence demonstrates how to use the apostles in interpreting prophecy, and establishes a hermeneutical principle for the proper understanding of Old Testament prophecy.

## EXEGESIS OF THE TEXT

### The Decree of the Seventy Weeks
### (v. 24)

**Verse 24** *Seventy weeks are decreed upon thy people and upon thy holy city, to finish transgression and to make an end of sins, and to make reconciliation for iniquity, and to bring in everlasting righteousness, and to seal up vision and prophecy, and to anoint the most holy.*

The literal seventy year period of Babylonian world oppression which included Judah was revealed by Jehovah through Jeremiah (Jer. 25:11-12; 29:10) and was now drawing toward an end (v. 2). The future of the people, city, and sanctuary of Daniel's interest (vv. 7, 19), was covered by the events of seventy symbolic weeks (490 days). As one reads the various efforts of commentators to make the 490 days 490 literal years, he is impressed by the failure of all such efforts. No satisfactory beginning point leads to a satisfactory inclusion and conclusion of the events of the seventy weeks passage. In light of the symbolic interpretation of Daniel's visions, it seems perfectly reasonable to believe that the seventy weeks are figurative also, and symbolize various periods of time in the history that lay ahead for the Jewish people. The future that lay before them, covered in the vision of seventy sevens, but is now behind us, should make it possible for us to reach a reasonable solution to our problem of the vision and its meaning. That which was "decreed upon" the people and city was from Jehovah, therefore authoritative. "The verb [*hātak*] translated, **are determined** (KJV), **decreed** (ASV) appears only...in Daniel 9:24, the famous 'seventy weeks' passage" (*TWOT* I 334). It applied only to Jehovah's decree. Another word was used of Cyrus' decree.

Considering Isaiah's testimony to the Messiah's relation to the transgression, iniquity, and sin; the appeal to the prophets and the apostles for help in interpreting prophecy is established; and the three words considered, it is time to discuss the verse. The "seventy weeks" symbolize the entire period from the Decree of Cyrus allowing the Jews to return to Jerusalem and rebuild the temple, to the destruction of Jerusalem by the Romans (v. 25 below). Although the city lay in ruins, Jerusalem was called "the holy city" because it was the city where Jehovah dwelt among His people and in which His sanctuary was located.

"To finish transgression" means "**to restrain**" (margin, ASV), and also Leupold (p. 410) and Young (p. 197). "The basic meaning of this root is to restrict the flow or movement of a thing or person." The Hebrew word "seems to indicate the interruption of what is in progress or would be naturally in progress" (*TWOT* I 438). This applied to the people of God under the Messiah who have been "born of water and the Spirit" (John 3:5); in whom is the reign of God in their hearts (Luke 17:20-21); who are "led by the Spirit of God" (Rom. 8:14); who have put off the old man and put on the new (Eph. 4:22-24). These are the ones in whom transgression is restrained. The spiritual power provided through Christ holds in check the passions of the flesh that lead to transgression.

"To make an end of sins" - "to seal up [sins]" (margin ASV) which is preferable to the text "make an end." "The basic meaning of the root [of the Hebrew word] is to seal" (TWOT I 334); e.g., "My transgression is sealed up in a bag" (Job 14:17), being reserved for judgment and punishment. Young prefered the King James translation, "To make an end of sins" (p. 199); but Leupold translated the phrase, "to seal up sins," applying it to the sins of the wicked (p. 413). Leupold's position is better because it is consistent with scripture. Isaiah said that God would make the Servant's "soul an offering for sin" (Isa. 53:10); and that "he [the Servant] bare the sins of many" (v. 12; cf. Heb. 9:28). Of the "many," not all received Him, but those that did receive Him received "the remission of sins" (Acts 2:38, 41). Their sins were "blotted out" (Acts 3:19), and remembered "no more," never to be brought before God or themselves (Heb. 8:12). But not so for the wicked. The sins of the nation were sealed up until the bag was filled by the rejection of Jesus and their assumption of responsibility for His crucifixion (Matt. 27:24-25). But their personal sins remained sealed up until they are revealed and faced at the great final judgment (Rev. 20:11-15; 21:8).

"And to make reconciliation for iniquity." Iniquity is defined as crooked behaviour, deviation from God's way, which is the only right way. Both Gentiles and Jews were guilty of this sin. Both had wandered far from God, thereby becoming God's enemies. "Reconciliation is bringing again into unity, harmony, or agreement what has been alienated" (ZPEB V 44), alienation brought about by the sins of both branches of the human race. It was God who took the initiative as the apostle Paul said, "All things are of God, who reconciled us to himself through Christ [the Messiah of promise], and gave unto us the ministry of reconciliation; to wit that God was in Christ reconciling the world unto himself, not reckoning   unto them their trespasses [for these had been blotted out through the blood of reconciliation], and having committed unto us the word of reconciliation" (II Cor. 5:18-19). And now, as ambassadors "on behalf of Christ, as though

God were entreating by us [i.e., on behalf of Christ and God]: we beseech [not **you**, which is interpolated, but **the alienated**] on behalf of Christ, be ye reconciled to God" (II Cor. 5:20). The plea was to the alienated world to whom the apostles were ambassadors with Christ's message, urging them to be reconciled.

Reconciliation in Christ included the Gentiles, as was often promised in the prophets, who are brought near through the reconciliation "in the blood of Christ," whereby the enmity is abolished and the two, Jews and Gentiles, are made one. The "anointed one" the Messiah (Dan. 9:26), through the apostles, came and preached peace and reconciliation to both Jews and Greeks (Eph. 2:14-18). To the Colossians Paul said that God has "reconciled all things unto himself, having made peace through the blood of his cross [the sacrifice of the **crushing** (Isa. 53:5-6, 10)]...in the body of his flesh through death" (Col. 1:20-22).

With the transgressions restrained, the sins blotted out, sealed up, and reconciliation made for iniquities, God revealed to Daniel three positive blessings. He would bring in "everlasting righteousness," "seal up vision and prophecy," and he would "anoint the most holy" (Dan. 9:24b).

"To bring in everlasting righteousness" would be during the seventy weeks, through the "anointed one" toward the end of the period. The words "everlasting" and "eternal" are from the same Hebrew word *ôlām* and Greek *aiōn*, which "came to be used to refer to a long age or period" (*TWOT* II 672f), and therefore could be defined as "age lasting." The Hebrew word is translated **eternal, everlasting, forever, perpetual, old, ancient, world,** and others. The use of the word indicated its "age-long" or "age-lasting" meaning: God (Ps. 90:2) and the Messiah (Mic. 5:2) are from eternity, therefore outside of time - eternal in the strict or absolute application. The "everlasting mountains [and] perpetual hills" (Hab. 3:6) pertain to the geological period or age. The covenant, priesthood, Sabbath, land of their possession are spoken of as everlasting, but belong to the Mosaic or Old Testament age. When the dispensation ended, these ended. Consequently, our "everlasting righteousness" must be determined by Biblical usage.

**Righteousness,** "In its general use,…represents any conformity to a standard whether that standard has to do with the inner character of a person, or the objective standard of accepted law. Thayer suggested the definition, 'the state of such as he ought to be'…The Biblical [Old Testament] approach preeminently concerns itself with the man whose way of thinking, feeling, and acting is wholly conformed to the righteousness of God" (*ZPEB* 5 104). It seems obvious that only Christ can fulfill this, which is what Daniel's vision pointed to. Stephen charged the Jews with killing "the Righteous One" of whom the prophets spoke (Acts 7:52); and Ananias told Saul that it was God's will that he know His will and see "the Righteous One" (Acts 22:14).

An unnamed psalmist wrote, "Thy righteousness is an everlasting righteousness" (Ps. 119:142). Isaiah said, "Israel shall be saved by Jehovah with an everlasting salvation" (Isa. 45:17); and he added latter, "By the knowledge of himself shall my righteous servant justify many" (53:11). Biblical justification means to reckon or account the individual as righteous. Paul's epistle to the Romans was devoted to the theme of justification by faith in Christ Jesus (3:21-26; 4:6-8; 5:1-2, 8-11; etc.; see also II Cor. 5:17-21; where Paul said, "that we might become the righteousness of God in him [Christ, v. 21]." This "everlasting righteousness" which was "brought in," was brought into the world of lost men through Jesus Christ, the anointed one of God.

"And to seal up vision and prophecy." The "seal" has the same relation to "vision and prophecy" that it has to the sealing up of "sin" in the foregoing passage. If this assumption is correct, then it referred to the sealing up of the visions and prophecies of Jesus and the apostles which would be sealed up until the time of their fulfillment at the end of history. Jesus' prophecy of Jerusalem's destruction was fulfilled in that generation (Matt. 24, cf. v. 34; Mark 13, cf. v. 30; Luke 21, cf. v. 32). The book of Revelation was words of prophecy (Rev. 1:3), was not to be sealed up, for he said, "The time is at hand" (Rev.

22:10). The words were beginning to be fulfilled at that time.

In John's vision of "the little book" he was told to take and eat, and said, "In the days of the voice of the seventh angel [of the vision of the bowls of wrath HH], when he is about to sound, then is finished the mystery of God, according to the good tidings which he declared to his servants [Old Testament] the prophets" (Rev. 10:7). The fulfilling of this mystery was the permanent establishment of the kingdom of God, and the destruction of the fourth world empire. This means the prophecies of Jesus and the apostles are sealed, and these pertain primarily to His final return and subsequent events.

Jesus said he would raise the righteous unto eternal life at the last day (John 6:39, 40, 44, 54). He told of his appearing with His holy angels and the judgment at which He would sit as Judge, the separation of those before him into two groups, destined for eternal life or eternal destruction (Matt. 25:31-46). Paul spoke of the end when we shall all appear before Him (II Cor. 5:10), and of Christ's delivering the kingdom back to God the Father, and becoming subject to Him (I Cor. 15:24-26). He told of the resurrection of the righteous and the change of the living (I Thess. 4:13-18), the nature of the resurrected body (I Cor. 15), and the destruction of the wicked (II Thess. 1:6-12). Peter described the passing of the present order and the new heavens and the new earth (II Pet. 3:8-13). John revealed the destruction of Satan, the final judgment, and the new heavens and the new earth (Rev. 20:10-15; 21:1-8). All of these are sealed, ready to be revealed at the end of the days.

"**And to anoint the most holy.**" According to *Cruden's Concordance,* the expression "most holy" occurs forty-two times in the King James Version of the Old Testament; but occurs only here in the New Testament scripture, "Your most holy faith" (Jude 20). In the Old Testament "most holy" described places, the altar, sacrifices, days, persons, and other things. And the word "anointed" was used of the anointing of numerous items: a pillar, the furniture of the tabernacle, shields, captains, and etc. The two words do not of themselves render help in interpreting Daniel. However, the word anoint was used of kings, priests, and in one passage it was used of the anointing of a prophet.

The anointing of a prophet was Jehovah's instruction to Elijah to anoint Elisha (I Kings 19:16), where the word seemed to be used symbolically. When he found Elisha, Elijah only "cast his mantle upon him" (v. 19). And when Elijah was "taken up into heaven," his mantle, which fell from him, was taken up by Elisha (II Kings 2:1, 13). Keil expressed a narrower view when he said that Isaiah 61:1 "Is the only [passage] in which there is any allusion to the anointing of a prophet" (K & D, Kings, p. 260). However "anoint" and "most holy" may be used in the Old Testament, it seemed obvious that Daniel was writing of the anointing of the Messiah who should come at the termination of the seventy weeks.

The passage referred to by Keil, "Jehovah hath **anointed** me to preach good tidings" (Isa. 61:1) was quoted by Jesus, translating the Hebrew by the Greek *chirō*, and applying the passage to Himself (Luke 4:18). *Chirō* occurs only five times in the New Testament, and was used of the anointing of Jesus four times; the fifth time it was used of three of His preachers (II Cor. 1:21), and in each of the five incidents the action of anointing was ascribed to the Lord (God). David described "Jehovah's Anointed" as King (Ps. 2:2), which was quoted by Peter and John and their "whole company," who ascribed the anointed one of the passage to Jesus (Acts 4:26-27). In his sermon to Cornelius and his household, Peter said of Jesus whom John the Baptist immersed, "How God anointed him with the Holy Spirit and with power" (Acts 10:37-38). The writer of Hebrews, quoted Psalm 45:7, applying it to Jesus, saying, "God, thy God, hath anointed thee / With the oil of gladness above thy fellows" (Heb. 1:9). The "oil of gladness" is probably a metaphor for "the Holy Spirit and Power" (Acts 10:38). If He was considered "above thy fellows" who were addressed as "holy brethren" (Heb. 3:1), then He must be "the most holy" of Daniel's prophecy. It was the anointing of the "most holy [one]" that the purpose of God was realized, and the prophecies of His prophets were fulfilled.

# Periods of the Seventy Weeks
## (v. 25)

**Verse 25** *Know therefore and discern, that from the going forth of the commandment to restore and to build Jerusalem unto the anointed one, the prince, shall be seven weeks, and threescore and two weeks; it shall be built again, with street and moat, even in troublous times.*

It was stated in verse 24a that these are not literal weeks, or symbolic of 490 years, but time periods of different lengths symbolized by seven sevens, sixty-two sevens, and one seven (or heptad). These periods correspond with the three remaining empires: the Persian, Greek, and Roman; Babylon will have fallen when these begin.

Apparently the angel anticipated a problem with his message to Daniel, for he said, "Know therefore and discern." That is, Take the message into your heart with the intent of being instructed to a practical use. And discern, comprehend, understand its bearing on the future history of the city and people, which was the mission of the angel (vv. 22-23).

**The seven sevens.** Immediately a problem is encountered. From a grammatical point of view the seven and the sixty-two weeks are from the decree of Cyrus to the anointing of the prince, which can be none other than the Messiah, one period. But this clearly falls into two periods of seven and sixty-two weeks. In the face of learned discussions to the contrary, it seems that Young's view is preferred by accepting the two period position of seven weeks, one period; and sixty-two weeks, a second period.

The seven weeks period would be from the commandment of Jehovah through the decree of Cyrus, issued in the first year of Cyrus' reign (Ezra 1:1-2; 6:14). It should be observed that in the various records of the commands and decrees, Jehovah emphasized the city and people, whereas Cyrus emphasized the house or temple. In his proclamation, Cyrus said, "Jehovah, the God of heaven…**hath charged me** to build him a house in Jerusalem" (Ezra 1:2). God could have charged him directly, or, Daniel could have read the charge from Isaiah to him (Isa. 44:28). This was followed by a direct statement from Jehovah to Cyrus telling him what He would do for Cyrus that he might render this service (Isa. 45:1-7). Jehovah said that it was for this purpose that He raised up Cyrus to the position of world ruler (v. 13).

The angel's message contained news, both good and bad. The good news was, "It shall be built again," complete with walls, gates, and streets, i.e., a broad space within the gates for civic meetings; and with "moat," a man-made ditch filled with water for a city's protection. Since the terrain about Jerusalem does not lend itself to such a ditch, it was probable that the word was used figuratively, a symbol of completeness. The bad news was, "even in troublous times"; and troublous times followed them from their arrival until the destruction of the city by the Romans.

Although the dates suggested by some scholars may differ slightly from these which are the ones generally accepted. Cyrus issued his proclamation in 538 B.C.; the first contingent of the exiles arrived, built the altar and laid the foundation of the temple in 536 B.C. For sixteen years the work was hindered by internal indifference and external opposition. Jehovah raised up Haggai and Zechariah, prophets who urged continuation of the building (Ezra 5:1-2). Four years later (516 B.C.) the building was completed (Ezra 6:14-15).

Ezra brought a second group from Babylon (458 B.C.) whose special contribution to the return was the restoration of public scripture reading at the Feast of Ingathering (Neh. 8, et al.). Nehemiah was relieved from his service at the king's court and came to the city where he served as governor for twelve years (444-432 B.C.), during which time the walls of the city were rebuilt. During all this period the Jews were troubled from without by the inhabitants of the land, and from within by corrupt and rebellious Jews."[2]

---

[2]"For the history of this period see the histories: Ezra and Nehemiah; and for the spiritual conditions, read Haggai, Zechariah, and Malachi. For the period

**The Sixty-two Weeks.** This period of time covered the history and events from Nehemiah's leadership in building the walls of Jerusalem, which completed the physical restoration to the coming of the anointed one, the prince or the Messiah. The sixty-two weeks period and its events are revealed in chapter eleven.

## After the Sixty-two Weeks
## (v. 26)

**Verse 26** *And after the threescore and two weeks shall the anointed one be cut off, and shall have nothing: and the people of the prince that shall come shall destroy the city and the sanctuary; and the end thereof shall be with a flood, and even unto the end shall be war; desolations are determined.*

The phrase, "And, after the threescore and two weeks" marks a difference between the seven weeks and the sixty and two weeks of verse 25, making two periods, not just one. The angel passed over the events of the sixty-two weeks for the present; but dealt with the events of that period in chapter eleven. Following the sixty-two weeks, "Shall the anointed one be cut off." As stated, the anointing may be applied to various things. But in verses 24 and 25, it was applied to "the most holy...the anointed one, the prince," which is none other than Jesus the Christ.

"Be cut off" is "to bring to an end,...destroy by a violent act of man or nature" (*TWOT* I 457). The same phrase, "cut off," was used by Isaiah of the Servant in a Messianic passage (Isa. 53:8), and quoted by Philip, as referring to Jesus (Acts 8:32-33). "And shall have nothing." When "the anointed" one was "cut off" from the living by a violent death on the cross, He had nothing save the clothes He had been wearing; and for these the soldiers cast lots (Matt. 27:35). He had no church or kingdom as yet, but would receive or establish these after His

---

of the sixty-two weeks, read *Between the Testaments,* Charles F. Pfeiffer, Baker Book House, Grand Rapids, 1959.

resurrection (Matt. 16:18; Dan. 7:13-14). During His crucifixion His disciples forsook Him and fled from the scene
(Matt. 26:56). And following His death He was buried in a
borrowed tomb, with only a stone for a pillow (Matt. 27:59-
60). Though Creator of all, He died a pauper.

"The people of the prince that shall come" were the Roman
soldiers under Titus, the son of Vespasian, emperor of Rome.
These would destroy the city of Jerusalem, and the temple in
its midst. The city, temple, and people as a nation or kingdom,
came to an end in A.D. 70 when these were destroyed by
Roman legions. This would be "with a flood," a flood of
destruction. A similar threat was made by Jehovah against
ancient Judah and Jerusalem, a flood from Assyria that would
come only to the neck but would not take the city (Isa. 8:5-8).
Wars and desolations were determined against the Jewish people by the Lord unto the end. As a people, the Jews would
never be brought to an end, but would continue throughout
time (Jer. 30:11; 46:28). But as a nation which was destroyed
by Babylon and Rome, it would never again exist (Jer. 22:24-
29; Ezek. 21:25-27; I Cor. 15:20-28).

## The Final Week: The End
## (v. 27)

**Verse 27** *And he shall make a firm covenant with many
for one week: and in the midst of the week he shall cause
the sacrifice and the oblation to cease; and upon the wing
of abominations shall come one that maketh desolate;
and even unto the full end, and that determined, shall
wrath be poured out upon the desolate.*

The entire seventy week period is Messianic, dealing with
events from the period of Cyrus and the Persians to the coming and anointing and death of the Messiah, the destruction of
Jerusalem, and the end of the Jewish nation. In developing an
exegesis of the present verse and the events recorded here, a
careful examination of this verse and those scriptures that shed
light upon it will be made. Many of the interpretations of

commentaries rest on unfounded speculation.

The first question to be asked is, who is the "he" that pertains to the covenant? Since the angel passed over the sixty-two weeks period which included the person and deeds of Antiochus, that eliminates him as a possibility. The two possibilities within the scope of the text are the anointed prince, the Christ (v. 25), and the prince of the people who destroyed the city and the sanctuary (v. 26). But since the text emphasized "the people of the prince," and not the prince, that eliminated the latter, leaving only the anointed prince, the Messiah. To Him the evidence points as the most probable or possible one.

The ASV translation, "He shall **make** a firm covenant," seems to be a faulty translation. "**Confirm** a covenant" (KJV, NKJV, NIV) is better, but not the best. The root of the Hebrew word from which the English word is translated is *gabar*, which means "**prevail, be mighty, have strength, be great**" (*TWOT* I 148). It is translated, "And he hath **strengthened** a covenant" (*Literal Translation of the Bible*, p. 552, Robert Young); and, "He shall make **to prevail** a covenant" (Edward J. Young, *op. cit.* p. 209; c.f. also p. 213).

So, "he" does not "**make** a covenant," but "causes to prevail" or "to be strengthened," one already made. Jesus did this by making "to prevail" the covenant made with Abraham (Luke 1:2, 52; Acts 3:25; Gal. 3:16-17). This He did by His teaching the true meaning of the law of the covenant made through Moses at Sinai (Matt. 5 - 7 et al.); and by perfectly living it before the people (John 8:46). In so doing He magnified "the law [of the covenant HH], and made it honorable" (Isa. 42:21). As the angel passed over the events of the sixty-two weeks, so also he passed over some events of this last week which will be discussed at the proper time.

The "many" of the covenant who prevailed would be from the "great multitudes" that followed and gave heed to Jesus, and later gave heed to the apostles, until the number became so great that it aroused the jealousy of the Jewish leaders (Acts 13:45; 25:24). The period, "For one week," was the period which continued from the end of the sixty-two weeks until the destruction of the city, AD 70. "And in the **midst** of the week"—"**half, middle**...[with] a broad range of usage" (*TWOT* I 514) - "he," the one who caused the covenant to prevail, "shall cause the sacrifices and oblations to cease." **Sacrifices** generally referred to the killing and offering of animals to God; and oblations were the various bloodless offerings - meal-offerings, peace-offerings, which were offered to Jehovah according to the Mosaic law. The ceasing of these was an effect, the cause of which was the death of the Messiah which fulfilled the purpose of these sacrifices and took them away. They did not cease to be offered until the temple was destroyed but they ceased to be effectual. These pertained to the first covenant, the Mosaic, which He took out of the way that He might establish the second (Heb. 10:9).

"And upon the wing of abominations shall come one that maketh desolate," is difficult, and has been subjected to many untenable interpretations. The meaning of "**wing**" used here is uncertain. A presentation of the varied efforts to explain its meaning would be of little value. (It should be noted that Jesus did not include "wing.") "**Abominations**": "detestable things," is used of idols in particular, and of those who worship idols (Hos. 9:10); of unclean animals and birds, etc. (*TWOT* II 955). This one who so comes makes "**desolate**." The word is used of land: dust, dry, barren forsaken, of a city in ruins; of a locality, or place, unfit for God to be sought or found; of offerings, likewise unfit to be offered to Deity (*Ibid.*, 936f.).

Because of the difficulty of the passage and the confusion of commentators and their interpretations, one need not be discouraged. For in Jesus' explanation of the destruction of Jerusalem, the temple, and the people, we have a divine commentator and His interpretation of Daniel's prophecy (Matt. 24:15). Upon these one can depend. Before appealing to His discussion of the city and temple, read again the introduction of this chapter, noting carefully the message of the heavenly messengers. Their mission was to make Daniel understand God's message of the people, city (Jerusalem), and sanctuary (temple), in the end days, the latter days - the things on which Daniel had been thinking. Since Daniel's visions pertained to these, and Jesus told of them, why look further and depend on speculations about antichrists and such?

When Jesus left the temple for the last time, He said to the Jews, "Behold, your house is left unto you desolate" (Matt. 23:38). It was no longer a place suitable for the "presence" of God to abide, or in which He could be worshipped; it was fit only for destruction. As in the days of Ezekiel when the temple was given over to idolatry and the glory of Jehovah left it, it was fit only for destruction by the Babylonians (Ezek. 11:22-25).

As He was leaving the temple area, certain of His disciples called Jesus' attention to the beauty of the buildings. Jesus replied, "There shall not be left here one stone upon another, that shall not be thrown down" (Matt. 24:1-2). This would be the ultimate end - the final end - of the material sanctuary. The disciples responded by asking these questions, "**When** shall these things be? **What** shall be the sign of thy coming? and of the **end** of the world [the consummation of the age (margin)]" (v. 3). Jesus' answer to the first question must be considered carefully for it involved a large number of incidents (vv. 4-14; Mark 13:5-13; Luke 21:8-18). To the second, the sign of His coming, He said, "When therefore ye see the abomination of desolation, which was spoken through Daniel the prophet, standing in the holy place (let him that readeth understand)" (Matt. 24:15); "Standing where he ought not" (Mark 13:14); "When ye see Jerusalem compassed with armies, then know that her (Jerusalem's) **desolation** is at hand" (Luke 21:20). The answer of Jesus, recorded by three inspired men, parallel records, gives us the answer to our question regarding Daniel's statement: "Upon the wing of abominations shall come one that maketh desolate." It was the armies of Rome that compassed Jerusalem, standing in the place where they ought not, even upon the holy ground sanctified by Jehovah. That the three men - Matthew, Mark, and Luke - were speaking the same thing is confirmed by the added exhortation of each, "Let him that is in Judea flee unto the mountains."

Jesus further described this destruction of Jerusalem, the temple, and the people, saying, "For then shall be great tribulation, such as hath not been from the beginning of the world until now, no, nor ever shall be" (Matt. 24:21; Mark 13:19; Luke 21:22). This shall mark "the coming of the Son of man" (Matt. 24:27, 30, cf. v. 3; Mark 13:26; Luke 21:27). This will be the coming of Jesus in the clouds of judgment against the city, sanctuary, and the people—not His final coming, but His coming in judgment against these.

Jesus added this word which gives further evidence to the accuracy of this interpretation: "Wheresoever the carcass is, there the eagles [vultures] will be gathered together" (Matt. 24:28). The carcass was the desolate, spiritually dead city; and the vultures were the Roman armies set on the desolation - destruction, making the city and temple a place of ruins. Added to these things spoken by Jesus are three more events: Before these things shall all come to pass, "The gospel must be preached unto all the nations" (Mark 13:10), which according to Paul, was done (Col. 1:23). 2) All three writers affirm that Jesus said, "Verily, I say unto you, This generation shall not pass away till all these things be accomplished" - all the things written above. And He did not mean "race," but the people living at that time (Matt. 24:34; Mark 13:30; Luke 21:32). 3) And Jesus said of the days of which He had been speaking, "For these are days of vengeance, that all things which are written may be fulfilled" (Luke 21:22). They were being fulfilled at that time, and were completely fulfilled in A.D. 70 when the city was destroyed.

Daniel concluded his record of the seventy weeks with this final word, "And even unto the full end, and that determined, shall wrath be poured out upon the desolate." Jesus' description of the city, temple, and nation that had become a spiritual waste, unfit to continue longer, would be brought to a full and complete end. So, the seventy weeks that began with Cyrus and the return of the Babylonian captives to Jerusalem, ended with the complete destruction of the nation, a city, and the temple. But these would be supplanted by a far greater spiritual kingdom, people, sacrifices, and covenant, in the joy of the new order, the things of the old shall be forgotten (Isa. 65:17). To offer animal sacrifices, and burn incense to Jehovah beyond the installation of the Messiah as King and high priest would be an abomination to Him (Isa. 66:3).

# CHAPTER X

# A Vision of Introduction
# To Chapters Eleven and Twelve

Throughout the period of the Babylonian captivity (chs. 1—5), Daniel served as the interpreter of dreams for Nebuchadnezzar, and of the handwriting on the wall for Belshazzar. When the fall of Babylon occurred, and the Persian Empire began, with "flashbacks to the first and third years of Belshazzar's reign" (7:1; 8:1), dreams and visions, and their interpretations, are revealed to Daniel. In these there was a noticeable progressive development of the divine judgments upon the nation Israel for its spiritual and general condition in Babylon until its final destruction as a nation and the destruction of its city and sanctuary. Also, there was a progressive glory in the description of the heavenly beings who revealed the meaning of the visions to Daniel.

To this point in time the prophets had condemned the sins and idolatry of heathen nations, pronouncing the judgment of God upon them, and declaring their eventual destruction. But of God's kingdom (the nation Israel), the prophets had condemned their sins and idolatry, pled with them to repent and serve God faithfully, and threatened them with captivity by foreign kingdoms if they did not: Israel in Assyria and Judah in Babylon. Israel was carried into Assyria (722 B.C.) never again to exist as a nation or separate people; and the captivity of Judah in Babylon was now drawing to a close. What was to be the future of the nation, city of Jerusalem, and the temple? This was the question that deeply concerned the prophet.

Daniel was the last of the two captivity prophets, and the last to deal with the destruction of specific heathen kingdoms. He had dealt with the future of the nation Israel after his time in a vague manner, but not in specific detail. What God had revealed stirred an intense desire within the prophet to know what would be the future of the nation: its people, city, and temple. God's intimate relation to these, and His claim that they were His own, made the answer to this question of extraordinary and supreme importance.

In the four visions revealed to Daniel, God progressively set forth the answer to questions concerning the four great world empires, their relation to the Jewish kingdom, and its future. Answers to Daniel's questions were made known by God's messengers of progressively greater degrees of greatness. A brief summary of the prophet's visions reveal the following facts.

**Chapter 7.** In his first vision four beasts symbolically reveal four empires and their judgment (vv. 1-12). The explanation of the vision was made known by an angel, "one of them that stood by" (v. 16). And the word of encouragement to the faithful was, The saints would possess the kingdom (vv. 18, 22), "an everlasting kingdom" (v. 27).

**Chapter 8.** In the vision of a conflict between a ram and a he-goat, in which the ram was defeated, there was symbolized the conflict between Persia and Greece in which Persia was destroyed. A little horn out from among four horns, involved itself with the Jewish nation in an effort to destroy all that pertained to God, His worship, law, and sanctuary (vv. 9-13). The angel Gabriel, one of high rank, was directed to instruct Daniel in understanding the vision which pertained to the appointed "time of the end" (v. 17). In a later time, a time of transgression of the people, a king of fierce countenance would appear against the Jews (vv. 23-26).

**Chapter 9.** In the light of these two visions, Daniel set his heart by fasting and prayer to learn the meaning of the two visions. Before he had completed his petitions, the angel Gabriel appeared to give him understanding (vv. 1-23). This was done by the third vision, the vision of seventy weeks which, in capsule form revealed what would be the history of the people from Cyrus until the destruction of Jerusalem (vv. 24-27).

**Chapter 10.** And now for the fourth and final vision to appear to Daniel. Chapter ten is an introduction to chapters eleven and twelve, which contain the most specific details of any prophecy among the prophets. But this need not be surprising, because of its importance of the three visions that led to it; because of its revelation of the future of the people, city, and temple of God; and because of two laws of God discussed below. Because of the importance of this vision, it was introduced to Daniel by the most majestic heavenly personage yet to appear to a prophet. Daniel's final chapter to his book brings us to the end of the Jewish economy. Chapter eleven has probably aroused more adverse criticism than any prophecy yet made by the prophets.

God always has a reason for what He does; and the possible reason for being specific in the future history described in chapter eleven, was to test faith. We believe that Daniel received the visions at the dates he designated, because he said that he did. The two principles mentioned above are these: 1) Jehovah said through Moses that the test of a prophecy was in its coming to pass, or its failure to come to pass (Deut. 18:20-22). By the coming to pass of the things spoken in chapter eleven some three hundred years before, they should believe the prophecies fulfilled in Jesus as the Messiah when He came. This leaves no excuse for rejecting Him. 2) In Isaiah's record of God's conflict with the idols, Jehovah challenged them to tell something they had done, or do something now, good or evil. Or, let them tell of something they would do (Isa. 41:21-24). Jehovah concluded the conflict with these false gods of the people by saying, "Therefore I have declared it to thee from of old; before it came to pass I showed it thee; lest thou shouldest say, Mine idol hath done them…hath commanded them" (Isa.

48:5). So when the specific prophecy of chapter eleven was fulfilled to the letter, as were those of Jesus the Messiah, they would be without excuse for not believing Him.

## Introduction to Chapter Ten
## (vv. 1-3)

**Verse 1** *In the third year of Cyrus king of Persia a thing was revealed unto Daniel, whose name was called Belteshazzar; and the thing was true, even a great warfare: and he understood the thing, and had understanding of the vision.*

Since Babylon had fallen to Cyrus in 536 B.C., by the third year of his reign the remnant would by now have been in Judea. The question as to why Daniel had not returned with them is neither raised nor answered; but we can offer three possible reasons why he remained in Persia: 1) His age. By now he would be ninety or more years of age and time would have taken its toll on his physical condition. 2) God had further work for him to do. The revealing of the fourth vision, the receiving and writing of it which could better be accomplished where he was than either on the road or amidst the turmoil of getting settled in Judah. 3) He could better serve his people at the Persian court than he could amid the ruins of Jerusalem.

Daniel spoke in the third person by way of introducing this new vision as he spoke in the earlier chapters of his book (chs. 1—6). It was over seventy years since he had been given the name Belteshazzar by the prince of the eunuchs under Nebuchadnezzar the king of Babylon (1:7). He was now under a different king in a different kingdom. This identified him to a new generation, but it also connected him with the first group who were brought into the captivity.

"A thing...the thing" was revealed unto him. The word "thing" from the Hebrew noun *dābār*, "stretches all the way from anything that can be covered by the word thing or matter to the most sublime and dynamic notion of the word of

God" (*TWOT* I 179). Knowing that "the thing" revealed would be challenged, the Holy Spirit added, "the thing was true,"— God's "Amen" to the revelation. The various translations of "the thing" indicate the difficulty of its meaning: "A great warfare" (ASV), "A great war" (NIV), "A great conflict" (RSV), "And the appointed time was long" (KJV, NKJV), "And of a great conflict" (NKJV, margin).

If one accepts the translation, "the great warfare [or] conflict," then the thing revealed was the great conflict between Persia and Greece (Macedonian) and that of Antiochus Epiphanes and the Jews. However, the introduction of Michael (vv. 13, 21) suggested that this conflict was a phase of the great spiritual conflict from Eden to the establishment of the kingdom and salvation of God, and the authority and rule of the Christ (Rev. 12:7-12). His understanding of the vision probably rested on the revelation of the former visions.

> **Verse 2** *In those days I, Daniel, was mourning three whole weeks.* **3** *I ate no pleasant bread, neither came flesh nor wine into my mouth, neither did I anoint myself at all, till three whole weeks were fulfilled.*

"In those days," the days of the vision's revelation to him, Daniel mourned. No doubt the cause of his grief was the greater realization of the intense suffering that lay ahead for his people. His avoidance of flesh and wine during the three weeks of mourning suggested that the prophet no longer adhered to the rigid diet of his youth (cf. 1:8-16). Times had changed, and no doubt the significance of the various foods had changed with the times.

## The Vision of the Heavenly Personage
## (vv. 4-9)

> **Verse 4** *And in the four and twentieth day of the first month, as I was by the side of the great river, which is Hiddekel,*

If this was the period of Daniel's fast, which it appeared to be, then Daniel fasted during the Passover and the week of unleavened bread that followed (Deut. 16:1; Ex. 12:15). Why Daniel was by the river Hiddekel (the Tigris, margin; also cf. Gen. 2:14 and margin) is not revealed. But it was there that the vision appeared unto him.

**Verse 5** *I lifted up mine eyes, and looked, and, behold, a man clothed in linen, whose loins were girded with pure gold of Uphaz:*

In this vision the most glorious and wonderful of all the heavenly personages yet to appear, spoke to Daniel. This raises the question, Who is this gloriously majestic one? When the description of this one is compared with the description of the glorified Christ of John's vision (Rev. 1:13-16; 19:12), the reader is inclined to identify him as the pre-incarnate Word of God, the Messiah—the Son of God. However, two things must be considered: 1) the differences between the two which is noteworthy; 2) and the fact that Michael came to help him. It may be questioned whether that could be said of either the pre-incarnate Son of God or the glorified Son. And yet, concerning this latter point, at the end of His temptations and beginning of His ministry, "Behold, angels came and ministered unto him" (Matt. 4:11). And toward the end of His ministry as He prayed so fervently in the garden of Gethsemane, "There appeared unto him an angel from heaven strengthening him" (Luke 22:43). Also, when Peter drew his sword with the intent of defending Jesus against Judas and the mob that followed him, Jesus said to Peter, "Thinkest thou that I cannot beseech my Father, and he shall even now send me more than twelve legions of angels?" (Matt. 26:53). If one angel could slay one hundred eighty five thousand in one night, imagine what over twelve legions could have done (Isa. 37:36)!

If one chooses to accept the angel view and rejects the pre-incarnate view, then it seems to be a decision of identity between one of God's strong or mighty angels (cf. Rev. 5:2;

10:1; 18:21), or one of His angels with golden girdles from which to choose (Rev. 15:6). After considering the two possibilities, and the nature of the vision itself, it seems probable that the heavenly visitor was the pre-incarnate Messiah, the Son of God.

The angel appeared to Daniel as "a man clothed in linen," visible, and one with whom the seer could communicate. Linen is mentioned often in scripture as the apparel of individuals of noble or religious positions; and of the material in religious use. It was the clothing of the high priest when he went into the most holy place to offer the blood of the annual atonement (Lev. 16:4, 23); of the man with the inkhorn in Ezekiel's vision (Ezek. 9:2); of the wife of the Lamb at the marriage feast (Rev. 19:8); and of the heavenly armies that follow the King of kings in His great warfare against the forces of evil (Rev. 19:14). The "Uphaz" to which his golden girdle was associated (mentioned only here and in Jer. 10:9), is uncertain. It may be an unknown geographical location, a technical name for specially refined gold, or a confusion with Ophir (*ZPEB* 5 645).

**Verse 6** *his body also was like the beryl, and his face as the appearance of lightning, and his eyes as flaming torches, and his arms and his feet like unto burnished brass, and the voice of his words like the voice of a multitude.*

"The beryl," to which his body is likened, is a stone of various colors and qualities, possibly of uncertain modern identity; but it was of great beauty, strength, and value. His face was "as the appearance of lightning," flashing brilliantly. He had come to enlighten Daniel by making him understand the words of the vision, which he was thoroughly capable of doing (vv. 11, 14). "And his eyes [were] as flaming torches" doubtless symbolizing his penetrating insight of the things to come. "His arms [symbols of power] and feet [symbols of his ability to tread under foot, cf. Jehovah's power, Isa. 63:3] like unto burnished brass." That is, they sparkled brilliantly (cf.

Ezek. 1:7) like highly polished brass, probably from active use in the service of God. "And the voice of his words like the voice of a multitude," voluminous, capable of being heard by multitudes at great distances (cf. Rev. 19:6).

## Effect of the Vision on Daniel and Others (vv. 7-9)

**Verse 7** *And I, Daniel, alone saw the vision; for the men that were with me saw not the vision; but a great quaking fell upon them, and they fled to hide themselves.*

Only Daniel saw this great vision of the majestic heavenly personage; therefore it is on his testimony, and his alone, that we accept the vision as being authentic. If one cannot believe that it was in the third year of Cyrus king of Persia (v. 1), rather than in the second century B.C. how can we then accept as true the message of these last three chapters of the book? The men that were with him did not see the vision, nor is it said that they heard the voice. Instead, it is insinuated that only Daniel heard it. But they knew something supernatural was transpiring, for they were seized by a great quaking. **Quaking** is from the Hebrew word *hārad*, and may be translated "**quaking, trembling, fear** (a great panic [I Sam. 14:15 (RSV)]). [It] primarily describes human trembling before some strange, or fearsome event" (*TWOT* I 321). If men would flee to hide themselves from some unseen phenomenon such as this, what must be the terror of the visible reality! (cf. Hos. 10:8; Rev. 6:16).

**Verse 8** *So I was left alone, and saw this great vision, and there remained no strength in me; for my comeliness was turned in me into corruption, and I retained no strength.*

Being left alone, I repeat, it was upon his testimony, and his only, that one accepts or rejects these three chapters, or any other visions recorded in this book. The message of the vision was so impressive, and the majesty of the angel so striking, that, following the three weeks fast, Daniel was bereft of strength. His "comeliness" was changed to "corruption," is translated "My radiant appearance was fearfully changed" (RSV). It was now destroyed as if by the corruption of death.

> **Verse 9** *Yet heard I the voice of his words; and when I heard the voice of his words, then was I fallen into a deep sleep on my face, with my face toward the ground.*

But in spite of his weakness and sense of destruction as if by death, Daniel heard and understood the words of the voice that spoke to him. He was so overcome by the whole experience that he swooned, falling upon his face in a deep sleep.

## Daniel's Recovery
## (vv. 10-13)

> **Verse 10** *And behold, a hand touched me, which set me upon my knees and upon the palms of my hands.*

Daniel's recovery was gradual, not instantaneous. Whether the hand that touched him was that of the majestic messenger or that of another was not stated. When the hand of one sent from God touched the weary wayfarer he found strength to continue his work or journey. When that hand touches the sorrowing or suffering saint, he finds the spiritual power to believe that, "Weeping may tarry for the night, / But joy cometh in the morning" (Ps. 30:5). The hand that touched him set him upon his hands and knees, the beginning of an upright position.

> **Verse 11** *And he said unto me, O Daniel, thou man greatly beloved, understand the words that I speak unto thee, and stand upright; for unto thee am I now sent. And when he had spoken this word unto me, I stood trembling.*

With help from the angel, Daniel was instructed to "stand upright." Like the message of Gabriel (9:22-23), he was told about the love and esteem in which he was held, and the mission of the heavenly visitor. The messenger was sent with a message from heaven which Daniel was to hear and understand. At this word he stood by his own strength, "trembling." The trembling seemed to be from weakness; but whether from present fear, age, fasting, or the seriousness of what he witnessed, or all four of these, we are not told. But it was of those who "tremble at his word" that God would build His future spiritual temple (Isa. 66:2, 5).

> **Verse 12** *Then said he unto me, Fear not, Daniel; for from the first day that thou didst set thy heart to understand, and to humble thyself before thy God, thy words were heard: and I am come for thy words' sake.*

Though man is to fear God by holding Him, His name, and His word in reverence and awe, he is not to fear Him in the sense of His presence or response to prayer in His providential care. The prayers are heard and the response will be according to God's purpose and what is best for the one praying. Two things characterized Daniel's prayer that are essential to everyone's prayer is that the heart be set on understanding the will and purpose of the Lord, and a humble spirit that is perfectly submissive to that will. On these two principles his words were heard and the angel came because of them. His appearance was God's response to Daniel's words. (Study Heb. 1:14 in this light.)

> **Verse 13** *But the prince of the kingdom of Persia withstood me one and twenty days; but, lo, Michael, one of the chief princes, came to help me: and I remained there with the kings of Persia.*

Here we are faced with a question of identity. Are the princes of Persia and of Greece (v. 20) political leaders (kings) or are they good angels who guide kings, or wicked angels? The question may be settled by the fact that this prince of the kingdom of Persia resisted this angel of God who was assisted by Michael, "one of the chief princes." In Jude's epistle Michael was called "the archangel" (v. 9). And in Revelation Michael led his army of heavenly angels in the war against "the dragons and his angels" (12:7-9).

It seems here God draws open the curtain and gives a view of the great conflict between the spiritual forces of good and the forces of evil from Eden till the victory of Christ (Rev. 12:7-12). This conflict with the world kingdoms of Persia and Greece is a part of that conflict. Worship of and sacrifices to idols means to have communion with the demon spirits or fallen angels which they represent, as spoken of by Paul, (I Cor. 10:19-21). Paul also said, "For our wrestling is not against flesh and blood, but against the principalities, against the powers, against the world-rulers of this darkness, against the spiritual hosts of wickedness in the heavenly places" (Eph. 6:12).

The twenty-one days were equivalent to the time of Daniel's fasting. However, this seemed to be only one phase of the conflict, for he said, "And I remained there with the kings [plural] of Persia." The "kings" must have referred to the subordinate rulers, for it was in the third year of Cyrus and he was the only ruler of the empire (cf. 9:1, Darius, king of the Chaldeans). It was an ongoing conflict between the rulers of the world empires and their demon angels and the kingdom of God. This remained to the end of the empire, and then it was continued with the "prince of Greece" (10:20). A summary statement of the history of this conflict follows.

At some point in eternity, or early time, there was a rebellion in heaven, led by a high ranking angel, later called "the great dragon...the old serpent...the devil [slanderer or false accuser HH] and Satan [accuser], the deceiver of the whole world" (Rev. 12:9). These were the devil and his angels, cast out of heaven to Tartarus (II Pet. 2:4) ("darkness," which is complete separation from God because "God is light" I John 1:5), to be reserved unto judgment (II Pet. 2:4; Jude 6).

When God created Adam and Eve and placed them in the garden of Eden, Satan, the old serpent, was there ready to entice the two to join his ranks against God by their disobedience to the Creator. When the two sinned by eating of the forbidden fruit, God called a council and pronounced an enmity between Satan and his seed (probably those whom he would seduce, [cf. John 8:44]), and the woman and her seed (the Son of man and God, "he") (Gen. 3:14-16). This described the beginning of a great spiritual warfare between good and evil, symbolized in Revelation by Michael and his angels warring against the "old serpent," the dragon, and his angels (Rev. 12:7-11). One of the lessons taught in the book of Job is that Satan's power is limited by God. He can act only within divinely limited bounds (Job 1:6-12; 2:1-6).

It should be observed in the war between Michael and the dragon, that Michael had his angels and the dragon had his angels. It was of these angels of the two world kingdoms, Persia and Greece, that the angel discussed in verses 13 and 20. There are good angels and there are bad angels. The good are messengers or servants of God; the bad or wicked are servants of Satan. As angels they may work among nations; or among men they may work as ministers of righteousness, fashioning themselves into servants of Christ (II Cor. 11:13-15).

In the great conflict, Satan and his angels were defeated (Rev. 12:7ff.). This defeat was consummated in the coming and victory of Jesus. When the disciples of Jesus returned from one of their preaching excursions, they reported how that demons were cast out by the power of Christ's name. To this Jesus responded, "I beheld Satan fallen as lightning from heaven" (Luke 10:18). Did Jesus pause before answering, and with a faraway look in His eyes recalled by divine foresight the fall? That is very doubtful. More likely He referred to His first clash with Satan, immediately after His baptism, in which Satan was defeated for a season (Matt. 4:1-10). That signaled the devil's final and total defeat in Jesus' resurrection from the dead (Rom. 1:4). In a later speech, Jesus said, "When the strong man fully armed guardeth his own court, his goods are in peace: but when a stronger than he shall come upon him, and overcome him, he taketh from him his whole armor wherein he trusted, and divideth his spoils" (Luke 11:21-22). When the end came, and the judgment was finished, those who had served Satan instead of God, were cast into "the eternal fire which is prepared for the devil and his angels" (Matt. 25:41a; cf. also Rev. 20:10).

## The Message and Further Effect Upon Daniel
## (vv. 14-17)

**Verse 14** *Now I am come to make thee understand what shall befall thy people in the latter days; for the vision is yet for many days.*

The angel continued to explain his mission to Daniel which he introduced in verse 12. Daniel was exceedingly interested in the future lot of his people: What is to befall them, and what will be their end? The visions of chapters 7 and 8 aroused this interest concerning which he had prayed so earnestly in chapter 9. Again he prayed and fasted for three whole weeks. The mission of the messenger was to inform him "what shall befall thy people in the latter days." Not in every case, but most frequently, the phrase "latter days" referred to the Messianic age (Isa. 2:2; Dan. 2:28, et al.). The vision was not for the present or the immediate future, but would be fulfilled many days hence.

**Verse 15** *And when he had spoken unto me according to these words, I set my face toward the ground, and was dumb.*

What the angel said (vv. 11-14) left Daniel speechless, which probably consisted of three things: 1) God had heard his prayer and was responding to it immediately by sending such a majestic and awe-inspiring heavenly messenger to grant his petition (vv. 11-12). 2) The angel's description of the unseen spiritual warfare that was being waged shocked him; and the mutual help of God's angels, one for another overwhelmed him (v. 13). 3) And now he was to have his desire granted, knowledge of "what shall befall [his] people in the latter days," which information would be alarming, if not terrifying (v. 14).

> **Verse 16** *And, behold, one in the likeness of the sons of men touched my lips: then I opened my mouth, and spake and said unto him that stood before me, O my lord, by reason of the vision my sorrows are turned upon me, and I retain no strength.*

Whether the one who touched his lips and restored his speech was the angel sent to him, or another, is not stated. Evidently the message of the unseen conflict revealed more to Daniel than appeared on the surface. It may have included knowledge of the difficulties faced by the newly returned remnant disclosed in Ezra and Nehemiah. The returnees built the altar the first year, and laid the foundation of the temple the second year, but were otherwise hindered from continuing, "For fear was upon them because of the peoples of the countries" (Ezra 3:2-3, 8, 10). They continued to be hounded by neighboring enemies even to the completion of the walls around Jerusalem.

Upon receiving his speech, Daniel said to the angel, "By reason of the vision my sorrows are turned upon me." Sorrows is translated from a word meaning "pangs" (Isa. 13:8), which means, "a sudden, sharp feeling of pain or distress"; a pain so severe that it left him weak and breathless.

> **Verse 17** *For how can the servant of this my lord talk with this my lord? for as for me, straightway there remained no strength in me, neither was there breath left in me.*

Daniel's response to the angel is typical of Biblical speech used by inferiors in rank to their superiors. The difference in rank, the prolonged conversation and subject matter of the two put Daniel under great stress. The stress left him weak and breathless. He had neither breath to speak, nor strength with which to act.

## (Verse 18-11:1)

**Verse 18** *Then there touched me again one like the appearance of a man, and he strengthened me.*

The numerous times Daniel mentioned his weakness being relieved and his strength revived by the touches of the hand of an unnamed messenger from God, should impress all believers with the confidence that God is the source of spiritual strength. One may be touched by the word of God, by the word of a friend, by the act of a friend, but in whatever the manner, God is the source.

**Verse 19** *And he said, O man greatly beloved, fear not: peace be unto thee, be strong, yea, be strong. And when he spake unto me, I was strengthened, and said, Let my lord speak; for thou hast strengthened me.*

This is the third time Daniel was addressed as "greatly beloved" (cf. 9:23; 10:11), which revealed God's estimate of him which is an estimate earned, not bestowed carelessly. "Fear not," neither be afraid of me, the angel, nor of the message and its imputation; rather, "Peace be unto thee." Of **peace** it is said, "The general meaning behind the root *sh-l-m* is of completeness and fulfillment—of entering into a state of wholeness and unity, a restored relationship." And, the Hebrew word also "describes the state of fulfillment which is the result of God's presence" (*TWOT* II 930, 31). Whatever the future may hold, your state of wholeness will be sustained by the presence of God. As for you, "Be strong, yea, be strong" (twice for emphasis); that is, become strong. A few years later Haggai gave the same exhortation to the discouraged saints in Jerusalem, with the added word, "For I am with you, saith Jehovah" (Hag. 2:4; cf. also Paul, Eph. 6:10; to which he added, "in the Lord"). It is only "in the Lord" that such strength is found. Being strengthened by the words of the angel, Daniel was now ready for any revelation of the future trials that God might reveal. In the peace, the fullness of the Lord and His strength, the saint can face and survive any judgment that may come upon the world kingdom of the present or future.

**Verse 20** *Then said he, Knowest thou wherefore I am come unto thee? and now will I return to fight with the prince of Persia: and when I go forth, lo, the prince of Greece shall come.*

Some regard the angel's question as foolish, but not so. He told Daniel that he came in answer to the prophet's prayer (v. 11) and to tell him, make him understand what he had desired to know (vv. 12, 14). In the meantime Daniel was on his face, dumb. Before departing, the angel wanted to be certain that Daniel understood what he had come to reveal to him. He must now return to continue the spiritual war with the prince of Persia, for the battle would continue until the work of Nehemiah was completed. When the end of the Persian Empire came by destruction, the war against the forces of evil continued with the Grecian empire under the Macedonian opposition, followed by the conflict with Antiochus Epiphines.

**Verse 21** *But I will tell thee that which is inscribed in the writing of truth: and there is none that holdeth with me against these, but Michael your prince.*

"The writing of truth" is a figure of speech probably for God's eternal purpose which would include the victory for truth in all the conflicts met by His people. The symbolical book which would be completely carried out by the Lamb of God was in the hand of God (Rev. 5:1), and in His providence nothing could thwart its being fulfilled. Therefore all efforts of Satan's angels were doomed to fail. And in the conflict, only Michael, the archangel, the prince of the good angels, the leader in the war against Satan would stand with him. Under the two, the speaker and Michael, the victory would be won (Rev. 12: ff.).

## Chapter 11 verse 1, Continuation of Chapter 10

**Verse 1** *And as for me, in the first year of Darius the Mede, I stood up to confirm and strengthen him.*

This verse is a continuation of 10:21. The heavenly speaker concluded his speech concerning the princes of Persia and Greece, and concerning Michael the chief prince of God's people, that as Michael had stood up and helped him in his conflict with the prince of Persia (10:13), so two years later he had stood by Michael. This harmony, unity, and cooperation among the heavenly beings can be used as a commentary on Jesus' instruction regarding the phrase in the prayer he taught, "Thy will be done, as in heaven, so on earth" (Matt. 6:10).

# Between the Testaments

**It** has been said already that chapter eleven is probably the most specifically detailed prophecy of the entire Bible. But "specific details" is not contrary to visions or prophecy. Let the reader keep in mind that this is a prophetic vision, not related history past at the time of its being written. Moses was quite specific in some details when he foretold the consequential judgments should the nation turn from God in rebellion against Him (Lev. 26; Deut. 28). The later writing prophets were also explicit when they described the future judgments of the heathen world nations. Also, their prophecies of the coming Messiah were sufficiently specific in details that had the people looked at them with an open mind and honest heart, they should have recognized Jesus as the Messiah of God.

Although Daniel did not state a reason for the detailed nature of his prophecy, the three reasons given already bears repeating. 1) No specific details of the political nation's future, its people, city, temple, and conflicts, had yet been revealed. And the important relationship of these to God and His purpose merited a minute description of what lay ahead of the Israelites in their dark days and final end. 2) The fulfillment of these prophecies of specific historical events, made three to four hundred years earlier, should be great faith builders to the people: God always fulfills His word. 3) When Jesus came as predicted, lived as foretold, revealed God and taught as He did, and was put to death as so graphically described in Psalm 22, they should have believed the report of His resurrection and accepted Him as the Messiah. Even now, nearly two thousand years after His coming, a fresh study of such prophecies and their fulfillment in Him should convince the Jews and the Gentiles as well.

## The Four Kings to Come
### (vv. 2-4)

**Verse 2** *And now will I show thee the truth. Behold, there shall stand up yet three kings in Persia; and the fourth shall be far richer than they all: and when he is waxed strong through his riches, he shall stir up all against the realm of Greece.*

The speaker's statement, "Now will I show thee the truth," indicated the probability that the vision would be questioned or denied by future skeptics. His word was either truth, or a deception; and if it is to be rejected as a fraudulent vision, the entire book is under question. Cyrus was king at the time; the three kings that followed him were Cambyses, Smerdis, and Darius Hystaspis (Darius the Great, the great organizer of the empire). This makes Xerxes, the Ahasuerus of the book of Esther, the fourth. To "stand up" was to come to power. It is thought that the six month festivity when his sub-rulers and servants were gathered to the palace (Esther 1:4) was the occasion of his plans to invade Greece. In his effort to subdue Greece Xerxes was ingloriously defeated, though he inflicted much suffering upon that nation. There were many other rulers over Persia, but these would exert the greatest influence on Israel's future.

**Verse 3** *And a mighty king shall stand up, that shall rule with great dominion, and do according to his will.*

Slightly over two hundred years passed from the fall of Babylon by Cyrus to the rise of the "mighty king," Alexander the Great, who should "stand up"—come to power (539 -334 B.C.) and invade Persia. This was introduced earlier (8:20-21). And although he had twelve able generals, his victories were primarily the result of his own genius and leadership. The extent of his dominion extended from Greece and Macedonia to the border of India.

**Verse 4** *And when he shall stand up, his kingdom shall be broken, and shall be divided toward the four winds of heaven, but not to his posterity, nor according to his dominion wherewith he ruled; for his kingdom shall be plucked up, even for others besides these.*

The message of the prophecy was that Alexander's kingdom would come to a sudden end, which it did by the untimely death of the young world conqueror at the age of thirty-four years. Following his death, a power struggle ensued between his generals, which resulted finally in a general four direction division, but "not to his posterity," for his two young sons were slain by a conspiracy among certain of the generals. Others among them received small territories. Alexander's four generals were Cassander, who received Macedonia, Lysimachus received Thrace, Egypt went to Ptolemy Soter, and Antigonus, whose son was Seleucus, acquired Asia.

## Conflict between the Kings of the North and South (vv. 5-20)

(The careful reader of this commentary has observed that where possible I have let Scripture interpret the Scriptures of the book of Daniel. But this is impossible in this chapter which deals with the period between the Testaments. My knowledge of intertestamental history is general. Consequently, what follows is taken verbatim from H. Deane's comments from his Commentary on Daniel.[1] The only exceptions will be the insertion of the Scripture texts from the American Standard Version at the proper places, and the change in format of his references. Let the reader keep in mind that Daniel is writing the words of the heavenly speaker, telling of events to come, both near and distant; whereas Deane is dealing with the events of the prophecy as they were being fulfilled.)

"The four generals of Alexander among whom his empire was divided, so far as especially concerned the fortunes of Israel, were Cassander, Lysimachus, Seleucus, and Ptolemy. The last two respectively reigned over Syria and Egypt, and from this period of the revelation onward the kings of these two countries are severally called the King of the North and the King of the South.'

## The Kings of the South and the North (vv. 5-6)

**Verse 5** *And the king of the south shall be strong, and one of his princes; and he shall be strong above him, and have dominion; his dominion shall be a great dominion.* **6** *And at the end of years they shall join themselves together; and the daughter of the king of the south shall come to the king of the north to make an agreement: but she shall not retain the strength of her arm; neither shall he stand, nor his arm; but she shall be given up, and they that brought her, and he that begat her, and he that strengthened her in those times.*

"The first two kings to whom Daniel is supposed to refer are Ptolemy Lagus and Seleucus Nicator. Ptolemy, as it appears, was a powerful king, and succeeded in increasing the territory which he obtained at the death of Alexander. The Northern king Seleucus, on the other hand, was "strong above him and had dominion" (Dan. 11:5). He indeed may be looked upon

---

[1] H. Deane, B.D., Men of the Bible, Daniel His Life and times (New York: Fleming H. Revell Company, 1888), pp. 182- 187.

as the only one of the four generals who was a worthy succes-
sor to Alexander."

### Their Successors (vv. 7-9)

**Verse 7** *But out of a shoot from her roots shall one stand
up in his place, who shall come unto the army, and shall
enter into the fortress of the king of the north, and shall
deal against them, and shall prevail.* **8** *And also their
gods, with their molten images, and with their goodly
vessels of silver and of gold, shall he carry captive into
Egypt; and he shall refrain some years from the king of
the north.* **9** *And he shall come into the realm of the king
of the south, but he shall return into his own land.*

"Nothing further appears to be stated with regard to these
two kings (Dan. 11:6). We appear to pass over from them to
their successors, Antiochus Theos and Ptolemy Philadelphus.
It appears that after a considerable time had been spent by
these two kings in war, an attempt was made by them to come
to terms. Philadelphus, with this in view, gave his daughter in
marriage to Antiochus, and a large dowry was given with her
to secure peace between the two kingdoms. But the help of
Berenice, the king's daughter, availed little; both her suite and
the princess herself were "given up," that is, betrayed; Berenice
herself was murdered; all the complicated plots failed, and hostilities between the two kingdoms commenced afresh.

Berenice had a brother, Ptolemy Euergetes, who on suc-
ceeding his father determined to avenge his sister's death (Dan.
11:7-9). Accordingly he marched against Seleucus Callinicus,
who had succeeded Antiochus Theos; put to death Laodice,
who had instigated the murder of Berenice; took part of the
northern provinces belonging to Seleucus; and returned to
Egypt carrying with him the gods and the treasures which he
had captured in his expedition. For some time war ceased
between the two kingdoms. Euergetes "continued more years
than the king of the North;" he survived him, according to the
ordinary chronology, some four years.'

### Renewal of Hostilities (vv. 10-12)

**Verse 10** *And his sons shall war, and shall assemble a multitude of great forces, which shall come on, and overflow, and pass through; and they shall return and war, even to his fortress.* **11** *And the king of the south shall be moved with anger, and shall come forth and fight with him, even with the king of the north; and he shall set forth a great multitude, and the multitude shall be given into his hand.* **12** *And the multitude shall be lifted up, and his heart shall be exalted; and he shall cast down tens of thousands, but he shall not prevail.*

"At length circumstances combined to effect a renewal of hostilities (Dan. 11:10-12). The sons of Seleucus Callinicus, namely, Seleucus Ceraunus, and Antiochus the Great, collected a large army. One of the sons only is mentioned by Daniel, which is Antiochus, for Ceraunus was killed shortly after setting out upon the campaign. Antiochus took his army with him, and went to attack the Asiatic provinces of Ptolemy Philopator, the son of Euergetes. He was successful in his military expedition, and then returned to Syria. Shortly afterwards he got together a large army, and marched against Philopator himself. Philopator, "moved by choler," met him on the frontier at Raphia, where some four hundred years previously Sargon had overcome Egypt, and inflicted a serious defeat upon her king. Yet no permanent fruits remained even to so great a victory as this. Philopator "was not strengthened by it." He returned to his home and spent the rest of his life in the greatest luxury and excess, by which indeed he shortened his days.'

### Events Which followed (vv. 13-14)

**Verse 13** *And the king of the north shall return, and shall set forth a multitude greater than the former; and he shall come on at the end of the times, even of years, with a great army and with much substance. 14 And in those times there shall many stand up against the king of*

*the south: also the children of the violent among thy peo-*
*ple shall lift themselves up to establish the vision; but they*
*shall fall.*

"Some fourteen years later (Dan. 11:13-14) "the king of the North," Antiochus the Great, returned with a larger army than that which he had brought upon the former occasion. Philopator had been succeeded by Ptolemy Epiphanes, who was a mere child of four years of age. His tender years enabled many enterprising persons to enrich themselves at the expense of the country. One of those thus enriched was Antiochus himself. Another out of the "many who stood up against the king of the South," was Philip III, King of Macedonia. The provinces subject to Egypt and a part of Egypt itself rose in revolt against the regents of Egypt, and some of Daniel's own countrymen deserved the name of "robbers" for joining in the insurrection and supporting the cause of Antiochus against Ptolemy Epiphanes. Unconsciously these seditious Jews accomplished a part of this revelation, "establishing the vision," but in the end they fell. Josephus gives the following account of this matter— "When Antiochus had beaten Ptolemy he seized upon Judea; and when Philopator was dead, his son sent out a great army under Scopas, the general of his forces against Coele-Syria, who took many of their cities, and in particular of our nation; which, when he fell upon them, went over to him. Yet was it not long afterward when Antiochus overcame Scopas...and afterward the Jews of their own accord went over to him, and received him into Jerusalem, and readily assisted him when he besieged the garrison which was in the citadel of Jerusalem" (Josephus, "Ant." XII.iii.3). In this striking way, if credit may be given to Josephus, the Jews brought upon themselves the very troubles which they were forced to undergo in the time of Antiochus Epiphanes.'

## Continued Hostilities (vv. 15-19)

**Verse 15** *So the king of the north shall come, and cast up a mound, and take a well-fortified city: and the forces of the south shall not stand, neither his chosen people, neither shall there be any strength to stand.* **16** *But he that cometh against him shall do according to his own will, and none shall stand before him; and he shall stand in the glorious land, and in his hand shall be destruction.* **17** *And he shall set his face to come with the strength of his whole kingdom, and with him equitable conditions; and he shall perform them: and he shall give him the daughter of women, to corrupt her; but she shall not stand, neither be for him.* **18** *After this shall he turn his face unto the isles, and shall take many: but a prince shall cause the reproach offered by him to cease; yea, moreover, he shall cause his reproach to turn upon him.* **19** *Then he shall turn his face toward the fortresses of his own land; but he shall stumble and fall, and shall not be found.*

"The next move is that the Syrian king, Antiochus, went out to attack the fortress of Sidon (Dan. 11:15-19). This was held by Scopas, who had retreated thither after his defeat by Antiochus. Ptolemy sent troops to relieve Sidon, but it was to no purpose. Scopas was forced to surrender: Antiochus took the Asiatic portions of the Egyptian territory, and disposed of them as he pleased; he then entered the Holy Land (the glorious land as it is described in this revelation), with a view of gaining all the possessions of his southern rival. Hence, again, he set his face to march against Egypt. He had not only a large army, but also "upright ones" with him—that is, he had various plausible schemes and diplomatic arrangements by which he trusted that he should succeed if force failed. One of these plans was to betroth his daughter Cleopatra [I],"[2] who was only a child, to the young king, expecting in this way to allure the young king to his destruction. Rightly is such conduct on

---

[2]"Cleopatra I was queen of Egypt (193-176 B.C.), wife of Ptolemy V Epiphanes and regent for her minor son, Ptolemy VI Philometor. She is not

the part of Antiochus stigmatized as "corrupting his daughter." However, this plan proved a singular failure, as his daughter, Cleopatra, not only refused to comply with his request, but actually at a later time took the opposite side to him. Still Antiochus lost none of the ambition with which he had commenced his reign. He "turned his face to the isles," making a descent upon the Mediterranean coast, upon Asia Minor, and some of the Greek islands. He met with some success, taking some cities and islands, but the Romans, whose power was daily increasing, considered that "a reproach was offered" to them by his conduct; and they inflicted upon him a series of defeats, finally crushing him in a battle near Magnesia. The result of this defeat was that his son, Antiochus, was sent to Rome as a hostage for the future good behaviour of his father, who was forced to retreat within the fortresses of his own land, Antioch, and other places, and while going through the provinces, attempting to raise money, was slain in the act of plundering a temple at Elymais.'

### Heliodorus, the Tax Collector (v. 20)

**Verse 20** *Then shall stand up in his place one that shall cause an exactor to pass through the glory of the kingdom; but within few days he shall be destroyed, neither in anger, nor in battle.*

"Antiochus the Great was succeeded by his son Seleucus Philopator (Dan. 11:20). A heavy tribute was due from him to the Romans amounting to no less than a thousand talents annually. With the object of paying this charge he was compelled to raise a large amount of money by taxation, and if we may trust the writer of the Second Book of Maccabees, he actually sent the tax collector, Heliodorus, to plunder wherever he could (2 Macc. iii.2-7). For about twelve years Seleucus carried on his government in this miserable fashion, but at last

---

as famous as Cleopatra the VII who ruled Egypt 69-30 B.C. and married Mark Antony. For further information on the Cleopatras of Egypt see *The Encyclopaedia Britannica.*

he fell "neither in anger nor in battle." His death was not occasioned by revenge or by war, but by the treachery of the same Heliodorus whom he had employed as his tax collector.'

## Antiochus Epiphanes
## (vv. 21-35)

### The Contemptible Person (vv. 21-24)

**Verse 21** *And in his place shall stand up a contemptible person, to whom they had not given the honor of the kingdom: but he shall come in time of security, and shall obtain the kingdom by flatteries.* **22** *And the overwhelming forces shall be overwhelmed from before him, and shall be broken; yea, also the prince of the covenant.* **23** *And after the league made with him he shall work deceitfully; for he shall come up, and shall become strong, with a small people.* **24** *In time of security shall he come even upon the fattest places of the province; and he shall do that which his fathers have not done, nor his fathers" fathers; he shall scatter among them prey, and spoil, and substance: yea, he shall devise his devices against the strongholds, even for a time.*

"At this point the most prominent person in the chapter, Antiochus Epiphanes, is brought before us (Dan. 11:21-24). He was the younger brother of the late king, and had resided for some years at Rome as a hostage, (I Macc. i.10) and knowing that he was not legally entitled to the kingdom, obtained it by flattery and by stealth. Having once become master of the situation, he determined to act in the most tyrannical manner, his power becoming greater day by day. His troops rushed on as a torrent that none could stem, overwhelming all that were brought into contact with him, even "the prince of the covenant," that is, the priests and rulers of Jerusalem. He succeeded in making a league with one high priest, but broke it, and gave the high priesthood to another. Notwithstanding, all that he accomplished at Jerusalem was done by the aid of a very small number of men. By means of his "peaceable" or stealthy policy, he succeeded in overcoming hostile troops which were brought against him, and annihilating them. In this way he defeated the army of Ptolemy Philometor, son of Ptolemy Epiphanes; and then coming into the richest of his provinces, scattering among his followers large quantities of spoil and plunder, would form plans for reducing the fortresses of other neighbors. such is his conduct to be "even for a time," that is as long as God will allow him to succeed with this policy of craft.'

## His War Against Egypt, and the Great Spoil (vv. 25-28)

**Verse 25** *And he shall stir up his power and his courage against the king of the south with a great army; and the king of the south shall war in battle with an exceeding great and mighty army; but he shall not stand; for they shall devise devices against him.* **26** *Yea, they that eat of his dainties shall destroy him, and his army shall overflow; and many shall fall down slain.* **27** *and as for both these kings, their hearts shall be to do mischief, And they shall speak lies at one table; but it shall not prosper; for yet the end shall be at the time appointed.*

**Verse 28** *Then shall he return into his land with great substance; and his heart shall be against the holy covenant; and he shall do his pleasure, and return to his own land.*

"At last, following in the steps of his predecessors, he resolved upon conducting a war against Egypt (Dan. 11:25-28). The king of this country was Ptolemy Philometor, son of Cleopatra, nephew to Antiochus Epiphanes, who overcame him at Pelusium (I Macc. i.16-19). It appears that the Egyptians had amassed a large number of troops, but that the devices that were planned against them were of so crafty a nature that they were forced to yield. By some act of treachery it may have been that the battle was lost, and the strong cities of Egypt and a considerable amount of spoil came into the hands of the Syrians.

A singular change in the course of events occurred at this juncture. The two kings profess mutual friendship for each other, and hold apparently the most friendly relations, but all the while each was seeking for some secret opportunity of destroying the other. Neither of them, however, obtained his object, for the time appointed by God had not yet arrived. The Syro-Egyptian troubles could not be brought to a finish before "the end at the time appointed." Elated by his conquest, Antiochus returned to his home loaded with spoil; his heart was stirred up against Jerusalem on his return, (I Mac. i.20-28); and it was upon this occasion that he commenced his persecutions of the Jews; the holy vessels were taken away, a large number of persons were massacred, a large number sold as captives, and the Temple itself was defiled. Having accomplished this much of his impious purpose he returned to Antioch.'

### His Effort to Extinguish All that Pertains to God (vv. 29-35)

**Verse 29** *At the time appointed he shall return, and come into the south; but it shall not be in the latter time as it was in the former.* **30** *For ships of Kittim shall come against him; therefore he shall be grieved, and shall return, and have indignation against the holy covenant and shall do his pleasure: he shall even return, and have regard unto them that forsake the holy covenant.* **31** *And forces shall stand on his part, and they shall profane the sanctuary, even the fortress, and shall take away the continual burnt-offering, and they shall set up the abomination that maketh desolate.* **32** *And such as do wickedly against the covenant shall he pervert by flatteries; but the people that know their God shall be strong, and do exploits.* **33** *And they that are wise among the people shall instruct many; yet they shall fall by the sword and by flame, by captivity and by spoil, many days.* **34** *now when they shall fall, they shall be helped with a little help; but many shall join themselves unto them with flat-*

*teries.* **35** *And some of them that are wise shall fall, to refine them, and to purify, and to make them white, even to the time of the end; because it is yet for the time appointed.*

"Two years afterwards, "at the time appointed," (Dan. 11:29-35) he renewed his attack upon Egypt, but this time with a very different issue from the last. After he had almost completely attained his object, in spite of the machinations of Ptolemy, ships came from Chittim [Kittim] that is, from the West, bringing a Roman envoy named Popilius, who met Antiochus near Alexandria, and requested him to give up his expedition against Egypt without delay. The story is well known in Roman history. Antiochus pleaded for time to consider what course he would adopt; but the Roman promptly drew a circle around him, and forbade him to withdraw from that small space until he had given a satisfactory answer. Antiochus had no other alternative open to him but to obey the imperious summons of Rome. Greatly discouraged he withdrew, and vented his wrath once more upon the people of the covenant, gaining the assistance of many apostate Jews in his attempts to persecute those who continued faithful (I Macc. i.11-15; ii.18)."[3]

## The Identity of 'The King' (vv. 36-39)

Daniel's shift from a discussion of Antiochus' effort to destroy the whole of divine semblance in the land of Judah to "the king," with no explanation for the shift, has given occasion for much speculation as to the king's identity. Young names nine different views taken (pp. 246f.); some seems absurd, and only one fits in the context of the total prophecy of Daniel. Probably the most absurd and least tenable view is that advocated by Jerome, and followed by many writers since, is that it refers to a "the antichrist" yet future, of which the Scriptures know nothing. See Appendix B.

---

[3]The material quoted from Deane ends here.

Any position that one seeks to defend presents problems. This is freely admitted. But in light of Daniel's development of the fourth world empire, the Roman, this view seems most reasonable. It seems most justifiable that the proposition that "the king [v. 36]" is not an individual, but was used symbolically for the empire and its emperors. The argumentation will be developed from three points of view: 1) A summary of Daniel's development of the character and nature of the fourth kingdom—the Roman; 2) the text of the present passage and John's characterization of the emperors who represented the empire in the book of Revelation; and 3) some sustaining evidence from the history of the empire. The procedure will be to let Scripture interpret Scripture.

## A Summary of Daniel and the Fourth Empire

**Chapter 2.** In interpreting Nebuchadnezzar's dream of the great image of gold, silver, brass, iron, and iron and clay, Daniel said that God was making known to him "what shall be in the latter days" (Dan. 2:28; cf. Isa. 2:2-4). This defined and limited the time period. The fourth element of the image—iron and iron and clay—symbolized the fourth empire, the Roman, that would be "strong as iron," breaking in pieces crushing and subduing all before it. But it would be weak in its inability to fuse its conquests into one homogeneous body (Dan. 2:40-43). The king had likewise seen a stone cut out without hands that struck the feet of the image, broke it to pieces, ground it to powder; and the stone became a great mountain that filled the earth (Dan. 2:35). In the days of those kings God would set up a kingdom that would never be destroyed; but it would break in pieces those kingdoms, "and it shall stand for ever" (Dan. 2:44). This claim would be challenged by the fourth kingdom in a gigantic contest between the two kingdoms—the kingdom of God and the Roman world empire.

**Chapter 4.** In a second dream in which Nebuchadnezzar was deprived of his kingdom, and was given the heart of a beast, until seven times passed over him. This dream and its realization was "to the intent that the living may know that the Most High ruleth in the kingdom of men, and giveth it to whomsoever he will, and setteth up over it the lowest of men" (Dan. 4:17, 25, et al.). This rule over the kingdoms of the world will be demonstrated again and again.

**Chapter 7.** In this chapter Daniel revealed his dream and visions of four great beasts from the stormy sea (vv. 1-7). The fourth was described as, "Terrible and powerful, and strong exceedingly; and it had great iron teeth; it devoured and brake in pieces, and stamped the residue with its feet; and it was diverse from all the beasts that were before it; and it had ten horns" (v. 7). It was judged by Jehovah and destroyed by fire (v. 9-12). This was followed by a vision of Christ's receiving his kingdom—the kingdom of God (vv. 13-14), "In the days of those kings" (2:44).

From among the ten horns there came forth another horn which "made war with the saints, and prevailed [for a time HH] against them; until the ancient of days came, and judgment was given to [on behalf of] the saints of the Most High, and the time came that the saints possessed the kingdom" (vv. 19-22). This foretold the conflict that would arise between the Roman Empire and the Kingdom of God described in 11:36ff.

Note carefully the following: "These great beasts, which are four kings, that shall arise out of the earth" (v. 17). But "The fourth beast [which is a king, v. 17] shall be a fourth **kingdom** upon earth, which shall be diverse from all the kingdoms, and shall devour the whole earth, and shall tread it down, and break it in pieces" (v. 23; cf. v. 7). This vividly described the conquests of the Roman Empire as it conquered the world. The little horn seemed to represent the persecuting element of the emperors, for not all of them persecuted the saints. The conflict was in reality between God and His Kingdom and the deified emperors and their kingdom of earth (v. 25); but the Kingdom of God shall be victorious (v. 27). Later discussion will focus on 11:36ff. in the light of these passages.

**Chapter 9.** In response to his prayer, Jehovah sent the angel Gabriel to give Daniel "wisdom and understanding" (v. 22) that he might "understand the vision" of the seventy weeks (v. 23). In the vision (of the seventy weeks), the angel answered the desire of Daniel's heart that he expressed in his prayer. What will be the end of the nation, the people, the city, the temple, and the promise of the coming Messiah (vv. 24-27). Verse 27 definitely pertains to the Roman's destruction of the city and temple, for Jesus so described it in Matthew 24.

**Chapter 10.** The messenger sent to Daniel upon this occasion seemed to have been one of special honor and rank (vv. 5-9). His mission was "to make thee [Daniel] understand what shall befall thy people in the latter days; for the vision is yet for many days" (v. 14); not the latter days of time, but of the Jewish economy, which occurred in the days of the Roman Empire and its world domination. In chapter 8 the second and third kingdoms were dealt with, and in chapter 11:5-35 the contemptible one, Antiochus Epiphanes and his effort to destroy the kingdom of God were revealed. So, beginning with verse 11:36 the Holy Spirit was ready to bring the book to a conclusion with the fourth kingdom, the Roman, and to deal with its end.

### The King, the Fourth Beast, the Roman Empire and its Emperors (vv. 36-39)

**Verse 36** *And the king shall do according to his will; and he shall exalt himself, and magnify himself above every god, and shall speak marvelous things against the God of gods; and he shall prosper till the indignation be accomplished; for that which is determined shall be done.*

Objections have been made to making verses 36 and following, apply to the Romans on the ground that there is no indication of such a change between verses 35 and 36. But the same, even stronger objection could be made to applying verse 36 and following, to the antichrist. For my comments on this, see Appendix B, "Antichrist.'

It seems that the "the king" is used here as it was used in chapter seven (review Summary, chapter seven, above). "The four beasts are four kings" (7:17); "The fourth beast shall be a fourth kingdom" (v. 23). The conclusion is that the beast equals king equals kingdom; therefore the king is a kingdom, the fourth empire. If king was used to designate the Roman Empire in chapter seven, why can it not be used here of the same kingdom? According to its usage, it is used in both places collectively to indicate the kingdom and its emperors and people. He did "according to his will" as did Nebuchadnezzar (5:19), Alexander the Great (11:3), and probably Antiochus the Great (11:16). The emperors magnified themselves above every god by deifying themselves, or allowing the people to deify them. The emperors and their magistrates spoke "marvelous things against the God of gods" by forcing the people to confess, "Caesar is God," or, "Caesar is Lord" under the penalty of death. The empire and its people would prosper until the wrath of God against His former people should be accomplished and the testing of the question, "Is the new spiritual kingdom being preached really the kingdom of God?" This would be determined at the time appointed by God, and not by the emperors per se.

**Verse 37** *Neither shall he regard the gods of his fathers, nor the desire of women, nor regard any god; for he shall magnify himself above all.*

The disregard of "the king" (the fourth empire and the emperors who represented it) of its former gods, the desire of women, and the magnifying of themselves above these, is exemplified to its supreme extent in Nero. The following statement is a good commentary of the verse: "He was cowardly, and committed one crime to cover up another. He caused Britannicus to be poisoned in A.D. 55, and four years later had his own mother slain by swordsmen. He divorced and later put to death his wife Octavia. He killed his second wife Poppaea Sabina in a fit of rage. A third woman who refused to marry him was slain, and he killed the husband of a fourth woman so she might become his wife. He was insanely suspicious of all his associates. Upon discovering a plot against him, he had Seneca put to death, together with many other famous men." [4]

> **Verse 38** *But in his place shall he honor the god of fortresses; and a god whom his fathers knew not shall he honor with gold, and silver, and with precious stones and pleasant things.*

"In his place"—"a person's position or office" (*TWOT* I 444)—as the world conquering empire and emperors, "the king" would honor the god of fortresses, the symbol of war and conquest. This would be a far cry from the character, ambition, and "god" of the early Roman ideal and object of the city state. Upon this "god" of fortresses—the "god of world conquest"—the nation would spend its treasures and wealth which would be to its final destruction. The following is an excellent summary of the empire's decline:

"But though the Roman peace (*pax romana*) spread its beneficent aegis over the civilized world, though the remotest lands were ransacked to supply the wealthy citizens with luxuries and delicacies, though art and letters were prized and fostered, the national character was steadily decaying. Gone was the fundamental seriousness (*gravitas*) of attitude which marked all the conduct of Romans of the antique mold. Gone was the old reverence for the family, for the state, and for the gods. Prosperity had brought in the leaven of corruption. In place of a Brutus, offering up his sons on the altar of duty to the state, we find a Nero, murdering his mother and his wife at the prompting of a Poppaea. Selfishness became the first law of life. The passion for a life of luxurious ease ruled in all classes. The rich amused themselves by giving feasts of unparalleled splendor; the poor had their *panem et circenses*—free bread and free shows. Slave labor degraded the once sturdy peasantry to the status of serfs or beggars. The backbone of the nation, the

---

[4] *Compton's Pictured Encyclopedia*, Vol. 10, p.64. with gold, and silver, and with precious stones and pleasant things.

middle class, almost disappeared; there were only the very rich and the very poor."[5]

> **Verse 39** *And he shall deal with the strongest fortresses by the help of a foreign god: whosoever acknowledgeth him he will increase with glory; and he shall cause them to rule over many, and shall divide the land for a price.*

"The king" (11:36) continued to be the subject of Daniel's prophecy. His successes in conquering the strongest of fortresses "shall be by the help of a foreign god"—a god foreign to the Roman Empire. This evidently was Jehovah, for, "The Most High ruleth in the kingdom of men, and giveth it to whomsoever he will, and setteth up over it the lowest of men" (4:17). The emperors may have thought they were conquering by their own power, dividing the glory with conquered nations, causing individuals to rule over many, dividing land for a price, but it was not they who made the final decision. For the wise man said, "The righteous, and the wise, and their works, are in the hand of God" (Eccl. 9:1). God always has the last say, He casts the deciding vote.

## The Time of the End
## (vv. 40-45)

This is admittedly a difficult passage, and is so indicated by the varied interpretations of it. In my view the popular antichrist theory of interpretation is among the most untenable of all. If one keeps within the bounds of Daniel's total context of his visions, he may reach a reasonable and possible understanding of the passage.

> **Verse 40** *And at the time of the end shall the king of the south contend with him; and the king of the north shall come against him like a whirlwind, with chariots, and*

---

[5] *Op. cit.*, vol. 12, p. 135.

*with horsemen, and with many ships; and he shall enter
into the countries, and shall overflow and pass through.*

"The time of the end" is neither the end, nor near the end
of time. The vision of the seventy weeks was God's answer to
Daniel's prayer in which he showed concern for the nation,
its people, city, and temple. Upon these would come a "full
end, and that determined," determined by the God of heav-
en (9:27, see comments; cf. also 11:27, 35). The "him" of
this verse is "the king"—the Roman kingdom and its emperors and people of verse 36, which continued to be the subject
of Daniel's vision. History provided no single operation of
such a fierce character as that ascribed to Syria, or of Egypt;
since the book of Daniel abounds in symbols and metaphors,
it is possible that Daniel summarized the total opposition of
these two kingdoms to the advances of the Roman legions"
invasions. But there would be no success in their opposition.
The legions would overrun the countries and move on to
other conquests.

**Verse 41** *He shall enter also into the glorious land, and
many countries, shall be overthrown; but these shall be
delivered out of his hand: Edom, and Moab, and the
chief of the children of Ammon.*

"He," the Romans, would enter "the glorious land" the land
of Judea. In 63 B.C. two brothers were fighting over the position of High Priest and King when Rome intervened. Pompey,
the Roman general stationed in Syria, entered the picture to
help settle the quarrel. He settled it by annexing the Jewish
kingdom to Rome. He continued the conquest by overthrow-
ing many countries, but Edom, Moab, and portions of the
children of Ammon escaped. Many think that this was because
of their opposition to the people of Israel. This, however does
not seem to be creditable.

**Verse 42** *He shall stretch forth his hand also upon the
countries; and the land of Egypt shall not escape.*

**43** *But he shall have power over the treasures of gold and of silver, and over all the precious things of Egypt; and the Libyans and the Ethiopians shall be at his steps.*

In "the king's" march toward world conquest Egypt would not escape; however, it seemed that the conquest of that portion of the world was gradual, rather than sudden and devastating, though it would have its occasions of destruction. In its control of Egypt and the adjoining countries, Rome would have power or control over their wealth and its use to Rome's benefit. One historian has well expressed Rome's attitude toward Egypt, when he said, "Rome regarded Egypt merely as a valuable granary and burdened the natives with cruel taxes. Among others, there were grain taxes, sales taxes, poll taxes, and inheritance taxes. Three centuries of Byzantine misgovernment followed the rule of Rome and left the Egyptians in a mood to welcome the Saracen conquest (A.D. 641) which came nine years after Mohammed's death. Ever since Mohammedanism has prevailed in the land of the Pharaohs."[6]

**Verse 44** *But tidings out of the east and out of the north shall trouble him; and he shall go forth with great fury to destroy and utterly to sweep away many.*

Whether this prophecy was fulfilled by the threat of invasion by barbarians from the north and east, that is, the Huns, Goths, and other invaders, or threats of rebellion among Roman possessions, is uncertain. Rome could tolerate neither, so it could have been either, or both. At any rate, Rome would respond to the threat in its usual vigorous and crushing manner.

**Verse 45** *And he shall plant the tents of his palace between the sea and the glorious holy mountain; yet he shall come to his end, and none shall help him.*

---

[6] *op. cit.*, vol. 4, p. 211.

"The king" would enter the glorious land, which he did in the person of Pompey (v. 41). But he would also plant his tents between the Mediterranean Sea and the glorious mount Zion. This he did when Titus brought his Roman troops and besieged the city in A.D. 70, destroying the people as a nation, the city, and the temple. But like all heathen world powers, he would come to an end. And like the passing of Nineveh as "a great at last!" (see Nahum 3:19), so would come the passing of the Roman Empire, the forth beast of Daniel's dream.

This prophecy should be supplemented by a few observations from John's Revelation. The Revelation revealed a conflict between Jehovah and the gods of the pagan world powers which came to a final showdown in the conflict between Christ and the deified rulers of the Roman Empire. When Satan failed in his effort to devour the man-child born to the radiant woman, he sought to destroy the woman (Rev. 12:1-6). He found an ally, a helper, in the beast out of the sea, a symbol of political power in the Roman Empire (Rev. 13:1-10); and another in the beast out of the earth, the symbol of false religion, specifically emperor worship (Rev. 13:11-18). The war between these and the Messiah, the King of Kings and their being cast into the lake of fire (Rev. 19:11-20), proves conclusively that the kingdom preached by the early preachers was and is the kingdom of God.

In summary: the first seven weeks of the seventy weeks vision of Daniel covered the period from Cyrus to the building of the temple and walls of the city in the days of Nehemiah and Malachi. The last week, the seventh, was dealt with in Daniel 9:27, and will be covered more fully in chapter twelve. That left the sixty-two weeks in between which now have been covered by the between-the-testaments-period in chapter eleven. Also, this deals with the four beasts of Daniel's vision. The first beast represented the Babylonian kingdom, fulfilled in the death of Belshazzar. The second and third beasts, the Persian and Macedonian empires, and the beginning of the fourth, the Roman, were covered in chapter eleven; and the closing period of the Jewish and Roman kingdoms in the twelfth chapter.

# CHAPTER XII

# The End

## The Final Tribulation
## (vv. 1-4)

**Verse 1** *And at that time shall Michael stand up, the great prince who standeth for the children of thy people; and there shall be a time of trouble, such as never was since there was a nation even to that same time: and at that time thy people shall be delivered, every one that shall be found written in the book.*

"**At** that time," the time of the siege of Jerusalem by the Romans (see comments above, 11:45), "shall Michael stand up," that is, to fulfill his role as the angelic prince of Daniel's people, who has been introduced already (see comments, 10:13). And the angel whom Michael helped had "come to make thee [Daniel] understand what shall befall thy people in the latter days" (10:14).

A further word needs to be added about Michael. In the great spiritual conflict from the garden of Eden (Gen. 3:14-16) to the victory of Christ, he was the prince that led God's people to the final victory when the "old serpent" was cast down (Rev. 12:7-9). With that defeat of Satan came "the salvation, and the power, and the kingdom of our God, and **the authority of his Christ:**...And they [the brethren, 12:10] overcame him [the 'old' serpent] because of the blood of the

Lamb, and because of the word of their testimony; and they loved not their life even unto death" (12:11). We know that this applies to the victory through Christ because He claimed this authority after His resurrection (Matt. 28:18).

This chapter deals with those things of "the latter days." Daniel described the condition to come in the latter days, "And there shall be a time of trouble, such as never was since there was a nation [apparently a Jewish nation] even to that same time." Compare Jesus' statement in which He identified the word of Daniel with what is to come upon the people of His generation (Matt. 24:15-20), "For then shall be great tribulation, such as hath not been from the beginning of the world until now, no, nor ever shall be" (Matt. 24:21). This confirmed the position taken that Daniel 11:36-45 was a prophecy of the Roman Empire and its rulers and people; and that verse 45 pertained to the destruction of Jerusalem by the army of Titus.

"And at that time thy people shall be delivered, every one that was found written in the book." But of what book was the angel speaking? and who will be found written in it? Not all the Jews, but only those faithful to God. Malachi, the last book in the Old Testament, provided an excellent commentary on Daniel's statement: "Then they that feared Jehovah spake one with another; and Jehovah hearkened, and heard, and a **book of remembrance** was written before him, for them that feared Jehovah, and that thought upon his name. And they shall be mine, saith Jehovah of hosts, even mine own possession, in the day that I make [the day of judgment]; and I will spare them, as a man spareth his own son that serveth him. Then shall ye return and discern between the righteous and the wicked, between him that serveth God and him that serveth him not. For, behold, the day cometh [the day of judgment], it burneth as a furnace; and all the proud, and all that work wickedness, shall be stubble; and the day that cometh shall burn them up, saith Jehovah of hosts, that it shall leave them neither root nor branch. But unto you that fear my name," they that are written in the book, "shall the sun of righteousness arise with healing in its wings [beams]"; the word is s-u-n, not s-o-n, which means the light of righteousness—the brilliance of righteousness that God will provide in Christ (Mal. 3:16—4:2). This was spoken of by Daniel where he refers to God's bringing in "everlasting righteousness" in the Messiah (Dan. 9:24). This paragraph in Malachi dealt with all who fear the name of Jehovah and whose names are written in a book. When the day of this calamity comes, these will be delivered. These are the ones who belong to God. When the Jewish kingdom rejected Christ, He brought it to an end, they were no longer His people as a nation, for He has a new kingdom. And though the time of the fulfillment of this prophecy would be a time of great tribulation, it would also be a time of great deliverance. But the deliverance would be to those only whose names would be found in the book. (For further passages referring to the "book," see Ex. 32:32-33; Luke 10:20; Phil. 4:3; Rev. 3:5; 13:8; 17:8; 20:12, 15; 21:27).

**Verse 2** *And many of them that sleep in the dust of the earth shall awake, some to everlasting life, and some to shame and everlasting contempt.*

This prophecy, which applies to the time of the Messiah's teaching, has its parallel in Ezekiel's prophecy of the dry bones and their resurrection (Ezek. 37:14), neither of which, Ezekiel or Daniel, refers to the final resurrection. Ezekiel's prophecy referred to a spiritual resurrection of the Jews in Babylon and their return to Judea; for Jehovah added, "Son of man these bones are the whole house of Israel" (v. 11f.; read also vv. 12-14), and the resurrection of Daniel's prophecy referred to the spiritual resurrection of the people under the teaching of Jesus and the apostles. Jesus spoke of two resurrections when He said, "The hour cometh, and now is, when the dead [the spiritually dead] shall hear the voice of the Son of God; and they that hear shall live" spiritually (John 5:25). Matthew spoke repeatedly of the great multitudes that followed Jesus; but Jesus said, "The love of the many shall wax cold. But he that endureth to the end, the same shall be saved" (Matt. 24:12-13). It was of these that Daniel spoke, for he limited the number to "many"; whereas Jesus said, when he spoke of the second group, "Marvel not at this: for the hour cometh, in which **all** that are in the tombs shall hear his voice, and shall come forth; they that have done good, unto the resurrection of life; and they that have done evil unto the resurrection of judgment" (John 5:28-29). Daniel's resurrection and Jesus' first resurrection were limited to "many"; whereas Jesus' final resurrection included "**all** that are in the tombs." To make Daniel's statement refer to the final resurrection at the end of time is to do violence to his language and to Jesus' words.

The better explanation is that through the preaching of the word by Jesus, many were brought to spiritual life. But because iniquity abounded, the love of many waxed cold, they gave up the faith and went back into Judaism, or back into the world. They were raised by the Gospel, some to everlasting life, some to everlasting contempt, so not all of them remained faithful to Jesus Christ.

**Verse 3** *And they that are wise shall shine as the brightness of the firmament; and they that turn many to righteousness as the stars for ever and ever.*

Out of this furnace of affliction, trouble, and tribulation (v. 1), and they that rise in the spiritual resurrection to everlasting life (v. 2), there will emerge a new people of God. These are the wise, those who have insight and understanding of what God had done, was doing, and is doing. They shall shine as the brightness of the heavens; they shall be "the light of the world" (Matt. 5:14); they shall be "seen as lights in the world, holding forth the word of life" (Phil. 2:15-16) in a land of darkness, filled with peoples "in gross darkness" (Isa. 60:2). This shall be the people who hear and do the words of the Messiah, the wise who build their house on the rock of truth (Matt. 7:24). The interest of these include the turning of many to righteousness, who will say to the lost, "Come ye, and let us go up to the mountain of Jehovah, to the house of the God of Jacob: and he will teach us of his ways, and we will walk in his paths: for out of Zion shall go forth the law, and the word of

Jehovah from Jerusalem" (Isa. 2:3). They will brighten the world of darkness as stars brighten the night; and this they shall do so long as the age lasts.

> **Verse 4** *But thou, O Daniel, shut up the words, and seal the book, even to the time of the end: many shall run to and fro, and knowledge shall be increased.*

And now the glorious messenger from God who was introduced in 10:1-10, who was the speaker from 10:11 through 12:3 (with a few minor exceptions), closed his mission with a final charge to Daniel. Daniel was told to "shut up the words," that is, bring them to a close; "and seal the book." To seal a document, in this case a book, was done "by affixing seal impressions from stamp or cylinder seals." This could be done by stamping into wax or clay; or by rolling a cylinder across it, leaving an impression (*TWOT* 1 334). "Even to the time of the end," the end of the Jewish economy, which had been the subject dealt with by the angel. The sealing was to preserve the accuracy of the prophecy and the integrity of its authorship. The phrase, "Many shall run to and fro" is difficult and has been the occasion of numerous interpretations. It could mean that many events would transpire before the fulfillment at the end, and that many would "come and go" before that time. However, viewed from the context, it seemed to mean that many would go here and there seeking knowledge. However, knowledge would increase by the historical fulfillment of the prophecies, by the teaching of the Messiah when He came, and by the Holy Spirit's revelation through the apostles and prophets. The personal growth in knowledge of individuals would depend on the application and effort of each, and the interest and quality of the teachers. Paul considered prayer a factor in learning (Phil. 1:9; Col. 1:9); and Peter considered it a matter of growth (II Pet. 3:18).

## The Angel's Final Message
## (vv. 5-13)

### The Angel Above the River (vv. 5-6)

**Verse 5** *Then I, Daniel, looked, and behold, there stood other two, the one on the brink of the river on this side, and the other on the brink of the river on that side.*
*6 And one said to the man clothed in linen, who was above the waters of the river, How long shall it be to the end of these wonders?*

Although the majestic messenger of 10:5-6 is not spoken of as being "above the waters of the river" in chapter ten, yet Daniel's description of the one in each passage being "clothed in linen" (10:5 and 12:6) seems to identify the one in each passage as the same. And the two men [angels] one on either side of the river, are not mentioned in chapter ten, but it may have been the hand of one of these that touched Daniel and gave him strength (10:10, 18). This is suggested because the special messenger was above the water, and the hand that touched Daniel appeared to have been on the ground beside him. The question asked of the one above the waters was, "How long shall it be to the end of these wonders?" Of the word "wonders," it may be said, "Preponderantly both the verb and substantive refer to the acts of God, designating either cosmic wonders or historical achievements on behalf of Israel" (*TWOT* II 723). Likely, in this instance it referred to the latter.

### The Angel's Oath (v. 7)

**Verse 7** *And I heard the man clothed in linen, who was above the waters of the river, when he held up his right hand and his left hand unto heaven, and sware by him that liveth for ever that it shall be for a time, times, and a half; and when they have made an end of breaking in pieces the power of the holy people, all these things shall be finished.*

"The man clothed in linen" is the speaker from 10:5 who revealed to Daniel what was to come to pass. The holding up of the hands, when taking an oath was an appeal to God to witness, or testify to the solemnity of the oath being taken, a practice found numerous times in the scriptures. The "time, times, and a half" was a period of trials, testing, and tribulation (see comments, 7:25). When the two are compared, it seems that this text referred to the Roman Empire. There would be troublous times ahead for the nation and its people; these would be finished at the end of the breaking of the power of the people who had been God's people. Probably the best commentary on this passage is found in John's statement in Revelation 10:5-7: "And the angel that I saw standing upon the sea and upon the earth lifted up his right hand to heaven, and sware by him that liveth for ever and ever, who created the heaven and the things that are therin, and the earth and the things that are therin, and the sea and the things that are therein, that there shall be delay no longer."

It should be observed that the angel in Daniel's vision lifted up both hands and the angel in John's vision lifted up only one hand (Rev. 10:5) which probably signified that much of what the angel in Daniel's vision revealed had come to pass already; whereas by the time of John's angel there remained only the completion of the mystery by its total victory in Christ, and the complete breaking up of the Jewish nation and people. A more solemn oath could not be made than that found in Revelation 10:6.

In order that the reader may get a fuller picture of the relation between Daniel's vision and that of John, the quotation of Revelation 10:7, and my comments on the verse follows.

"But in the days of the voice of the seventh angel, when he is about to sound, then is finished the mystery of God, according to the good tidings which he declared to his servants the prophets" (Rev. 10:7). In the interpretation of this verse there is a continuation of the problem introduced above (Dan. 12:6). Is this verse speaking of the end of time and the point of entrance into eternity, or is it dealing with the end of delay for the fulfillment of the divine purpose respecting the church? The angel's words fall into three sections: 1) the days of the voice of the seventh angel; 2) the finishing of the mystery; and 3) the good tidings which He declared by His servants the prophets.

The view that this passage is not speaking of the final end of time is supported by the angel's introduction of the seventh angel's sounding, which would bring to pass the third Woe. Following the vision of the measured temple and the victorious mission of the two witnesses (Rev. 11:1-13) it was said, "The second Woe is past: behold the third Woe cometh quickly" (11:14). The word "quickly" (*tachu*) is defined by the lexicons to mean "quickly, speedily, without delay, at once" (A & G; Thayer). The third Woe was to come quickly, but the end of time did not come speedily, at once, or without delay; in fact, after nineteen hundred years it has not yet come. Therefore, what was to be without delay was something other than the end of time; thus, it must have been the completion of the mystery.

"Then is finished the mystery of God." This mystery was God's plan for human redemption, conceived in His mind, after the counsel of His will, and summed up in Christ (Eph. 1:9-11; 3:8-11). It was revealed by the Holy Spirit (Eph. 3:1-5; I Cor. 2:6-13; I Peter 1:12), made known to the Gentiles (Col. 1:26f; 2:2), and preached by the apostles to all men (Eph. 6:19; Col. 4:3; I Peter 1:12). This mystery was something that man could not know until it was revealed. In the gospel Christ was being preached, "according to the revelation of the mystery which hath been kept in silence through times eternal, but now is manifested, and by the scriptures of the prophets, according to the commandment of the eternal God, is made known unto all the nations unto obedience of faith" (Rom. 16:25-26). This complete fulfilling of God's mystery and its revelation was about to be finished. To finish (from *teleō*) means "to bring to an end, complete something...to carry out, accomplish, perform, fulfill" (A & G; Thayer and Vine); hence, that purpose which the prophets looked forward to and the apostles preached was about to reach the completion of its fullness, it would not terminate, but carried out in its entirety.

"According to the good tidings which he declared to his servants the prophets." What prophets are in the angel's mind? Of the 143 times the word "prophet" (including *prophētikos*, Rom. 16:26) occurs in the Gospels, Acts, and the Epistles, New Testament prophets are definitely spoken of fourteen times; but these never have the prominence ascribed to the apostles. John spoke of prophets eight times in Revelation, but it is difficult to determine whether he has in mind those of the Old Testament or of the New. Twice he spoke of "his servants the prophets" (Rev. 10:7; 11:18), an expression used by Jeremiah six times, Ezekiel once, Daniel twice [cf. Dan. 9:6], Amos once, and Zechariah once. This special identification of prophets as "his servants" occurs only here in the New Testament, which leads to the conclusion that in these two instances the angel referred to the Old Testament prophets.

If this is a valid conclusion, then this statement pointed to the completion of God's plan, and not to the end of time and entrance into eternity. The good news which was declared to those servants the prophets was the news of salvation provided by God's grace in the suffering Servant. The prophets sought and searched diligently for this, but it was reserved to be announced by the apostles through the Holy Spirit (I Peter 1:10-12). The end to which they looked was now being finished or completed. The Old Testament prophets never dealt with specific events beyond the coming redemption, the permanent establishment of the spiritual kingdom, the termination of the Jewish theocracy, the persecution of the saints, and the destruction of the fourth world empire (the Roman Empire—see Dan. 2, 7). This point considered further in the light of Revelation 11:15-19 seems clearly to establish the fact that this angel's message looked not to the end of time but to the completion of God's mystery, the gospel, the firm establishment of His kingdom and power, and the destruction of world powers.[1]

---

[1] Homer Hailey, *Revelation. Introduction and Commentary* (Grand Rapids, Michigan: Baker Book House, 1979), p. 245-246.

For a discussion of time, times, and a half time, see comments, Daniel 7:25.

## The Future Acceptance and Rejection of God's Message (vv. 8-10)

**Verse 8** *And I heard, but I understood not: then said I, O my Lord, what shall be the issue of these things?*

Daniel heard and wrote but did not understand what he was writing. And no marvel! The Persian Empire was just coming into power; and Macedonia was probably in its infancy at that time. What could he understand of Alexander's greatness, his death, and his kingdom being divided into four major powers, and two of these engaging in a long state of war? And how could he understand that out of one of these would come a leader of fierce countenance that would attempt to destroy all semblance of that which was holy and pertained to God? And how could he understand the development of the most powerful nation ever to exist to that time, the outgrowth of a small city-state in north Italy probably unheard of at the time of his writing? But, to make a present day application to the things written by the apostles of the second coming of Christ, the resurrection of the dead, the new glorified bodies of the saints, the judgment, heaven and hell, how much did the writers understand, and how much do we understand about these? Like Daniel, one can accept it all by faith and wait for its realization in its proper time. This raised a question in Daniel's mind: "What shall be the issue [end, KJV] of these things?" In this instance, "issue" or "end" probably means, What shall follow the fulfillment of the things discussed thus far?

**Verse 9** *And he said, Go thy way, Daniel; for the words are shut up and sealed till the time of the end.*

Daniel had been told already to "shut up the words, and seal the book, even to the time of the end" (12:4)—the end of the

Jewish nation. This is virtually repeated by the angel. In figurative and symbolic language Revelation takes up where Daniel stops. It (John's Revelation) was not to be sealed, for the beginning of its fulfillment was at hand (Rev. 22:10).

> **Verse 10** *Many shall purify themselves, and make themselves white, and be refined; but the wicked shall do wickedly; and none of the wicked shall understand; but they that are wise shall understand.*

"Many," not all, "shall purify themselves"; this will be a work of the individual; it will be a purification of the heart. "Blessed are the pure in heart, for they shall see God" (Matt. 5:8). This standard of purity will be revealed in the Messiah; "And every one that hath this hope set on him purifieth himself, even as he is pure" (I John 3:3). "And make themselves white," the symbolic color for purity. "And be refined," from a word that means to be tested, be tried; this is passive; it is the work of God, and He does this through the furnace of affliction and the floods that threaten to overflow and drown the saint. In contrast to the "many" who purify themselves, the wicked shall continue in their wickedness, waxing "worse and worse, deceiving and being deceived" (II Tim. 3:13). They shall not understand the teaching of truth, nor the love of God manifested in the Messiah. But the wise, those who set their heart to learn, will understand.

## Two Periods of Time (vv. 11-12)

> **Verse 11** *And from the time that the continual burnt-offering shall be taken away, and the abomination that maketh desolate set up, there shall be a thousand two hundred and ninety days.*

These two verses are certainly difficult. But if one keeps in mind that the angel whose words Daniel recorded is writing of the time of the fourth world empire, the Roman, and not a continuation of the time of Antiochus, this will facilitate. Neither is he writing of the distant future just prior to the second coming of the Messiah; nor is he writing of a yet future mythical antichrist, but he is writing of the end days of the Jewish nation and its people; this will also help. The precise phrase, "abomination of desolation" is not found in the Old Testament scriptures, but the idea occurred four times in the book of Daniel. Consider the four passages where the idea appears.

Daniel heard the question asked, "How long shall be the vision concerning the continual burnt-offering, and the transgression that maketh desolate..." (Dan. 8:13). This referred to Antiochus Epiphanes. The second time the idea was expressed is in Daniel 9:27, where it would be applied by Jesus to the Roman destruction of Jerusalem (read the comments on 9:27 for argumentation defending the position). The third time of its occurrence is Daniel 11:31 where it occurs as prophesy of what Antiochus would do. And in Daniel 12:11 it appears with reference to Antiochus, but only as a historical reference, and not that the speaker is still in the time bracket of Antiochus.

Examine the events that occurred before the time of Daniel 12:11. In his opposition to the people of God, "the people that know their God shall be strong, and do exploits" (11:32). This prophecy was fulfilled by the Maccabees, many of whom died in the struggle, but were victorious in the end, the time appointed by the Lord (Dan. 11:32-35).

Many expositors think that verse 36 through verse 45 is a continuation of the days and events of Antiochus; but it appears that verse 36 introduced the Roman Empire and its exploits through the present verse (Dan. 12:12). Read the argumentation for the position taken, beginning with Daniel 11:36.

In the verse under discussion (Dan. 12:11), the angel said from the time of Antiochus to the breaking in pieces of the holy people, the destruction of Jerusalem, that all things in between "shall be finished" (Dan. 12:7). This included the wars between the kings of the north and south, the oppressions of Antiochus, the war of the Maccabees, and the intervention of Rome; an indefinite period seems to be symbolized by the number, "a thousand two hundred and ninety days." I know of no significance attached to the specific number, and that of the following verse, except their proximity to the period of time, "a time, times and half" (v. 7), a troublous time for the people of God.

**Verse 12** *Blessed is he that waiteth, and cometh to the thousand three hundred and five and thirty days.*

This would be another period of indefinite time, but slightly longer than the former, "the thousand three hundred and five and thirty" beyond the breaking in pieces, the destruction of Jerusalem and the Jewish nation. The blessing signified that for those "who wait" is not specified, therefore it must be left in the realm of the unrevealed.

## The Angel's Last Words of Instruction to Daniel (v. 13)

**Verse 13** *But go thou thy way till the end be; for thou shalt rest, and shalt stand in thy lot, at the end of the days.*

"The end" and "the end of the days" referred not to the end of time, but to the end of the Jewish theocracy. The time for Daniel to stand in his lot would come at the end of the days of the Jewish nation, and God's judgment of the Roman Empire and the nations that were under its rule and opposed God's kingdom. This would be the time to render judgment on behalf of the dead, those who had died in defense of His kingdom; "And the time to give their reward to thy [God's] servants the prophets [i.e., the prophets of the Old Testament Period]" (Rev. 11:17-18). It was at this time that Daniel would stand in his lot as a prophet. His lot was with God's servants whose reward would be in seeing their prophecies fulfilled in the destruction of the heathen nations that had opposed their word, the word of God. Their reward would be in seeing the kingdom that God established in victory and triumph.

## Summary of Chapter Twelve

The chapter revealed what would be an almost continuous history of trials and tribulations ahead for Daniel's beloved people. It points to the time of the Messiah and what would be the reception of the people to His teaching and preaching. The angel introduced in chapter ten continued to be the spokesman through this final chapter. He gave Daniel the information he desired, and then instructed him to shut up the words and seal the book till the time of the end. But at the end of the time Daniel would stand up with the prophets in receiving the reward of his work, which is the realization that his prophecies were fulfilled. Amen!

# A Summary of the Book

**It** has been a long and exciting journey to travel with Daniel
through six hundred years of yet unlived history. The journey began with Daniel just a youth, a Jewish captive brought
from his homeland in Judea to a foreign land many miles away,
destined never to return. But by God's providence, he was destined to be among God's greatest prophets. He began the
journey as a student of Babylonian language, science, customs,
politics and court manners under Babylonian "wise men." He
"graduated" with honors, and was awarded a place in Nebuchadnezzar's court of advisers. But he was determined to
maintain his Jewish faith and ordinances (ch. 1).

He served the king as interpreter of his dreams; interpreting
them faithfully as God revealed the meaning to him, though
they might be to the detriment of the king. In this role he
revealed the future of world kingdoms and of the kingdom of
God, which would be above all others, breaking and grinding
the world powers, but the kingdom of God would fill the
whole world (ch. 2).

His three friends shared the faith of Daniel, their mentor,
defying the king's command to worship an image he erected
on penalty of death for refusal. Their faith was rewarded by
God's sending an angel to deliver them from the fiery furnace

into which they were thrown. Their heroic faith was rewarded also by a eulogy from the king to the Great God whom they worshipped and served. Their demonstration of faith has been a source of encouragement to thousands since, who, under the consequences of divine judgment on the world, have had to suffer for the sins of others in similar consequential judgments. In the midst of idols and people of the world of wickedness, they faithfully represented the God whom they worshipped (ch. 3).

Daniel continued to act as interpreter of dreams to the king when he dreamed a dream that foretold God's judgment upon him, except he humble himself before the God of heaven. The seer added the role of counselor to the king as he advised him what to do to avert the humbling fulfillment of the dream. The king ignored the advice and suffered the consequence, spending "seven times" among the beasts of the field until he learned that God, not the kings, rule in the kingdom of men; and that He sets up as rulers those who will serve His purpose. This elicited from the king his greatest praise of Jehovah; but he never acknowledged Him as "the only God" (ch. 4).

With the passing of Nebuchadnezzar from the scene, Daniel served at the court of Belshazzar, king of Babylon, who seemed to be a grandson of the former great king, whether by marriage, adoption, or birth, is unknown. While engaged in a drinking banquet, the king summoned Daniel to interpret handwriting that appeared on the wall, written by fingers of a man. The message: the kingdom would pass to the Medes and Persians, bringing the Babylonian kingdom and its rule to an end. That night Belshazzar was slain, and Darius, king of the Medes, assumed the rule for Cyrus, the great king who was now conquering the world (ch. 5).

With the fall of Babylon to the Persians, Darius not only retained Daniel among his administrators of government, but exalted him to a higher position. This aroused the envy and jealousy of his fellow administrators who determined to destroy Daniel. This they tried to do by persuading the king to make a decree that all petitions to gods or men should pass his review and receive his endorsement. The king made and signed the decree, which Daniel ignored, continuing to pray three times each day as usual. And although the king tried diligently to revoke the decree, he failed and Daniel was cast into the den of lions. God sent His angel to shut the mouth of the lions thus delivering Daniel. The lions got their meal by the king's casting his deceitful administrators into the den, an act of administrative justice. Daniel had stood firm in his faith from his youth to this point in old age. He would not fail Him now, but would become an example of faith to all. God's faithfulness to His true saints under all circumstances of life would likewise be remembered. So Daniel prospered through the reigns of the kings of Babylon and of Darius and Cyrus of the Persians (v. 28, ch. 6).

Our journey with Daniel through his career as interpreter of dreams and counselor to kings terminated at the end of chapter six. He now became an amanuensis to God and angels in recording his own dreams and visions, and the revelations from both. During the late Babylonian rule, in a dream, God revealed the coming of four beasts which represented four great empires to arise out of the upheavals in society; they would be judged and destroyed by Jehovah. At some point in the time of these kingdoms, One like the Son of man would return to heaven and receive the kingdom of God. This vision paralleled that of Nebuchadnezzar of the four empires in chapter two. The fourth beast challenged the special interest of Daniel which impressed its importance throughout the remainder of the book (ch. 7).

Two years following the dream of the four beasts, while yet in the Babylonian period, Daniel had a second dream. It consisted of a he-goat and a ram, symbolizing the destruction of the Medo-Persian empire by the Greek-Macedonian Empire which occurred some two hundred years later. Out of the breaking of the horn of the he-goat (Alexander the Great) there would arise four lesser kingdoms; and out of one of these would emerge a king of fierce countenance that would oppose all that is holy and pertained to God. This was fulfilled in Antiochus Epiphanes. In response to Daniel's desire to know the meaning of the vision, Gabriel was dispatched from heaven to make him understand things that would come to pass in the latter times (ch. 8).

In the first year of the reign of Darius, by a study of "the books" Daniel realized, that according to Jeremiah the captivity would terminate at the end of seventy years, which period was now coming to an end. Whereupon Daniel prayed one of the most fervent prayers found in the Old Testament. What was to become of the nation, the city, and the temple? In response, God showed him the vision of the seventy weeks (or sevens). This portrayed in a few words the future history from Cyrus to the Messiah and the destruction of the city of Jerusalem (ch. 9).

Two years later, after Daniel watched the departure of the remnant to Jerusalem and their homeland, there was revealed unto Daniel the coming of a great warfare—both physical and spiritual. The revealing and understanding were made to Daniel by the most majestic personage yet to appear to him. The incidents of chapter ten served to introduce chapter eleven and twelve. This heavenly being was the chief speaker from that time to the end of the book (ch. 10).

This chapter is a vision and explanation by the angel of chapters eleven and twelve, which dealt with the sixty-two weeks between the first seven weeks, which would be fulfilled between the return of the remnant under Cyrus, and the last week, which would be fulfilled under the Romans. The vision of chapter eleven revealed the conflict between the descendants of two of Alexander's generals, between the nations of Syria and Egypt. It also developed more fully the craft, cruelty, and constant hatred of Antiochus Epiphanes for God and all that pertained to Him. And at verse thirty six the angel introduced the coming and conquest of the fourth beast of Daniel's earlier vision, the Roman Empire (ch. 11).

This final chapter continued to deal with the Roman Empire, the fourth, and things to occur under the Messiah and the final destruction of the city, and the indefinite time to the end of the Roman power. What shall become of Daniel? He will sleep the sleep of death, but at the end of these wonders that have been discussed and promised by the two (or more) angels, he will stand in his lot with the faithful prophets, and will be rewarded by seeing his prophecies and visions fulfilled (ch. 12).

Thank God for the book of Daniel! Let the liberals and skeptics be ashamed and hang their heads in disgrace for their attacks upon it.

# The Numerical Symbolism
# of the Seventy Weeks

Phil Roberts

## Daniel 9:24

The third, and most neglected, key to understanding this prophecy is the numerical symbolism of the seventy weeks. If the context establishes the beginning of the seventy weeks at the decree of Cyrus in 539/8 B.C. and if the stated goals of the seventy weeks fix the end of the period in the first century A.D., then why is it designated as a period of seventy weeks, or 490 years, when, in fact, it is somewhere between 500 and 600 years? The answer lies in the fact that the numbers are symbolic and were never intended to be taken literally.

In order to understand the symbolism, let us begin with the seventy years of the Babylonian captivity, which form the backdrop to this vision of seventy weeks. Why was this period designated as seventy years when, in fact, it was only about 66 or 67 years? (Old commentaries often get the seventy years by figuring the captivity from 606 B.C. to 536 B.C., but the dates of the first deportation and the fall of Babylon are now well established at 605 B.C. and 539 B.C.) We could say the seventy is only a round figure. But that would miss the real meaning of the captivity for the Jewish people.

The Babylonian captivity, as an instrument for punishment, was rooted in the Sabbath law of the O. T. It was based on the special status of the sabbath as a sign of the covenant relationship between God and Israel. "You shall surely observe my Sabbaths; for this is a sign between me and you throughout your generations, that you may know that I am the Lord who sanctifies you" (Exod. 31:13). And remember that this sabbath law also included the sabbath year, requiring that the land "rest" from cultivation every seventh year, and the Jubilee celebration of a "double sabbath" every forty-nine years (the sabbath of sabbaths) (Lev. 25:1-34). This whole complex of sabbath keeping—days, years, and Jubilees—was especially well-suited to be a sign of the covenant because of the faith it demanded on the part of the Israelites. Consider the faith required for the people of an agricultural economy to go without cultivating their land for an entire year, not to mention the two years of the Jubilee. Surely one of the first laws to be ignored during periods of unfaithfulness would be the sabbath, and especially the seventh-year sabbaths.

The importance of the sabbath law to the legal stipulations of the covenant is especially apparent in Leviticus 26. This chapter summarizes the entire covenant relationship in terms of the blessings that would come upon the nation if they were faithful and the curses that would come if they were unfaithful. In specifying the curses, God decreed that the ultimate penalty for unfaithfulness would be for the Israelites to be stripped away from their land and carried into captivity. Now this was not just some random form of punishment. It was based on the role of the sabbath as the sign of the covenant. It was specifically designed to allow the land to enjoy an extended sabbath rest to make up for sabbath years not observed during the period of unfaithfulness. "Then the land will enjoy its sabbaths all the days of the desolation, while you are in your enemies' land; then the land will rest and enjoy its sabbaths" (Lev. 26:34). And note that this twenty-sixth chapter of Leviticus immediately follows the twenty-fifth chapter that had initially spelled out all the sabbath laws.

Thus, when the Chronicler finally tells of the carrying away of the children of Israel into the Babylonian captivity, he explains that captivity not simply as punishment but as a time for the land to make up for the lost sabbath rest: "The land…enjoyed its sabbaths. All the days of its desolation it kept sabbath until seventy years were complete" (II Chron. 36:21). It is our contention, then, that the seventy years of captivity is a symbolic number highlighting their full sabbath rest due the land because of the fullness of their iniquity. By using a multiple of seven (the sabbath number) and ten (symbolizing fullness or completion), God was trying to get the Israelites to see the meaning—not the length—of the captivity. Although the number 70 approximates the actual length of the captivity, that is secondary. It was far more important for the Jews to know why they were going into captivity than it was for them to know the exact length of the captivity.

Now if this explanation is correct, further implications immediately arise. A seventy-year captivity would imply an epoch of 490 (70 X 7) years of unfaithfulness to accumulate a "debt" of seventy unobserved sabbath years. So the seventy years of captivity is the culmination of a 490-year epoch of unfaithfulness. (Again we should not press for an exact 490 years of unfaithfulness. But just as the seventy years of captivity approximates the historical reality, so may the 490.) This, then, suddenly illuminates the announcement to Daniel of the coming of a new epoch of 490, or 70 X 7, years. Just as the preceding epoch of Israelite history had culminated in failure and captivity because of the unfaithfulness of Israel, now a new epoch of seventy times seven will begin which will culminate in salvation and redemption because of the faithfulness of God to his part in the covenant.

But why would God choose 490 years to represent the past period of unfaithfulness as well as the new period of salvation? Again, the answer is found in the symbolism of the number, and that symbolism is rooted even more deeply in the sabbath law. We readily note that the number is 7 X 10 X 7, and thus inherently symbolic to the Jewish mind. Remember Jesus' charge to Peter to forgive his brother seventy times seven (Matt. 18:22). But, more importantly, it is not only seven times seven; it is also a period of ten Jubilees (7 X 7 = 49, a Jubilee). It is true that the Jubilee was the fiftieth year. But, while some rabbis reckoned Jubilees in fifty-year cycles, others reckoned the fiftieth year as overlapping with the first year of the next forty-nine-year cycle, thus keeping the entire cycle to forty-nine years. It seems clear that a forty-nine-year cycle for the Jubilee is being assumed here in Daniel. Compare also the Pentecost, which was the fiftieth day after a week of weeks yet which did not break the weekly cycle but was merely the first day of the eighth week.

A further clue to the 490 years representing ten jubilee cycles is the fact that the period is subdivided into units of 7—62—1. Notice that the first unit of seven weeks is precisely one Jubilee.

So ten Jubilees were appointed to accomplish the six things enumerated in verse 24 of our prophecy. But why ten Jubilees? And what did the Jubilee itself represent, to make it such an important symbol for the accomplishment of the goals of salvation defined in verse 24?

Inasmuch as the Jubilee was the grand culmination of all of the sabbath observances, we can only answer this question by going back to the basic meaning of the sabbath law itself. It is customary to downplay the sabbath as a law pertaining only to the Jews, and done away with in the New Covenant. This view is unfortunate. The sabbath is the most "Messianic" of all the Ten Commandments.

In the O. T. the sabbath (including days, years, and Jubilees) is associated with the commemoration of two things. First, in the giving of the Ten Commandments at Mt. Sinai, it is identified as a day of rest, commemorating the rest into which God entered when he had completed his work of creation (Exod. 20:11). This association is universally recognized. But, in the repetition of the Ten Commandments forty years later, Moses also says that it was a commemoration of the Israelites' deliverance from bondage in Egypt (Deut. 5:15).

Now these two concepts of rest and deliverance are closely connected. Israel is delivered out of bondage in order that she might enter into Canaan as the land of rest that God has prepared for her (Deut. 12:9-10). And that land of rest is but a type of God's own rest, which he entered after he had completed the creation and into which all who are delivered from the bondage of sin will ultimately enter (Heb. 4:1-11; see especially vv. 1, 3-4, and 10). This understanding of the sabbath as a sign of the rest and the deliverance that God was preparing for his people also helps us to understand the miracles that Jesus performed on the sabbath. He was not trying to prove that he could break the sabbath. He was trying to get the Jews to see the real meaning of the sabbath. Note his response to the Pharisees who had criticized him for healing a crippled woman on the sabbath: "Should not this woman, whom Satan has kept bound for eighteen long years, be set free on the Sabbath day from what bound her" (Luke 13:16). He was saying, in effect, that her deliverance from bondage and the rest she would now enjoy in her healing were what the sabbath was really all about: deliverance and rest from the ravages of sin and the power of Satan. And both the O. T. sabbath and her healing on the sabbath were signs of the rest and deliverance Christ was about to bring to mankind.

It is, in fact, the whole Messianic age that fulfills the promised rest and deliverance of the O. T. sabbath. This is the point of Hebrews 4:3 when the writer says that "we who have believed enter that rest." The "Sabbath rest" that "remains" for the people of God (v. 9) is the rest and deliverance that we have in Christ from the bondage of sin. That deliverance from sin is what the O. T. sabbath was all about. It was Messianic to the core. And that is not to say that there is not still a heavenly sabbath rest awaiting us as the people of God. Indeed, our entrance into God's rest is now by faith in Christ, but in the final stage of God's redemptive history we will enter by sight into God's sabbath, which he entered upon the completion of his work of creation, to rest with him through all eternity.

Every sabbath observance of the Israelites was intended as a reminder that God was preparing for his people a true and eternal rest. The fallow ground of every seventh-year observance was a reminder that, in that future rest, God would provide for their every need and that the curse of sin which made it necessary to till the ground (Gen. 3:17) would be no more. And every sabbath year observance that required the releasing of slaves and the remission of debts (Deut. 15:1-18) was a sign that in that day of future rest God would truly deliver his people from the bondage and debt of sin.

And the grand culmination of the O. T. sabbath law, the Jubilee, which would normally occur once in the life of every Israelite, was the occasion when the whole meaning of the sabbath law was summed up in the command to "consecrate the fiftieth year and proclaim liberty throughout the land to all its inhabitants" (Lev. 25:10). Down through the years it has been the poorer and enslaved classes of humanity, bearing the brunt of man's toil under the curse of sin, that have best understood the real meaning of the sabbath law and especially the meaning of the Jubilee. Note the prominence of the term "Jubilee" in the songs of black people in our own country, for example. And it is not without significance that this very passage of scripture is quoted and inscribed on our own "Liberty Bell," thus giving it its name. But the real Jubilee foreshadowed by these O. T. observances was not the granting of political liberty, but the gift of spiritual liberty in Christ.

Moreover, we should not think of the sabbath as an arbitrary sign. Nothing could be more ideally suited than rest—sabbath rest—to represent God's ultimate purpose to redeem man from the bondage of sin. It is because of sin that man has to labor by the sweat of his brow to obtain his food. Because of sin men and women are enslaved to sickness and disease, from which they long to be delivered, as was the woman of Luke 13:10-17. And because of sin the Israelites had to be sent into the bondage of the Babylonian captivity. In short, sin brings bondage and enslavement; deliverance from sin brings rest.

Now, to return to the 490 years of Daniel, if one Jubilee is an occasion to "proclaim liberty throughout the land," how much more the tenth Jubilee! Indeed, the tenth Jubilee would naturally symbolize to the Jewish mind the appropriate time for the proclamation of full and complete liberty and rest for the people of God. And that is exactly the point of the usage here in Daniel. Because of sin, the preceding epoch of ten Jubilees had not brought liberty, but a return to bondage—the very antithesis of what the sabbath law stood for. So now the angel announces to Daniel a new epoch of ten Jubilees to bring in the true salvation and deliverance from bondage that God was preparing for his people.

Such an interpretation of the 490 years was not foreign to the Jewish mind. In the Dead Sea Scroll, 11Q Melch, which is largely a commentary on the Jubilee law of Leviticus 25, we find that the Jews at Qumran, just before the time of Christ, anticipated the coming of the "Messiah spoken of by Daniel" (9:25) at the end of a "tenth jubilee" which they also identified as the "last Jubilee." It was further to be a time of "release," "liberation," "welfare," "peace," and "salvation." But it was especially to be a day of "atonement for iniquity" (9:24) and "vengeance and judgment" for the wicked. One could hardly ask for a better description of what the coming of the Messiah would mean for the nation of Israel.

Note that this explanation also helps us to understand why the seventy weeks is broken up into the pattern of 7 - 62 - 1. The first seven is the first of the ten Jubilees. It represents the period of time during which the first stage of restoration is to be accomplished—the rebuilding of the physical temple and city of Jerusalem. That physical restoration would then serve as a sort of down payment or guarantee of the full deliverance to come at the end of the tenth Jubilee. Such is often the case in fulfillment of Messianic prophecy; the first stage of fulfillment is physical and typical, whereas the final stage is anti typical and spiritual. Compare the promise to David of a son that would build the house of God, fulfilled literally in Solomon and then spiritually in Christ (II Sam. 7:11-16).

It is true that the rebuilding of the temple and the city did not occur exactly forty-nine years after the release from captivity. The release was in 539/8 B.C. and the temple was rebuilt by 516/5 B.C., or twenty-three years later. The city walls were not rebuilt until 445/4 B.C., some 94 years later, though some rebuilding of dwellings within the city precincts had no doubt taken place in the meantime. But we must remember that the significance of these numbers is symbolic and that they are not intended to predict exact dates. Indeed, the whole of the seventy weeks does not represent 490 literal years, but only symbolizes the period necessary for the full accomplishment of

God's plan to bring a true sabbath rest and a true Jubilee—true rest and deliverance from sin—to his people.

## Conclusions

Our analysis thus far has strong implications for all four of the major schools of interpretation described at the beginning of this paper. The symbolism of the seventy weeks obviously harmonizes well with either the Traditional Messianic Interpretation or the Church Age Interpretation. And the Traditional Messianic Interpretation seems to correspond best to the stated goals of the seventy weeks and to allow for the obvious correspondence of the destruction of the city and sanctuary (v. 26) with the destruction brought by the Romans in A.D. 70. It is also preferable on a grammatical basis since it locates the appearance of the Messiah at the end of the sixty-ninth week instead of at the end of the seventh week.

On the other hand, a correct understanding of the symbolism of the seventy weeks seriously undermines both the Maccabean Interpretation and the Dispensational Interpretation. Both of these interpretations assume (for different reasons) that there must be a literal correspondence between the seventy weeks and the events of history. Both engage in numerical gymnastics and contorted exegesis to make their respective schemes work out. But in these unnecessary exercises, both also miss the essential point of the symbolism and the essential point of the prophecy.[1]

---

[1] For brevity sake the first few pages of this paper were omitted. For an in depth study it can be ordered from Florida College Bookstore, Temple Terrace, Florida 33617; *The Doctrine of Last Things* by Phil Roberts, Florida College Annual Lectures 1986; Edited by Melvin D. Curry.

# John's Antichrist and Paul's Man of Sin

## The Antichrist

Several times in the process of writing this book, and in other writings, I have taken exception to men's presentation of the antichrist. It is needful therefore, to make clear what I object to, and what my position is on the question. Rather than introduce the views of a number of men, since Professor H. C. Leupold has much to say about the antichrist in his commentary on Daniel, and well represents the view, I shall let him represent the points to which I object.[1]

## Leupold's View

In commenting on Daniel 8:17, Leupold says of the end, "So the 'end' referred to the absolute end"—the end of time. But the end to which Daniel was interested, and the angels referred to was the end of the Jewish nation, Jerusalem, and the temple. He then observes, "King Antiochus is seen to be a kind of Old Testament antichrist like unto the great antichrist [of the New Testament HH]". He would thus make him an individual, a person, a man (261-262; see also p. 428).

In his comments on Daniel 9:27, the professor said, "The

---

[1] H.C. Leupold, *Exposition of Daniel* (Columbus, Ohio: The Wartburg Press, 1949).

person [individual, man, HH] under consideration as making the covenant is naturally still the Antichrist" (p. 431). And, "As the Lord made a covenant with His own to give them strong assurance as to what He would do, so antichrist will inaugurate a covenant that shall prevail, that is to say, compel the masses to accept it and to abide by it" (p. 432; Cf. my comments on the passage).

In introducing the last paragraph in chapter 11, Leupold wrote in bold letters, "II. **The More Remote Future: the antichrist and His Overthrow and the Consummation**, 11:36 - 12:3." He proceeded to speak of him as, "this personage: Antichrist, i.e., 'against' the Christ" (p. 514)—an individual, person, a man. The writer identified the antichrist with Paul's "man of sin"; in referring to Second Thessalonians 2:3, he said, "This New Testament passage without a doubt speaks of the antichrist" (p. 513). I lean toward the same view, but do not believe that Paul is speaking of an individual, a person, a man, any more than I believe that John is speaking of an individual man when he writes of antichrist.

And so, I differ from two major positions taken by writers such as Leupold and others who advance such views: 1) The Bible does not sustain or uphold the view that the antichrist is a special human enemy of Christ who is to appear before the end of time, gathering together a world host in a last furious battle against the Christ. 2) Nor do I believe that Daniel ever referred to such a one as the antichrist at anytime in his prophecy.

## The Antichrist

The word "antichrist" occurs four times, and "many antichrists" once, all in two of John's epistles. Let us consider each passage in which the word occurs. "Little children, it is the last hour: and as ye heard that antichrist cometh, even now have there arisen many antichrists; whereby we know that it is the last hour" (I John 2:18). The source of their information concerning the coming of the antichrist was not divulged, but John accepted it as correct. Yet, even then there were many antichrists, those who had gone out from among the apostles because they were not of them (v. 19). John tells us the nature and character of such when he asks, "Who is the liar but he that denieth that Jesus is the Christ? This is the antichrist, even he that denieth the Father and the Son" (v. 22).

"The last hour" of John seems to be the "last days" that Peter referred to in Acts 2:17; "the last time" (I Pet. 1:5; Jude 18); "the end of the times" (I Pet. 1:20); and "the end of these days"—the days of the prophets through whom God had formerly spoken (Heb. 1:2). All of these terms apply to the period of the Messiah, the last period in which God would make an appeal to man. The antichrists would be those who opposed the Christ, denied Him, and the Father's testimony to His being the Messiah, His Son. One spirit characterized them all: "And every spirit that confesseth not Jesus is not of God: and this is the spirit of the antichrist, whereof ye have heard that it cometh; and now it is in the world already" (I John 4:3). That spirit, the spirit of antichrist that denies Him as God's anointed in word, deed, and life—denies Him in any aspect of its inclusiveness that the word "anointed of God" sustains, is to that extent of the spirit of antichrist.

John further identified his subject when he said, "For many deceivers are gone forth into the world, even they that confess not that Jesus Christ cometh in the flesh. This is the deceiver and the antichrist" (II John 7). It is quite probable that John had in mind a certain sect of his day. The spirit and its expression continues to live and be manifested in the lives of many today.

We now raise the question: What does one see in any of these passages that lead to the conclusion that towards the end of time a special individual, a person, a man will arise and gather the peoples of the world together into a unified group and make war on the Messiah and God? True, the definite article "the" occurred before "antichrist" each of the four times that "antichrist" appears in the singular. But even if John's antichrist and Paul's "lawless one" are the same; I do not accept the conclusion that either applies to one particular individual, a person, a special man that gathers all nations as one under his leadership in opposition to the Messiah and God.

## The Man of Sin

In First Thessalonians Paul concluded each of the five chapters with some reference to the coming of the Lord (l:10; 2:19; 3:13; 4:13-18; 5:23). What he said in these passages, and possibly what he had said while with them, led to a misunderstanding of his teaching by many. Furthermore, it is possible that false teachers had misinterpreted it for them, either by word or by letters purported to have been from him. This misunderstanding led to unapproved actions and conduct on the part of some, which Paul sought to correct in Second Thessalonians. In chapter one of this second letter he discussed "the revelation of the Lord Jesus from heaven" and "the righteous judgment of God" which would occur at His coming. He also told of the destiny of the wicked and the glory of the saints. Many of the brethren interpreted what Paul said or wrote to mean that they were to look for His return immediately, which he corrected in chapter two. In this part of the Appendix, our concern is with what Paul wrote in chapter two, especially concerning the lawless one.

**Two Things to Precede His Coming:** Two events must occur before the day of the Lord's coming; it would not be except:

1. "The falling away," or "apostasy" comes first, which was beginning already in Paul's day. It would be a continuously developing or growing movement through the centuries to follow, and continues even until now.

2. "And the man of sin be revealed," which is our present theme. He is called "the man of sin," "man of lawlessness" (alternate reading, margin, as found in some ancient manuscripts), it matters not which one prefers, for John said, "Every one that doeth sin doeth also lawlessness; and sin is lawlessness" (I John 3:4). Also, he is called "the son of perdition," considered below, and "the lawless one" (II Thess. 2:3, 8). These terms indicate that he is the very personification and fullness of sin and lawlessness, as Jesus is the personification and fullness of righteousness and truth.

Through the centuries since Paul wrote this letter, men have advanced many theories concerning this "man of sin," of whom or what was Paul writing? That he is an individual person who is to appear just prior to the Lord's coming can be ruled out by what Paul says of him. Instead of discussing men's theories I shall set forth what I believe is a valid exposition of the passage. The question has challenged Bible students through the years with no definitive answer reached. One can only consider possibilities, leaving each student to reach his own conclusion on the ground of his total understanding of the text and correlating Scriptures which throw light on the subject. It is said that when Paul came to Thessalonica he entered the synagogue and "reasoned with them from the scriptures" (Acts 17:2). However let it be said that any reasonable conclusion reached must be reached on the ground of scripture that appears to be related to the subject; otherwise any answer reached will be guess, and nothing more.

**Paul's Description of His "Man of Sin"**: Before discussing the possibility of who the man of sin might be, let us consider what Paul said of him in II Thessalonians; by this description we will learn something of what we are looking for.

1. He is to be "revealed" (2:3b), a word that "signifies to uncover, unveil" (W. E. Vine). As the coming of Jesus "at the revelation" (1:7) was future and indicated that Jesus is now veiled from sight, so the revealing of the man of sin signified that he was at that time veiled. But before Christ comes he would be revealed, i.e., unveiled or uncovered. The specific length of time is left open.

2. "The son of perdition" (2:3c), meaning one doomed for destruction. The word signified a total lack of well- being. The only other time the phrase occurred is when Jesus applied it to Judas (John 17:12), whose act was one of supreme sin or lawlessness, and whose end would be utter destruction from the face of the Lord and the glory of His might.

3. "He that opposeth and exalteth himself against all that is called God or that is worshipped" (2:4a). This described one in total rebellion against God and all that pertained to Him: altar, sacrifice, principles, and laws—wholly and entirely.

4. "So that he sitteth in the temple of God" (2:4b). The

word "temple" (*naos*) indicates the sanctuary, the most holy place in the temple complex. Paul used the word *naos* (temple) of the church (I Cor. 3:16; II Cor. 6:16) and of the individuals who constitute the building, a dwelling place for God in the Spirit (I Cor. 6:19-20; Eph. 2:19-22). This raised the question: is the man of sin an apostate member of the body, having been originally added by the Lord? or did he arrogate unto himself such a place that he would displace God from His holy position in the universe? Hendricksen says that the word *naos* (temple) "is here clearly used metaphorically" (N. T. C., Second Thessalonians, p. 178), which I believe accurately expresses the truth.

5. "Setting himself forth as God" (2:4c). When God and all that pertains to Him is rejected, then that which personifies lawlessness takes over and becomes the god of its devotees.

6. "And now ye know that which restraineth...only there is one that restraineth now," (2:6, 7). Paul said that while he was yet with them he told them these things (2:5); therefore they knew these things (2:6). If he explained these things to them, then they had an advantage over us, for he did not make an explanation at this point. If we learn what or who it was that restrained the total takeover by lawlessness at that time, it will have to be from some other source than this passage. Even then, our understanding of that which restrained at that time will depend on our understanding or conclusion as to who the man of sin was (or is).

7. He is restrained "to the end that he may be revealed in his own season" (2:6b). His season is the period of his operation, which would be prior to the coming of the Lord (2:1-3), during which he—the man of sin—will be revealed, unveiled.

8. Although "the mystery of lawlessness doth already work," it would not be revealed in its fullness until the "one that restraineth...be taken out of the way" (2:7). The word mystery designated something not known until it was revealed or made known by one who knows. Since only God knew the mystery and those to whom He revealed it, we can never know unless somewhere in His revelation He has made it known; for it was not here made known by Paul.

9. But when taken out of the way, "**then** shall be revealed the lawless one, whom the Lord Jesus shall slay with the breath of his mouth, and bring to nought by the manifestation of his coming" (2:8). The order was: the mystery of lawlessness was at work; there was one which restrained, therefore the lawless one could not fully operate or be unveiled at that time; but when the one, or that which, restrained was taken out of the way, then the man of sin would be fully uncovered; with his full revelation, the Lord Jesus would slay him with the breath of His mouth, thereby bringing him to nought or perdition.

10. "Even he, [the man of sin] whose coming is according to the working of Satan with all power and signs and lying wonders, and with all deceit of unrighteousness for them that perish" (2:9-10a). It is clear from this that the man of sin—the man of lawlessness—the lawless one—under the complete control and service of Satan; he will be deceiving the world by working pseudo-signs and wonders, for the devil can neither work bona fide miracles nor give the power to work them to others. All so-called miracles are deceptions pawned off on the world by the devil; but such efforts by him through the man of sin will be intensified before the end.

11. Why he will be so successful: "Because they received not the love of the truth, that they might be saved" (2:10b). When love of the truth dies that which restrains is gone; lawlessness takes over and the devil has a field day.

12. "And for this cause"—their lack of love for the truth—"God sendeth them a working of error, that they should believe a lie: that they all might be judged who believed not the truth, but had pleasure in unrighteousness" (2:11-12). When one rejects the truth the only thing left for him to believe is a lie. Man makes himself what he is; God allows that, and lets him believe a lie that he might be judged according to "the righteous judgment of God" (1:5), and suffer the consequence of such a choice (1:9).

## Paul's "man of sin" – John's Gog (of) Magog

Let us proceed in our reasoning from the scripture. Paul's prophecy is eschatological, the mystery of lawlessness at work when Paul wrote Second Thessalonians grows until near the end-time when the Lord will soon appear; and it will be fully manifested in John's Gog of Magog shortly before Jesus comes.

Stated as a proposition: I believe that the man of law- lessness is the personification of lawlessness which reached its fullness in John's Gog and (of) Magog, shortly prior to the Lord's coming at which time it will be brought to nought. In developing my evidence, I appeal to Ezekiel, chapter 38; for an explanation of John's use of Gog and Magog and to Revelation 20 for his use of it. And for that which restrained, I appeal to Revelation 12.

**Gog of Magog, Ezekiel 38:** In Ezekiel 38, Jehovah told the prophet to "set thy face toward Gog, of the land of Magog, the prince of Rosh…" (v. 2), and to prophesy against him. God would be against him and all his hordes because they would come up against God's people who had been gathered out of many peoples (vv. 7-9), to take the spoil and the prey (vv. 10-13). Then in the "latter days," a term designating the Messianic period, God would bring him against His land (v. 16), which apparently would be the destruction of Jerusalem A.D. 70, which foreshadowed the final destruction (Rev. 20).

Who are Gog and the people of Magog? The following verse provides the key, "Art thou he of whom I spake [Are you not the one I spoke of? NIV] in old time by my servants the prophets of Israel, that prophesied in those days for many years that I would bring thee against them?" (v. 17). But where is the word of any prophet, who at any time spoke of "Gog" or "Magog" being brought up against Israel by Jehovah? There is no such prophecy. But the prophets did tell over and over of Jehovah's use of heathen nations or forces being led by heathen kings against Israel. So then, we are led to conclude that "Gog, of the land of Magog" was a phrase used by the Lord to signify the sum of heathen rulers and nations, the anti-God forces of ancient times whom He would use, did use, and destroyed.

The destruction of those forces who were fitted for destruction is described in chapter 39.

**Gog and Magog, Revelation 20:** In Revelation 20, John recorded a vision in which he saw, "an angel coming down out of heaven, having the key of the abyss and a great chain in his hand," and that he bound Satan "and cast him into the abyss, and shut it, and sealed it over him, that he should deceive the nations no more, until the thousand years should be finished; after this he must be loosed for a little time" (vv. 1-3). Although the mystery of lawlessness was at work, it could not be revealed in all its evil work so long as its master was restrained.

During this thousand years souls of martyred saints sat on thrones ruling with Christ (vv. 4-6). "And when the thousand years are finished, Satan shall be loosed out of his prison [the abyss into which he had been cast], and shall come forth to deceive the nations which are in the four corners of the earth, Gog and [of] Magog, to gather them together to the war: the number of whom is as the sand of the sea" (vv. 7-8). These symbolized the forces of evil, heathen forces of lawlessness under Satan's control, now fully turned loose upon the earth, even as Gog of Magog of Ezekiel symbolized the Satanic forces of the ancient heathen nations. In John's Revelation they symbolized all the forces of evil toward, or just before the end.

Note their multitude, "as the sand of the sea"; and note the point of their attack, "And they went up over the breadth of the earth, and compassed **the camp** of the saints about, and the beloved city" (v. 9a), the spiritual city Jerusalem to which the saints have come (Heb. 12:22-24; Gal. 4:26). "And fire came down out of heaven, and devoured them" (v. 9b); the son of perdition, that sought the destruction of God's people, was now himself destroyed. The climax of the conflict is described next, "And the devil that deceived them was cast into the lake of fire and brimstone, where are also the beast and the false prophet; and they shall be tormented day and night for ever and ever" (v. 10). Then came the final judgment (vv. 11-15).

**That Which Restrained:** Let us retrace our steps from Revelation 20 to chapter 12, and consider that by which the saints overcame and thereby restrained the man of sin until that which restrained was taken out of the way. The great spiritual conflict between the forces of God and Satan is symbolized as a war in heaven, in which Satan was cast down to the earth (Rev. 12:7-9). Following this, John heard a great voice, saying, "Now is come the salvation, and the power, and the kingdom of our God, and the authority of his Christ" (v. 10). Inasmuch as Jesus claimed His authority following His victory over Satan in His death and resurrection, we conclude that the conflict pictured was that from Eden to His resurrection which brought in the long anticipated salvation and kingdom. This was His victory which left Satan bound. What now is the power by which the brethren overcome and restrain Satan? John continued, "And they [our brethren, v. 10] overcame him because of the blood of the Lamb, and because of the word of their testimony; and they loved not their life even unto death" (v. 11). By these—the blood in which they trusted, and the word of their testimony which was a confession of their faith; and their martyr spirit—they overcame; but when these cease to be the force of Christian life and faithfulness, the restraining force of lawlessness is removed; Satan is footloose and fancy free.

Therefore when Satan was free from his prison, that which held him captive, he was able to gather Gog and Magog to the war—lawlessness took over. When men no longer regard the blood of Jesus, nor are interested in the salvation which it procures; when they no longer respect the testimony of Jesus and the apostles, nor that of the martyrs who gave their life for it, nor their own testimony of faith; and they no longer love these sacred things of God dearer than life itself, then lawlessness has no restraint.

## A Summary

Let us now summarize our argument by comparing Paul's points in his presentation of the man of sin or lawlessness, and John's Gog and Magog:

1. Both were to be revealed, come to light when Satan was

loosed just before or shortly before Jesus comes.

2. Paul's man of sin was also the son of perdition, one who sought to destroy and was destroyed; John's Gog and Magog sought to destroy God's camp and the beloved city, and were destroyed in the attempt.

3. As the Gog of Ezekiel sought to destroy the concept of the true God by destroying the people of God, so did the Gog of Revelation and Paul's man of sin by totally rebelling against God and leading men to do so.

4. If God is overthrown, then lawlessness takes over and rules in His temple, in His stead. The movement of both tended to this end. In the effort today to dethrone God, to deny and reject Him, lawlessness is ascending to every high place in society attempting to take God's place.

5. If successful in destroying the camp of the saints and the holy city, Gog and "the man of sin" as lawlessness would then reign as God.

6. That which restrained them, and has continued to restrain the man of lawlessness, has been the spirit of martyrdom which trusts in the blood, the word of their testimony which they confessed that their belief was that He is the Christ, the Son of God, and their readiness to die for that faith.

7. "His own season" of both the man of sin and Gog of Magog is that season just prior to the coming of the Lord.

8. It was pointed out above that what restrained would be taken out of the way when the force that restrained was no longer active; this was true of both.

9. When that which restrained was taken out of the way then the man of sin was revealed in all his lawlessness; and it was then that Gog of Magog gathered his forces and made one last furious effort to destroy all that was holy.

10. Both were completely under the power and dominion of Satan, exercising his satanic power to achieve their purpose.

11. Each was successful because men no longer loved the truth; the forces of Gog were as the sand of the sea; the camp of the saints was just a camp.

12. And because of this lack of love and faithfulness, the man of lawlessness was able to deceive with Satan's devices, and

likewise Gog was totally under the control of Satan, the deceiver and the liar.

## Conclusion

In the light of Scripture, it seems reasonable to conclude that Paul's man of sin or lawlessness is John's Gog of Magog. At least this conclusion has Scripture on its side. Let it be added, however, this is not to say that the end is immediate, or that we know how near it may be. There is yet the restraining force of the love of truth living and active in the lives of many today. Furthermore, inasmuch as there have been numerous times in the past centuries when it seemed that Satan was loosed and the end was near, but there was a revival of faith and he was turned back. In the light of such occasions, there can even now be a turning back to God by a sufficient number to avert the complete take-over by "the man of lawlessness," a complete compassing about "the camp of the saints" by Gog that would lead to the revealing of the Lord. There will always be a faithful remnant, a "camp of the saints," and just how small it will have to be, and how complete the influence and take-over of the lawless one, is strictly in the determination of God. In this all that I have sought to establish is that Paul's man of sin (or lawlessness) is in all probability John's Gog of Magog, and that which restrains him is love and faithfulness to the truth of God. When this is no longer of sufficient force to restrain, then lawlessness takes over and the Lord will come.

So, neither John's antichrist, nor Paul's man of sin, are individual men, but each is a symbol of spiritual forces at work against God and His people. Each shall be brought to an end at the coming of the Lord.

## Commentaries

Barnes, Albert. *Book of Daniel.* New York: Leavitt & Allen, 1855.

Coleman-Norton, P. R. *Roman state and the Christian Church.* vol. III, London: S. P. C. K., 1911.

Deane, H. *Men of the Bible, Daniel His Life and Times.* New York: Fleming H. Revell Company, 1888.

Hailey, Homer. *Revelation, An Introduction and Commentary.* Grand Rapids, Michigan: Baker Book House, 1979.

Hailey, Homer. *God's Judgements and Puishments.* Reno, Nevada: Nevada Publications, 2002.

Hendriksen, William, *New Testament Commentary, I and II Thessalonians.* Grand Rapids, Michigan: Baker Book House, 1955.

Keil and Delitzsch, (Abr. K & D). *Commentaries on the Old Testament, 25 vols.* Grand Rapids, Michigan: Wm. B. Eerdmans Publishing Company, reprint, 1949.

Leupold, H. C. *Exposition of Daniel.* Columbus, Ohio: The Wartburg Press, 1949.

Pfeiffer, Charles F. *Between the Testaments.* Grand Rapids, Michigan: Baker Book House, 1959.

Pfeiffer, Robert H. *Introduction to the Old Testament.* New York: Harper & Brothers Publisher, 1948.

Roberts, Phil. *The Doctrine of Last Things.* Temple Terrace, Florida: Florida College Bookstore, 1986.

Whitcomb, John C. Jr. *Darius the Mede.* Grand Rapids, Michigan: Wm. B. Eerdmans Publishing Company, 1959.

Wilson, Robert Dick. *Studies in the Book of Daniel.* Grand Rapids, Michigan: Baker Book House, 1979.

Young, Edward J. *The Prophecy of Daniel.* Grand Rapids, Michigan: Wm. B. Eerdmans Publishing Co., 1949.

Young, Robert. *Literal Translation of the Holy Bible.* Grand Rapids, Michigan: Baker Book House, 1953.

# Encyclopedias and Word Studies

Arndt and Gingrich (Abr. A & G). *A Greek-English Lexicon of the New Testament.* Chicago: University of Chicago Press, 1957.

*Compton's Pictorial Encyclopedia.* Chicago: F. E. Compton & Company,1945

Cruden, Alexander, *Cruden's Complete Concordance.* Grand Rapids, Michigan: Zondervan Publishing House, 1968.

*Encyclopedia Britannica.*

*International Standard Bible Encyclopedia* (Abr. ISBE), 5 vols. Chicago: Howard Severance Co., 1937.

Keil C. F. Keil and Delitzsch, *Commentaries on the old Testament,* (Abr. K & D) Daniel. Grand Rapids, Michigan: Wm. B. Eerdmans Publishing Company, 1949.

*New Century Dictionary.* New York: D. Appleton-Century Company, 1936.

Thayer, Joseph Henry, *Greek English Lexicon of the New Testament.* New York: American Book Company, 1886.

*Theological Wordbook of the Old Testament* (Abr. TWOT), 2 vols. Chicago: Moody Press, 1980.

Vine, W. E. *Expository Dictionary of New Testament Words.* 4 vols. London: Oliphants, 1946.

*Zondervan Pictorial Encyclopedia of the Bible* (Abr. ZPEB), 5 vols. Grand Rapids: Zondervan Publishing House, 1982.

# Historians

Josephus, Flavius, *The Antiquities of the Jews.* Grand Rapids, Michigan: Kregel Publications, 1967.

# Version

ASV - Unless otherwise indicated, scripture quotations are from the American Standard Edition of the Revised Bible 1901 by Thomas Nelson and Sons, 1929 by International Council of Religious Education.

# OTHER BOOKS BY HOMER HAILEY

**A COMMENTARY ON THE MINOR PROPHETS.** After presenting the 12 minor prophets as a group, the author then treats their writings separately with general observations about each prophet, the date of writing and the message. There are outlines of each book followed by lively verse by verse commentary which unfolds the meaning in clear, understandable language. 428 pages, cloth.

**REVELATION, AN INTRODUCTION AND COMMENTARY.** The author clearly shows that the book of Revelation describes problems faced by Christians in 95-180 AD. Amid moral-spiritual forces, Revelation's message continues to instruct God's people, disclosing principles of victory through righteousness and the failure of the false. Since end-time events and judgements are still future, these aspects of Revelation are to be recognized. 438 pages, cloth.

**A COMMENTARY ON ISAIAH, WITH EMPHASIS ON THE MESSIANIC HOPE.** Through prudently and discreetly phrased commentary, the author hopes that the reader will "grasp something of Isaiah's insight into the glory and majesty of Jehovah, to appreciate God's infinite love for the people He chose as His own." Isaiah foresaw the coming of the Suffering Servant, Jesus Christ, a truth reverently handled by Hailey. 542 pages, cloth.

**A COMMENTARY OF JOB.** Subtitled *Now Mine Eye Seeth Thee,* this study successfully analyzes the subtle distinctions in the speeches within the book of Job to make them clear to the student. Among the difficult problems of life is that of human suffering, and author Hailey shows how the power of the hero Job endured overwhelming afflictions through patience and faith in God to accomplish the greater good. 386 pages, cloth.

**THE MESSIAH OF PROPHECY TO THE MESSIAH ON THE THRONE.** This book details the development of the messianic hope chronologically, tracing it through Moses' writings and David's Psalms to the prophets God sent to Israel and Judah, century by century. Then, in the fullness of time, came Jesus in fulfillment of the messianic portrait that had been painted by holymen of old. 283 pages, cloth.

**PRAYER AND PROVIDENCE.** Written to believers in God, this volume addresses prayer by showing that it is a privilege and an obligation—a vital part of Christian living. The author develops the subject of providence as the working of God through His providing all things in both the natural and spiritual realms. 223 pages, paper.

**THAT YOU MAY BELIEVE.** Subtitled *Studies in the Gospel of John,* this book lays a firm foundation of faith for a consistent Christian life. Not a verse by verse commentary, this book is a topical study packed with helpful material for individual or group use. 200 pages, paper.

**HAILEY'S COMMENTS,** two volumes. The first one begins in Genesis and touches upon the Exodus, the giving of the law, and the remnant of Judah in Babylonian exile. There are commentaries on Amos, Hosa, Isaiah, Daniel, Ezekiel, and Jeremiah. The problem of human suffering as it related to Job, closes out the first volume. The second begins with Jesus and the significance of His life. Hailey discusses evangelism, elders, stewardship, the need for a saviour, and the saints amid a secular world. Vol 1, 347 pages; vol. 2, 384 pages. Scripture and general indices. A matching hardbound set with color dust jackets.

**FROM CREATION TO THE DAY OF ETERNITY.** Seeing God in nature, in providence and in His Christ, this book recalls the story of creation, the introduction of man, and the fall. Lofty OT themes show God's system of redemption, disclosing a hope-inspiring promise after captivity and restoration. Studies of Christ's ministry, death and resurrection, as well as worship, godly character, the church, the "second coming," the resurrection and judgement, round out a well-written book, useful for readers of all ages. Indexed. 226 pages, paper.

**THE DIVORCED AND REMARRIED WHO WOULD COME TO GOD.** This booklet sets forth the author's position on the subject and reasons for holding it. It is the author's hope that the booklet will be read in the spirit in which it was written—an examination of what God said (and did not say) in a devout search for truth. Scripture and general indices, 80 pages.

**THE EDOMITES: SYMBOL OF THE WORLD.** Esau symbolizes worldly pride and wisdom and hatred of God. The historical conflict between him and his brother Jacob is analogous to the tension between the flesh serving sin and the spirit of holiness and submitting to God in righteousness. 117 pages, paper.

**GOD'S ETERNAL PURPOSE AND THE COVENANTS.** The author concisely expounds upon the book of Ephesians, discussing Christ, the Holy Spirit and the church in the eternal purpose of God. Also addressed are the subjects of holiness, unity, and ultimate victory in Christ. 234 pages, cloth and paper.

**CARRYING OUT THE GREAT COMMISSION.** Subtitled *According to the New Testament Pattern,* this book carefully analyzes the teaching and preaching recorded in the gospels, the epistles, but especially in the book of Acts. Therein the theme of this book is fully demonstrated. 141 pages, cloth and paper.

# OTHER BOOKS BY NEVADA PUBLICATIONS

**THE IDENTITY OF BABYLON AND THE DATING OF THE BOOK OF REVELATION,** by Stanley W. Paher. Church writers before AD 550 unanimously attest to the late (AD 95-96) date of the writing of Revelation. Such evidence is joined by the contemporary use of the term "Babylon" in Jewish literature. The politics, commerce and self-indulgence of Babylon are compared with Tyre, Ninevah and old Babylon. The 29 items of Rev. 18:12-13, which world traders supplied "Babylon," qualifies only Rome as the trader/harlot. Paher's study augments Hailey's commentary on the book of Revelation. 142 pages, paper.

**MATTHEW 24: FIRST CENTURY FULFILLMENT OR END-TIME EXPECTATION?** By Stanley W. Paher. Bible texts referring to the "latter days" and the "end time" refer not to yet future events but to those culminating in the fall of Jerusalem in AD 70. With the OT as precedent, the author reviews the symbols of Matthew 24 and shows that the end of the Jewish nation is in view in the tribulation and the Roman siege of Jerusalem. The book was sparked by class study with Homer Hailey. 192 pages, paper.

**NATURAL LAW: UNIVERSAL IN SCOPE, MORAL IN DESIGN,** by Stanley W. Paher. The Creator-God has revealed Himself to man *generally* in nature (which is also subject to physical and moral law) and *specially* through holy men of old, who set forth God's mind and will in scripture. The book discusses Romans 1-2, the conscience, and the law in the heart as in the person of Cornelius. Seeking, not rejecting truth, is the hallmark of a relationship with God. 72 pages, paper.

**THE DEVELOPMENT OF THE NEW TESTAMENT CANON,** by Stanley W. Paher. As a record of God's supernatural revelations to His covenant people, the New Testament faithfully preserves God's will and man's response to it. For this reason, the inspired canonized writings are to be loved and appreciated as God's heritage to His people. 88 pages, Color chart. $5.95.

**THE KINGDOM OF GOD, A RELATIONSHIP NOT AN INSTITUTION,** by Dean Spurlock and Stanley W. Paher. The kingdom (or reign) of God is not the church but a relationship into which one enters, through a Deliverer. The sovereign rule of Jesus over human hearts is the means of deliverance. It is a reign received from God. Such a relationship is based upon repentance, the forgiveness of sin, mercy, grace and love. 72 pages, paper.

*~ Write to the Publisher for a complete catalog~*

# MEMORIES SHARED...

## *Would you like to share your memories of Homer Hailey?*

HOMER HAILEY fought the good fight, finished his course, and kept the faith and is now enjoying the crown of righteousness which was laid up for him. Along this course, he touched many of our lives leaving us with special reflections that helped us along our way.

Since the world lost a pinch of its salt in November of 2000, I have been overwhelmed with people telling me what Homer Hailey meant to them and how he influenced their lives. These recollections should be shared and preserved in a book.

Some memories are of his wisdom in presenting his knowledge of God's word. Other recollections are just of an impromtu incident, humorous and otherwise. He impressed us with his        special interest in the individual and his concern about health. Neither his quick wit nor  his counsel can be forgotten. These were all benefi-cial to us. Please share your story with us.

We would like you to be part of this effort. The length of your anecdote can be up to 1,000 words. Please send your reminescence of our brother before June 30, 2002 to:

### Ruby Stroup
4101 E. Hawthorne, Tucson, AZ 85711
*~ or ~*
### joys2@flash.net
Subject: Homer Hailey Memories

*Please include WHO you are,*

*WHAT you want to share,*

*WHEN and WHERE you knew brother Hailey,*

*and HOW or WHY he influenced your life.*

 *This book is as yet untitled. To the individual who suggests the final name for this book, the publisher will send 5 copies of the finished work postpaid. To nine runners up, a complimentary copy will be awarded.*